Understanding Organizational Change

Understanding Organizational Change

The Contemporary Experience of People at Work

Patrick Dawson

SAGE Publications
London • Thousand Oaks • New Delhi

SAGE Publications Ltd
6 Bonhill Street
London EC2A 4PU

SAGE Publications Inc.
2455 Teller Road
Thousand Oaks, California 91320

SAGE Publications India Pvt Ltd
32, M-Block Market
Greater Kailash – I
New Delhi 110 048

British Library Cataloguing in Publication data
A catalogue record for this book is available
from the British Library

ISBN 0 7619 7159 9
ISBN 0 7619 7160 2 (pbk)

Library of Congress Control Number 2002109394

Typeset by Photoprint, Torquay, Devon
Printed in Great Britain by The Cromwell Press Ltd,
Trowbridge, Wiltshire

To Susan Joy Thomson

Contents

List of figures   ix

Acknowledgements   xiii

1 Change riders   1
   Beyond metaphor and the scientific snapshot   2
   Processual research on change   3
   Structure of the book   5
   Conclusion   9

2 Dimensions of change   11
   Perspectives on organizational change   11
   The triggers to organizational change   15
   The concept of organizational change   16
   Why do people resist organizational change?   19
   Flexibility: in search of new ways of organizing and working   21
   Conclusion   24

3 A historical overview of theoretical perspectives and change frameworks   26
   Change and the Industrial Revolution   26
   Scientific management and change   28
   The human dimension to change   29
   The Organizational Development model of change   30
   Change and socio-technical systems theory   32
   A situational approach to change   34
   Celebrity professors and consultants   35
   A time to question simple change products and accounts   39
   Making sense of change: a processual perspective   41
   Framework for data analysis   45
   Conclusion   50

4 Flexibility, workplace change and non-standard employment   51
   Shifting employment strategies in the drive for profits and flexibility   52
   Management of change and employee experience of work   55

Full-time employment and the push for flexibility: outsourcing and
   part-time work   58
The casualization of work, job insecurity and employee representation   62
Conclusion   67

5 **New technology and power relations**   69
  Technology and change at work: an overview of conceptual debates 69
  New technology at Dalebake Bakeries   72
  Consumer demand and customer power: a changing market   73
  The Mossdale facility: a factory after its time   76
  The power of the retailing giants and the future of Mossdale   79
  Conclusion   80

6 **The experience of supervisors and older employees under conditions of change** 83
  The 'problem' of the supervisor and workplace change   83
  The older supervisor and workplace change   85
  Older employees and workplace change   90
  Change initiatives and older employees: a question of hierarchy and position 93
  Conclusion   95

7 **Cellular manufacture and the politics of change**   98
  Cellular manufacture   98
  Teamworking   99
  Cellular work arrangements at Washdale Manufacturing   102
  Sleepers wake: stamping down on the custom and practice of night shift
   operations   103
  Management strategy and machine shop resistance to change   105
  Conclusion   109

8 **Globalization and strategic change**   112
  Globalization and organizational change   113
  The company: F.H. Faulding & Co. Ltd   116
  Human resource management and growth   118
  Going global: beyond the local perspective   119
  A global technology forum: the DBL acquisition   121
  Strategic objectives: towards the seamless organization   123
  Conclusion   125

9 **Trade unions and a shifting industrial landscape**   127
  The changing industrial landscape and the decline in union membership 128
  Gender, changing patterns of work and trade unions   132
  Change and trade unions: the case of the Australian Services Union 134
  Gender and trade unions: from male bastion to female friendly? 137
  The politics of union organization: vested interest, gender and trade union
   democracy   140
  Economic rationalism and the context of change   142

Trade unions, technology and the geographical dispersal of work   143
Conclusion   145

10 The quality management experience   148
Quality management: the new competitive advantage?   150
Complex outcomes: a processual analysis of case study data   153
Using case study data to identify practical guidelines for change   159
Conclusion   165

11 Living with change in the twenty-first century   167
Beyond the cookbook approach: the need for critical reflection   167
Elephant, flea, seal or gazelle? Change and the future of work   169
Practical lessons on change: beyond stories of success   173
Conclusion   177

Appendix: the TQM research programme and guide for interviewers   180

References   186

Author Index   201

Subject Index   205

List of figures

2.1   Change framework of Buchanan and Badham (1999: 181)   17
3.1   The process of organizational change   49

Acknowledgements

Many of the case studies reported in this book would not have been possible without the agreement and support of a wide range of people from all levels within the participating organizations. Acknowledgement is given to all those who helped facilitate this research that has been carried out in four different countries over a period of 22 years. The cases draw mainly on research conducted within Australia and the UK over the last ten years, but earlier studies on change have influenced the direction and design of the research, and draw attention to continuity as well as change in the world of work. In enabling company access and allowing research to be conducted, I would like to thank the Australian Services Union, Britax, Central Linen Service, Email, Faulding, General Motors, Shell Expro, the Fifth Business, Pirelli Cables, Laubman and Pank and Aberdeen Asset Management, as well as those companies who wish to remain anonymous. Although all these companies have not been used as individual case studies in the main body of the text, they have all informed the perspective developed in the book. While it is not feasible to provide individual thanks to all the participants in these organizations, I would like to thank them collectively, for without their willingness to take part in the research this manuscript would not have been possible. I would, however, like to acknowledge the ongoing support of Graham Eagles, John Gazzola and Anne McEwen.

In carrying out the research some studies were conducted by the author while others involved collaboration with academic colleagues. The Faulding study was a joint piece of research with Margaret Patrickson at the University of South Australia; the study at Shell Expro and the Fifth Business was carried out with Niki Panteli at the University of Bath. The studies on quality management in eight companies in Australia and New Zealand involved Gill Palmer and members of the Collaborative ARC-funded Research Programme on Total Quality Management at Queensland University of Technology, University of Adelaide, Edith Cowan University, University of Otago and the University of Wollongong. The ongoing study of Aberdeen Asset Management is being conducted with my departmental colleagues Martin Atkins and Nicky Gunson. I would like to acknowledge their support and contribution both to the research and in our general discussions on change management. I would also like to gratefully acknowledge Blackwell Publishing for granting permission to republish case material from an article entitled 'Technology and the politics of change at work: the case of Dalebake Bakeries', which was published in 2002 in *New Technology, Work and Employment* 17(1).

For commenting on drafts of the manuscript, I would like to thank Richard Badham, David Buchanan, David Collins, Bernard Fusulier, Jim Grieves, Nicky Gunson, Jeff Hyman, Russel Lansbury, Paul Luff, Darren McCabe, Malcolm MacIntosh, Lorna McKee, Ian McLoughlin and David Preece. I would also like to acknowledge the academic insights that arose from discussions and debates with Niki Panteli in Scotland, Dexter Dunphy, Elizabeth Kummerow and Margaret Patrickson in Australia, and with Christian Clausen, Christian Koch and Klaus T. Nielsen in Denmark (during my guest professorship on the Danish Research Programme 'Working Environment and Technological Development'). I would like to thank the team at Sage for their work and support from the initial submission of a book proposal through to the cover design and the professional and comprehensive copyediting. Although I have not had contact with all of the team, I would like to thank Seth Edwards, Kiren Shoman, Keith Von Tersch and Verity Wood. Finally, I would like to give special thanks to Sue Thomson who read and commented on all sections of the text and who has been an understanding companion during my late night typing in front of a computer screen when I should have been giving more attention to family matters (and of course for that final paragraph which generally took two hours rather than the proclaimed ten minutes). Sorry and thanks for all the support (it probably will happen again). On the family front, I must mention my daughter Rosie Mae Dawson who constructed Figure 3.1 to represent the process of organizational change. Also, I would like to thank Rosie and my two sons Robin and Gareth for accompanying me (however reluctantly) on our infamous walks into the Grampian Mountains. I enjoyed these excursions and I do appreciate that many ideas have been formulated on the cold windy reaches of the Cairngorms and during the long walks back to the car. Finally, I would like to thank Cous Cous and Ozy for purring away the long vigils at the laptop and by clearly demonstrating that any sane being would be asleep or resting.

Change riders

Rider, riders (noun)
  1. *A rider is a person riding on a horse or bicycle*
  2. *A rider is also an additional statement which changes or puts a condition on what has already been said*

This book is about the meaning of change for people in work and employment. It is about riding change in the ways that we seek to manage, steer or resist the change process and in the ways that we may be swept along as relatively passive passengers. 'Change riders' may take an active position and harness these processes in shaping the outcomes and direction of change, or they may play a less active role in accommodating changes imposed by others. The term 'change rider' also refers to the emergent and uncharted character of change processes, and the need to qualify even the most carefully planned change programmes. There are change requirements and conditions that cannot be foreseen; unanticipated quandaries are not uncommon in major change initiatives. Moreover, the experiences recounted in this book remind us that employees act as modifiers to change initiatives – organizational change must be seen as a dynamic process that may take unexpected turns. It is this processual and ongoing character of change that makes it a difficult yet fascinating area to explore. This book is as much about people (their emotions, views and responses) as it is about the theory and practice of managing change. My intention is to present informative and readable accounts that provide useful insights into the murky processes of change; stimulate critical reflection and discussion; and enable the distillation of practical lessons for harnessing, steering and responding to change. The main objectives of the book are:

1 To draw on the contemporary experience of change for people in work and employment, and to make their views and stories accessible to the reader.
2 To document empirical evidence drawn from an intimate knowledge of case study data which have been collected over 20 years.
3 To present a diversity of views and perspectives by analysing data from a range of different individuals and groups (for example, chief executive officers, part-time employees and older workers) in order to chart 'voices'

that cover a spectrum of experience, including the self-proclaimed 'winners' and the supposed 'losers'.

4 To provide, for advanced undergraduate and masters level students, a concise historical overview of developments in change management and new critical case study material.

5 To explain and demonstrate the benefits of processual theory for understanding the dynamics of change.

6 To identify and discuss practical lessons on living with change.

The book attempts to engage a range of readers (students, academics, practitioners) who have an interest in understanding change. Inevitably, necessary constraints impose limitations on the depth of theoretical analysis and the breadth of empirical discussion, but in the end, my intention has been to provide a book that stimulates interest both in raising questions for further debate and discussion, as well as offering insights into long-standing change management myths and ongoing debates.

BEYOND METAPHOR AND THE SCIENTIFIC SNAPSHOT

Although workplace change has a long history, many commentators advocate that the current climate of change is quantitatively and qualitatively different. The break-up of the old Soviet Union and the transformation of Eastern Europe, the launching of the single European currency, the growth in trade in the Asia–Pacific region, wars, terrorist attacks, technological advances, world recessions, the digital economy and changes in international trade agreements – all form part of our contemporary political and economic world. Similarly, in the world of work and employment, there has been a barrage of change initiatives and yet the failure rates of programmes such as Business Process Re-engineering (BPR) have been estimated to be as high as 70 per cent (Beer and Nohria, 2000; Knights and Willmott, 2000). Given the toll on change initiatives, it is no wonder that employee cynicism has increased as yet another three-letter acronym – whether JIT (Just-In-Time), TQM (Total Quality Management), CAE (Computer-Aided Engineering), TPM (Total Productive Maintenance) or SAP (from the Germany SAP software company) – is invoked by management as the ultimate organizational panacea. The growing cadre of business consultants who stress the need to create and sustain competitive advantage in 'an increasingly aggressive commercial market' reinforces this seemingly insatiable need for change.

However, this simple characterization of the business need for change fails to elaborate some of the more critical issues that question the launch of a never-ending raft of change initiatives. For example, if change is so important to commercial success, how is it that there are many 'successful' companies who have spent millions on failed change initiatives? Perhaps a central question in a world where change is viewed as essential to competitive business survival is how do we identify not only when to change, but when not to change? Scanning any of the many recipe approaches does not, unsurprisingly, tell us how to identify inappropriate change programmes. Clearly what is needed is a greater understanding of the change process which goes beyond honeymoon scenarios and 'how to' recipes that prescribe a number of sequential stages (n-step manuals) integral to the successful management of change. A central aim of this book is to achieve a more balanced view by drawing on the experiences of shop floor and office employees, senior executives, plant and branch managers, supervisors, union representatives and officials, and change agents. As Nilakant and Ramnarayan (1998: 9) note in their preface:

> Given the various manifestations of change, it is not surprising that it evokes a myriad of emotions. Some find the prospect and experience of change exciting, challenging and fulfilling. Others find it daunting, stressful and unpleasant. It can cause both hope and despair. Managing change involves simultaneously managing resources, processes and emotions. This is what makes change a complicated and challenging task.

In charting the experience of change of people holding different positions and located in a range of social contexts, I provide many examples that illustrate how change can create a climate of excitement and hope; how it can fail to capture the hearts and minds of staff and instead generate apathy and ambivalence; and how the uncertainty of change can trigger anxiety and fear. In using the insights and views of those who promote, implement and adapt to change, my intention is to go beyond simple determinist arguments based on economic imperatives to a greater appreciation of the sociological dimensions of change. While the metaphor of change rider provides a useful entry point for our initial consideration of what we mean by change, we need to go beyond this notion to a broader conceptualization of the change process, one that is also able to accommodate elements such as life experience, wider contextual influences and dimensions such as gender and age. To put it simply, change does not occur in a hermetically sealed bubble; rather, choices are influenced by values and beliefs developed and modified during a lifetime of interaction with family, friends and social groups, and are constrained by socio-economic circumstances and power relations. These changes are integral to all aspects of life and may be welcomed, ignored, accepted or actively resisted. They are a part of our lived experience of change and are a central concern of this book.

PROCESSUAL RESEARCH ON CHANGE

The recounting of individual and group experience of change draws on workplace research that I have conducted over the last 20 years. Following a Ph.D. in industrial sociology, I have maintained a long-standing interest in how people experience change over time, and how the process of change is managed and shaped from the initial conception of the need to change through to a period where operating under new work arrangements becomes largely a matter of routine. This interest in the temporal element of change has resulted in a number of research projects which have studied change longitudinally. In some cases, it has been possible to follow the change process 'as-it-happens' from the decision to initiate change through to the implementation and operation of new work practices and procedures. In other studies, time constraints and access issues have limited the extent of the research. Whenever possible, a longitudinal element has been built into each research design to ensure that data can be collected on how the process of change unfolds in practice. Throughout the change process there is an ongoing series of tasks, activities and decisions. In some cases decision-making may be influenced by outside agencies and groups, such as local and national governments, professional bodies and trade unions. In others, activities and tasks may result from the plans and preparations of management and/or the views, expectations and demands of employee groups or their representatives. In addition, certain individuals may act as major facilitators or inhibitors of change and prove instrumental to the 'success' or 'failure' of programmes. In practice, it is impossible to provide a definitive list of tasks, activities and decisions implicated in the management of change. It is essential to study change processes over time to identify and examine the contextual and temporal character of change. Consequently, in the studies reported in this book a processual research approach was used whenever possible in the collection and analysis of data on employee experience of change. This made possible the collection of longitudinal data on change ('as-it-happens') rather than relying on snapshots or retrospective case study accounts.

In studying people's experience of change a combination of observation and in-depth interviewing was used to enable the cross-validation of data and the integration of contextual and temporal observations with the more perceptional and attitudinal data gathered from the interviews. Non-participant observation generally involved periods of up to 12 hours at a plant or branch office observing and informally discussing work activities with employees. The length of observations varied considerably across the case organizations and was influenced by time constraints and the extent of company access. A programme of semi-structured interviews was arranged with all participating organizations which made it possible to probe more deeply into employee experience of change. Each interview lasted between 40 minutes and three hours (typically 60–90 minutes) with the majority being taped and transcribed. Where possible, interviews and repeat interviews were held with employees at all levels from the senior executive to branch personnel.

The collection and analysis of company documents also formed a central part of the research. Internal memos and general correspondence were useful in constructing a chronology of key events and providing material on initial and subsequent proposals for workplace change. Access to confidential correspondence (including e-mail) provided a useful record of issues and historical areas of sensitivity. However, as Gill and Johnson (1991) have noted, it is important not to take such documents at face value. Political motives are often part of the hidden agenda of the writers (being written with a particular audience in mind).

Although the research design and methods did vary across the studies reported in this book, the general methods used in the collection of data were initial familiarization visits to build relations, gather basic information and agree on the study; the collection of documentary data including annual reports, company newspapers, e-mail and other company documents; observation of work activities and interactions (normally non-participative); semi-structured interviews with employees from senior executives to shop floor personnel (some cases focused more on employees at the workplace, some on senior management decision-making and strategy, and some on all levels); engagement in group discussions; what can be termed 'research by wandering around' (a lot of information was obtained through these more informal channels); and attendance at various social functions.

Although the book draws on data collected over a 22-year period (1980–2002), most is drawn from studies carried out in Australia and the UK between 1992–2002. The general intention is to provide new empirical material that uses the insights from past research in detailing the dynamic processes of change.

STRUCTURE OF THE BOOK

The book is designed for advanced undergraduate and postgraduate students in organization studies, as well as for academics and practitioners who have an interest in change management. Chapters 1 and 2 provide a historical, conceptual and theoretical overview of the key debates and frameworks in the change management literature. In Chapter 2, a number of theoretical perspectives are identified and it is shown how our theoretical position influences the way we see, understand and explain our chosen phenomenon of study. Four key dimensions are used to characterize change and a simple definition of change is put forward. The chapter also examines the triggers to organizational change; why individuals and groups resist change; and some of the general trends that shape employee experience of work.

Chapter 3 builds on this introductory material to present a historical summary of the main models and frameworks that have been developed to further our understanding of change. Many of these have arisen within a particular context and time when certain theoretical perspectives were dominant. Although context is used to explain the emergence and uptake of certain managerial ideas, it is argued that there has not been a simple replacement of one approach with another. This literature review highlights how the development of change management theories serves to emphasize the complexity and diversity of this process, and how there will always be competing frameworks and models. The essential elements of the processual approach adopted in this book are then outlined and the importance of clarifying the perspective of those studying change is stressed.

These summary chapters are necessarily selective but they provide a useful overview of perspectives and frameworks for understanding organizational change. Readers who are already familiar with this literature may wish to skip ahead to the empirical chapters that draw on new data collected in the UK and Australia. The data derive from a range of research programmes broadly concerned with the process of organizational change and how it is experienced by shop floor employees, branch personnel, supervisors, trade unionists, managers and senior company executives. In some studies I was fortunate to gain long-term access to employees ranging from the CEO to middle management and shop floor operators. In other examples, access was limited in terms of time and personnel. As a result, some chapters focus on the experience of workers while others are concerned with the implementation strategies of middle management or the development of strategic initiatives by the senior executive group.

In Chapter 4, interview data from a variety of case settings are used to draw out some of the more general as well as atypical views and experiences of change by branch personnel and shop floor workers. The intention is to examine the lived experience of change of those at the lower levels of an organization. The focus is on employee experience rather than the management of change, with attention being given to the effects of the general shift towards non-standard forms of employment. It shows how change fatigue and employee cynicism are on the increase as the rhetoric of change is, in practice, too often inconsistent with worker experience.

Chapter 5 is the first case study of change that focuses on a particular plant. The importance of customer–supplier power relations in understanding processes of change in the local reconfiguration of new technology at work is examined in the case of Dalebake Bakeries (a pseudonym). The findings illustrate how the strategic decision to invest heavily in a state-of-the-art bakery in 1991 tied the company to mass production in the face of a shift in the product market. Customer demand for a broader and more diversified product range did not match the technical configuration of the bakery (with a capacity to produce 13,000 loaves per hour). The customer – in the form of powerful supermarkets – reassessed their product demand and sought increasingly frequent product deliveries, squeezing the already narrow profit margins of Dalebake Bakeries. This chapter addresses the issues of power and customer–supplier relations as well as the need to reconsider strategy and to reinterpret the fixity of technical–structural arrangements (our concept of technology). How this is managed and the consequence of change for Dalebake Bakeries are analysed and discussed.

In Chapter 6, the place of the older worker and the role of the supervisor are examined. Once again, empirical evidence comes from older employees and supervisors working in different industries. It is shown how established supervisors (who have often worked in a company for a long time) are often inappropriately identified as barriers to change. This view can lead to a self-fulfilling prophecy whereby the supervisor who finds their authority undermined and their advice ignored actively resists these changes and thereby confirms the view held by management that s/he is a 'problem' that requires action. In exploring this myth of change management, assumptions about the inability of older supervisors to adapt to change are shown to be based not on empirical evidence, but on the commonly held views of senior management and broader social stereotyping.

Chapter 7 examines the experience and strategy of local managers in the introduction of cellular work arrangements in a company that manufactures washing machines (Washdale). The views of plant-level management highlight the hostilities and conflicts that can arise in the implementation of shop floor change. The Washdale case is a good example of how change initiatives may be used by management to eradicate traditional custom and practice. As the story progresses the sense of 'revenge' and 'management payback' is clearly illustrated. Although the company has not requested anonymity, due to the 'bloody nature' and sensitivity of some of the material a pseudonym is used.

In Chapter 8, our attention turns to the views and experiences of senior management in managing the transition from a locally-based Adelaide pharmaceutical company (F.H. Faulding & Co. Ltd) to an international corporation. The Faulding case study began in July 1997 with the aim of examining the process of managing the transition from a local organization manufacturing predominantly non-prescription pharmaceuticals to a global company manufacturing both prescription and non-prescription drugs, and distributing them to a global market. The research was carried out over a three-year period and consisted of two main parts. Part one addressed past changes by soliciting reminiscences and searching archival records. Part two addressed the present state of the company and its plans for the future. It integrated information from in-depth and repeat interviews, company documents and media reports. Essentially, documentary evidence and senior management interviews conducted over a number of years were used to capture the experience of managing strategic change from a senior executive perspective and to address the issues of growth and globalization.

A rather different and somewhat idiosyncratic methodology emerged in the trade union study on change reported in Chapter 9. The research into the Australian Services Union (ASU) was carried out in South Australia between November 1998 and January 1999 before, during and after the ASU annual convention in Adelaide. Prior to this, contact was made with the union to see if they would be willing to present material on change issues facing the ASU to students at the University of Adelaide. These frank and illuminating presentations (made in 1996 and 1997) highlighted dimensions to change management that are often absent from courses on organizational change. They also pointed to an interesting research area, one that would draw out some of the political processes of change (both internal and external) and the influence of tradition and culture on issues such as gender, change strategies and trade union amalgamation. The union made a number of documents available and provided open access to officials and members. I attended a number of social events, work dinners and branch barbecues, and was also welcomed at the branch office in Rundle Street, Adelaide. General observations and discussions were recorded as a series of notes and further questions were generated during the course of the study. Over a five-year period, contact was maintained with the union by e-mail, telephone and face-to-face discussions. The main fieldwork was conducted over two years involving taped interviews with a range of ASU members. This included the ASU National Secretary and the Secretary and Executive President, and the Senior Industrial Officer of the South Australian and Northern Territory Branch (SANTB) of the ASU. Interviews were held with industrial officers and workplace representatives (shop stewards) covering betting organizations, airlines, financial services, the automotive industry, higher education and local government. A small concluding set of interviews and discussions was conducted in Adelaide during December 2000 and November 2001.

The two main areas addressed in Chapter 9 are: the responses and strategies of trade unions in the changing business environment and workplace change initiatives; and the extent to which trade unions are themselves changing in order to renew their relevance. Linked to these broader areas are issues such as membership decline, deunionization, changing legislation, technology, shifts in the nature of employment, union organization and the barrier of male unionism to union renewal. The case of the SANTB is used to highlight some of these elements by drawing on the experience and reflections of a number of union members and officials. This trade union provides a pertinent example as it is not only having to deal with the problem of declining union membership; and a range of political changes associated with union amalgamation but is also trying to redress the tradition of male unionism through promoting the place of women. These changes are seen as both problematic and central to the development of union strategies and alternative approaches to meet the challenge of trade union renewal in the twenty-first century.

Chapter 10 investigates the long-standing corporate and political concern with quality management. Data are drawn from a TQM research programme that was carried out over a period of three years between 1989 and 1992. It involved detailed case studies on the introduction and effects of TQM in eight Australian and New Zealand organizations. The main methods used were in-depth interviews with key personnel; management, union and shop floor interviews; participant and non-participant observation; and document analysis. A longitudinal element was built into the research strategy and where practicable repeat interviews have been carried out at a number of stages during the process of organizational transformation. Each interview lasted approximately 60 to 90 minutes and covered topics such as the spread of TQM and the influence of change agents, the employment and industrial relations implications of change and the process of change. The interview schedule used in the study is outlined in the Appendix.

Data from the case studies are used to draw attention to the variety of change reforms under the label of TQM and to highlight the importance of context in understanding the scope and nature of change. The degree to which these programmes brought about a change in culture, enabled employees to be more empowered, or simply imposed heavy layers of bureaucracy on existing work practices is critically appraised. I argue that quality management cannot be captured in a simple definition and that this ambiguity has enabled it to endure over time. In practice quality management ideas have been variously adopted and shaped within the context in which they exist. The chapter concludes by presenting some practical lessons on the management of organizational change.

The final chapter uses the views developed in the main body of the text to discuss the lived experience of change in the twenty-first century. The management of strategic change and the views of senior executives, the implementation of change initiatives by divisional and plant managers, worker and supervisor experience of change, and their views – all raise interesting questions about change processes and what the future holds for work, employment and society. The chapter examines the tendency for commentators to focus on either negative or positive possibilities, and identifies five interrelated elements on the future of change. This is followed by a critique of recipe approaches in which it is argued that there is a need to go beyond stories of 'success' in order to fully appreciate and understand change. Some of the practical lessons on change – based on the data analysed in previous chapters – are identified. The chapter concludes with a reaffirmation of the need for a broader conception of organizational change, one that is able to accommodate the complex and dynamic nature of change.

CONCLUSION

For many business writers, an organization's ability to manage change is seen as central to its competitive position and ultimate survival, even though the majority of change initiatives fail. What does this tell us? For a start, it indicates that the assumption that change per se is a good thing needs to be challenged and critically appraised. It is ironic that the more we study change, the less we seem to learn. The popularity of shortcut answers testifies to the short-sighted character of many change management decisions. Long-haul frameworks that do not provide neat solutions to complex problems may be far less attractive and easy to package, but they do offer more insight into the process of change. In this book, I argue that a processual perspective provides a framework that can contribute to both our theoretical and practical understanding of change, as well as highlighting areas that require further study.

One such area is how the continuing barrage of change initiatives may heighten employee concerns and lower staff morale. In such an environment (not uncommon in many companies today), employees may become disillusioned and wearied by an ongoing torrent of change programmes and feel unable to shape change processes or engage in any meaningful discussions about the future direction of their areas of operation. Healthy critical reflection may turn to tongue-in-cheek cynicism and act as a barrier to change. This is more than a change management problem. Company employees are an important source of knowledge and their expertise should be used in shaping processes of change. By using employees rather than treating them as 'barriers', the expertise for change can be developed within the company rather than being the remit of an external change consultant or an internal project implementation team. By increasing their knowledge about change processes, employees would be better able to question and debate consultant change packages, reconfigure initiatives to meet local conditions, and develop their own potential skills as change agents. In developing local expertise and a culture of critical reflection, the appropriateness of change programmes can be evaluated and greater control over change (and importantly when not to change) can be achieved. Staff would not feel overwhelmed by the velocity, variability and personal vulnerability consequent on manifold change projects. Rather, they could assess the value of the change and take an active role in the redesign, abandonment and/or development of projects and by so doing actively influence change processes. Although this is only one area that requires further consideration, investigation and debate, there are many other change management myths and assumptions that deserve further attention. In the following chapters, some of these concerns are raised and discussed by drawing on the first-hand experience of people in work and employment.

Dimensions of change 2

Over the last 100 years a range of theories has emerged on how to manage change and organize work, this large body of knowledge has not provided any lasting answers. Perhaps the simple lesson is that there can never be a universal theory of organizational change, as change involves a movement to some future state that comprises a context and time that remain unknown. Even attempts to explain change 'after-the-event' remain partial and open to further revision as people seek to influence reconstructed accounts. Although the search for a theory that fully explains change may not be feasible, there is still great value in developing frameworks that further our understanding of change processes and the consequence of change for people's experience of work. While there may be little debate about the importance of change as an issue facing unions, employees, managers and change agents, there remains considerable debate about the speed, direction and effect of change, and about the most appropriate methods and concepts for understanding and explaining change. A central objective of this book is not to offer a further set of managerial prescriptions on how to 'successfully' implement change, but rather to provide insights into different lived experiences of change; to examine the way change unfolds in practice (including accounts of the harsh realities of change and not just *post hoc* 'success' stories); to provide a broader understanding of the nature and character of workplace change; to derive strategies and practical lessons on living with change (outwith the normal managerial 'how to' approach); and to provide a framework for making sense of and explaining the change process. But first, it is important to address the question: What do we understand by the term 'organizational change'?

PERSPECTIVES ON ORGANIZATIONAL CHANGE

At its simplest, organizational change can be defined as new ways of organizing and working, but as we shall see, much more is tied up with the concept of organizational change than this simple definition might at first suggest. As a growing area of study, organizational change has many of its theoretical roots in organization theory. For example, the conceptual developments of a number of modern management initiatives (such as knowledge management, the learning organization and best practice management) draw on an existing body of social science research to formulate 'new' approaches to change management. An essential concern is how best to organize the activities of employees to ensure that the goods or services provided by the company have a value in the market place. The pursuit of profit by private sector firms and the push for 'service excellence' by many public sector organizations oblige management to identify and implement new ways of organizing and working that can best harness employees' capacity to work. Typically, it is not simply the quantity of work that is important but also the quality. Where raw materials account for a high percentage of total operating costs, knowing when not to work (as in Just-In-Time [JIT] management) and when to tackle a recurring operational problem can be more important than the quantity of output (as evident under the old mass manufacturing piece-rate payment systems). Winning the hearts and minds of employees has also been seen as an important element in ensuring a committed and productive workforce. Different theories and change initiatives have emerged to tackle these issues. Among others, there has been a focus on formal structural arrangements (the technical organization of work); an interest in the effects of political processes and power relations on workplace behaviour (the political aspects of work); and an interest in shaping workplace beliefs and values (the cultural dimensions of work). As Rose (1988: 11) argues in his account of the most influential approaches to industrial behaviour in the organization and control of work:

> Methods of control may often work to produce among workers a sense of attachment to the workplace . . . some employers make strenuous and often sophisticated efforts to gain the positive consent of workers to the economic system, and to transform their reaction to being managed. But all techniques for controlling work behaviour embody an attempt to shape the experience of paid employment by influencing the meanings, values and sentiments given to work by workers, as well as programming and disciplining their behaviour directly through work organization and supervision.

Early theories often stressed the importance of goal-directed rational decision-making. Reed (1989) refers to this as the technical–theoretical perspective, where management is viewed as an instrumental tool, a means to obtain the efficiencies needed to achieve organizational goals. Although many adherents of this 'rational decision-making' approach now recognize that decision-making is often constrained (bounded rationality) by 'the information-processing capacities of the actor' (Simon, 1972: 162); by the extent to which decisions become institutionalized (Meyer and Rowan, 1977); and that the bounds of rationality may shift as new technologies or initiatives emerge, it nevertheless maintains a rather 'technical' and formal view of management. According to this perspective, managers may access various situational variables (contextual factors) to make rational decisions on their change management strategy for the purpose of achieving increased organizational efficiency and company performance. Morgan's (1997) organizational metaphor of a machine and Bolman and Deal's (1991) structural perspective are also related to these ideas.

This technical–bureaucratic perspective has been contrasted with a political perspective (see Dawson and Palmer, 1995) that recognizes the importance of 'the negotiating processes through which organizational structures are reproduced, are shaped by, and in turn shape, the prevailing pattern of power relations within an organization' (Reed, 1989: 8). Morgan (1997) describes those who adopt this political image of organization as emphasizing the importance of conflict and competition, particularly in understanding the way groups with different interests and values seek certain preferred outcomes from change initiatives. Unlike the previous perspective – where power is explained as formal and legitimate authority, associated with position, rationally determined objectives and organizational rules – the political approach does not assume that organizational objectives are unambiguous, or that those at the top of the hierarchy automatically have the political resources they need to implement change. A political perspective on management focuses on power relations and the processes involved in establishing and negotiating positions, and in gaining support for different policies. It looks for a plurality of interests and assumes that different interest groups will have a variety of resources with which to press their claims.

Another perspective on management, which has been fairly influential on change initiatives over the last two decades, is concerned with culture. A cultural perspective emphasizes moral order. Instead of management being concerned with establishing systems of bureaucratic administration or political accommodation, managers of culture are involved in the construction of moral systems of meaning and value (as encompassed by Bolman and Deal's [1991] symbolic frame of reference). During the 1990s, prescriptions for managing or changing organizational culture became a major feature of management thinking (Brown, 1995a). These prescriptions emphasize the importance of creating supportive, positive cultures that underscore organizational rather than sectional goals (Kanter, 1985, 1990; Peters and Waterman, 1982). In some cases, such as in the uptake of quality management programmes, these changes have been bolstered by prestigious quality awards, the development of national and international quality agencies, and the support of governments.

Each of these three perspectives (the technical–bureaucratic, the political and the cultural) provides a different lens through which we may examine company change and may direct our attention to certain key features or processes. As Jaffee (2001: 19) has indicated in his own threefold distinction between the contemporary sociological perspectives of functionalism, conflict theory and symbolic interactionism:

Functionalism highlights the functions played by parts of a single organization in advancing organizational survival as well as the functions played by different

Political Perspective

Cultural Perspective

social institutions in ensuring social order. Conflict theory denotes the competition and conflict among groups in organizations who struggle over valued resources. Symbolic interactionism directs our attention to the symbolic messages that are transmitted among organizational members and between organizations and environmental constituents.

In examining a range of theoretical frameworks, Collins (1998) also categorizes a number of perspectives and critically evaluates their contribution to understanding change. He criticizes top-down consensus-oriented views of the 'guru managers' and 'celebrity professors', and calls for greater attention to a more reflective bottom-up view which is able to deal with the complexity of the change process. He suggests that a way should be found between over-socialized models of change (which focus on culture change and the means to manage the attitudes and beliefs of diverse groups) and under-socialized models of change (which represent change as a rational response to economic and market forces). In discussing the latter, standard criticisms are levelled against its advocates who put forward an overly rational and prescriptive view on the management of planned change which is largely acontextual and apolitical. In his discussion of over-socialized models, Collins (1998) begins with a summary of the 'soft' Human Resource Management (HRM) approach (flexibility, quality and commitment) and suggests that 'competitive' HRM strategies (taken up by managers and business consultants) have drawn heavily on the culture literature. He pays particular attention to the work of Schein (1985), which he criticizes for presenting both an over-socialized and rather static psychological model in which culture is defined as a type of 'collective mental programming'. In drawing on the work of Pettigrew (1985), Dawson (1994), McLoughlin and Clark (1994) and Storey (1992), Collins provides a positive appraisal of theoretical models which can accommodate the contextual dynamics of change and move beyond 'single-shot studies' in providing historical processual accounts. Four prerequisites are outlined for this type of study: multi-level analyses (individual, group, organization, society); the need to study change over time (past, present and future); the importance of agency (action occurs within bounded social processes); and the integration of multi-level (contextual) analysis with horizontal (historical) analysis. In rejecting simple prescriptive models of change and celebrating frameworks that can accommodate the murky and sometimes contradictory nature of change, Collins usefully supports the value of processually informed and reflective approaches to the study of change. (This is the perspective I have adopted, although it should be noted that Collins is critical of any attempt to present guidelines or lessons on change as this book does.) As we shall see in Chapter 3, the perspective adopted by researchers directs attention to certain key elements of organizations which in turn shapes the development of change frameworks. But one area in which there is general agreement is on the drivers of change, which are seen to comprise some combination of factors that reside within a company and outwith organizations in the external business environment.

THE TRIGGERS TO ORGANIZATIONAL CHANGE

A range of 'triggers' to organizational change have been identified in the literature. They consist of elements both within and outside an organization. Some of the main external factors are:

- government laws and regulations (for example, legislation on age discrimination, world agreements and national policies on pollution and the environment, international agreements on tariffs and trade);
- globalization of markets and the internationalization of business (the need to accommodate new competitive pressures both in the home market and overseas);
- major political and social events (for example, September 11, the widespread European uptake of the euro in January 2002 and ongoing tensions between countries);
- advances in technology (for example, companies who specialize in high-technology products often encounter technological obsolescence and the need to introduce new technology);
- organizational growth and expansion (as an organization increases in size so may the complexity of the organization, requiring the development of appropriate coordinating mechanisms); and
- fluctuations in business cycles (for example, changes in the level of economic activity both within national economies and within major trading blocks).

Four internal triggers to change that are generally identified (Leavitt, 1964) are:

- technology (for example, in the uptake of video-conferencing, robotic technology or the computerization of management accounting and information systems);
- primary task (for example, in shifting away from the main product or service of a company into a new major field of core business);
- people (for example, in the development and implementation of new human resource management initiatives or through programmes of retraining and multi-skilling in the movement towards team-based work arrangements); and
- administrative structures (for example, in restructuring work and redefining authority relationships in the uptake of new forms of work organization such as best practice management and cell-based manufacturing).

Technology can be both an external and internal trigger to change. Within organizations, the term 'technology' can be used broadly to refer to the plant, machinery and tools, and the associated philosophy and system of work organization, which blend together in the production of goods or services. A change in an organization's technology may involve the installation of a single piece of equipment or the complete redesign of a production process. The primary task of an organization refers to its core business, whether this is providing a health service, refining oil or developing computer software. People (human resources) refers to the individual members and groups of people who constitute an organization. Administrative structures refer to elements pertaining to the administrative control of work, such as formalized lines of communication, established working procedures, managerial hierarchies, reward systems and disciplinary procedures. Essentially, both external and internal factors link and overlap in determining the speed, direction and outcomes of change.

THE CONCEPT OF ORGANIZATIONAL CHANGE

Although we can identify triggers to change, the question of how we differentiate types of change remains open to debate. At a general level, we could formulate a definition of organizational change that encompasses all aspects of change within any form of organization. Under such a broad definition, change initiatives could range from corporate restructuring and the replacement of key personnel through to the minor modification of basic operating procedures. One problem that arises from these commonsense definitions is that organizational change is not differentiated from the more general study of organizations. In other words, the study of organizational change becomes virtually the study of organizations. As already indicated, for our purposes a simple definition of organizational change is 'new ways of organizing and working'. However, this tells us little about the nature of the change in question. For example, should we differentiate between an individual's decision to use an electronic diary that is networked into the main office computer and the decision of a large corporation to delayer and downsize all major operations worldwide?

In tackling this conceptual problem and moving beyond lay definitions, academics have sought to identify a number of defining characteristics of organizational change. Although this has resulted in the development of competing conceptual frameworks, two common dimensions run through a number of these more sophisticated characterizations. They represent movement over time from a present state of organization to a future state (Beckhard and Harris, 1987) and they tackle the scale or scope of change (Dunphy and Stace, 1990). The main focus of this second dimension has been on the more permanent, influential, large-scale operational and strategic changes (Burnes, 2000). In examining these forms of organizational change the question arises as to whether change outcomes have been brought about through a rapid transformation or more incrementally over a longer period of time (Quinn, 1980). According to Buchanan and Badham (1999), strategies for

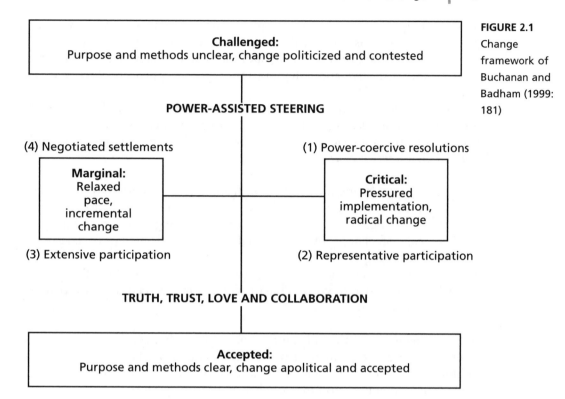

FIGURE 2.1
Change framework of Buchanan and Badham (1999: 181)

extensive participation may be used under apolitical programmes of incremental change as change is then accepted and occurs at a more relaxed pace. They argue that whether change is generally accepted or challenged is a central dimension and a key determinant of the type of strategy required to successfully manage the process. For example, they claim that radical change programmes, which are critical to the survival of the company and yet are highly politicized and contested, will need to be forcefully driven. They note that any form of contested change will necessitate political activity in dealing with opponents and building support for the initiative (Buchanan and Badham, 1999: 180–1).

By incorporating this third political dimension of change, the authors put forward a model that suggests that the degree of political intensity will vary under different settings and with different types of change initiatives. In their framework (see Figure 2.1), they argue that managing change in Quadrant 1 (where change is critical to survival but challenged) is likely to require power-coercive solutions. This form of radical change – which has wide implications and has to be managed fairly swiftly – is contrasted with marginal incremental change where there is time to negotiate disagreements and concerns (Quadrant 4). In both cases the authors identify the need for what they term 'power-assisted steering'. They further claim that change that is broadly accepted (whether radical or incremental) can be introduced in a more participative manner. If change is marginal, extensive participation is possible. If change is critical, then a strategy of representative participation may prove more appropriate. In Quadrants 2 and 3 they suggest what they term 'truth, trust, love and collaboration' types of approach (Buchanan and Badham, 1999: 181–1).

This model is similar to that advocated by Dunphy and Stace (1990) discussed in more detail in Chapter 3, although in this case political process is central to the approach. To summarize, the three dimensions that can be used to characterize change are:

1 The temporal element of transition from a present state to a future state (movement from A to B and the timeframe of change, for example, whether change is to occur quickly or over a longer period of time).
2 The scale of change (whether small incremental change or large-scale radical change).
3 The political dimension of change (whether change is generally accepted as being central and worthwhile or whether it is perceived as a threat and hence challenged).

A final dimension is the substantive element of change. This refers to the essential nature and content of the change in question. For example, are we talking about a cultural change programme, the introduction of new technology or the implementation of a quality assurance system?

In the literature, it is often some combination of these four dimensions that is used to define and classify organizational change. However, the dimensions that have been stressed and developed by authors vary considerably and, as a consequence, considerable debate and some conceptual confusion can occur. This is further exacerbated when certain elements of new theories and concepts are taken up by consultants in their drive to meet the growing demand for business solutions. As a result, the last decade has witnessed a mushrooming of consultants and consultant firms who variously modify, refine and repackage change concepts and theories. If they are successful in popularizing their change initiatives, then the high visibility of these programmes (especially if supported by government funding and taken up by large multinational corporations) can stimulate more widespread implementation. In practice, some of the consultant packages may differ considerably from the concepts and theories that were used in the initial formulation of the model. New change initiatives are often transformed from initial conceptualization, through to popularization, consultant or change agent modification, and eventual adaptation during implementation and uptake. A key area which many of these models address or attempt to offer solutions to centres on managing the people aspects of change and, in particular, overcoming resistance to change and winning the hearts and minds of employees. In the section below, the unwillingness of employees to accept change is briefly discussed. A more detailed discussion of change models and perspectives is then taken up in Chapter 3.

WHY DO PEOPLE RESIST ORGANIZATIONAL CHANGE?

One of the main reasons why people resist company change initiatives is that the proposed change may break the continuity of a working environment and create a climate of uncertainty and ambiguity. Under modern change initiatives it is not uncommon for old established relationships to be redefined, for familiar structures to be redesigned and modified, and for traditional methods of work to be replaced or modified. Understandably, some employees may seek to maintain the status quo and resist these changes. Typically, resistance has been identified as resulting from one, or a combination, of the following factors:

- substantive change in job (change in skill requirements);
- reduction in economic security or job displacement (threat to employment);
- psychological threat (whether perceived or actual);
- disruption of social arrangements (new work arrangements); and
- lowering of status (redefinition of authority relationships).

A substantive change in the nature of work and the skills required to perform certain functions is likely to engender distrust and resistance, particularly in situations where employees are not informed of the change prior to implementation. Even if these threats reflect an individual's perception of change rather than an actual threat, employee resistance is likely to result. Bedeian (1984) suggests that parochial self-interest, misunderstanding and lack of trust are common causes of resistance to organizational change. In addition, he notes that individuals differ in the way they perceive and evaluate change, and that some employees may have a lower tolerance for change (see also Carnall, 1999: 208–11).

In examining the reasons why employees resist change, Eccles (1994) identifies 13 possible causes. These are:

1 Failure to understand the problem.
2 The solution is disliked because an alternative is preferred.
3 A feeling that the proposed solution will not work.
4 The change has unacceptable personal costs.
5 Rewards are not sufficient.
6 Fear of being unable to cope with the new situation.
7 The change threatens to destroy existing social arrangements.
8 Sources of influence and control will be eroded.
9 New values and practices are repellent.
10 The willingness to change is low.
11 Management motives for change are considered suspicious.
12 Other interests are more highly valued than the new proposals.
13 The change will reduce power and career opportunities.

According to Collins (1998), there is a tendency for writers on change management to view employee resistance as a negative individual problem rather than a positive response to changing conditions that might require further consideration. As he states:

> Workers who 'resist' change tend to be cast as lacking the psychological make-up to deal with change, and so are said to be weak and fearful of change, whereas, those who support or manage change are regarded as 'go-ahead' chaps who have the 'right-stuff' for career success. (1998: 92)

It is perhaps ironic that, given the number of failed change initiatives, those who question the need for change are often cast as the villains of the piece, as 'unable' to adapt to the dynamic changing conditions of the modern world. Although change is an integral element within business organizations, change for change's sake, or to service the career agendas of certain individuals or groups, can result in employee cynicism and mistrust. It is as important to recognize when not to change as it is to identify when there is a need for change. This is perhaps one of the major myths that pervades the literature on change management – that, as changes are inevitable, change initiatives should not be questioned but embraced, as they are ultimately vital to the success of an organization. This approach can prove fatal to a company where inappropriate, large-scale strategic changes are enthusiastically endorsed and implemented by management. It is important to reflect critically on the need and reasons for change, and to take into account the concerns of others rather than to assume that, as resistance is inevitable, the reasons why people resist change should be ignored. There are many assumptions and dangerous myths about change that derive from particular examples which should not be generalized to all situations.

As will become evident from the case study chapters, major organizational change often takes years to achieve and during that time there will inevitably be casualties – those who feel disgruntled and hard done by by the change – as well as a range of other responses and positions. Although the champions of successful change are often hailed as the enthusiastic heroes and leaders of change, for those who lose their jobs or find their positions undermined it is a different story (some of these stories are told in the empirical chapters). However, for change agents who seek to overcome resistance to change, a number of strategies have been identified in the literature. Typically, these centre on participation, communication and support at one end of a continuum through to negotiation, manipulation and coercion at the other. As we shall see, change initiatives that adopt an organizational development approach have tended to opt for more participative methods, whereas those following a contingency perspective (and the power-assisted steering model of Buchanan and Badham) recognize the need for more coercive strategies when circumstances dictate. Some of the consequences of employee resistance are explored in Chapter 6, where acrimonious relations ensued between management and a particular group of workers. But before examining some of these lived experiences, the brief section that follows summarizes some of the major shifts that are occurring in the ways in which work is organized and in the growing emphasis on 'flexibility'.

FLEXIBILITY: IN SEARCH OF NEW WAYS OF ORGANIZING AND WORKING

In examining the change process, it is possible to identify in the literature some of the more common organizational trends that are shaping employees' experience of work. Although by no means an exhaustive list, these include:

- the movement from a union-based system of collective bargaining to a more individual contract-based system of employee relations;
- the uptake of management change initiatives that seek to secure employee participation and commitment;
- the delayering and downsizing of organizations with a concomitant devolution of control responsibility to employees for aspects of industrial engineering;
- outsourcing operations and developing flexible labour strategies (often involving the increasing use of part-time, temporary and casual labour);
- the replacement of demarcated single operator tasks with multi-skilled team activities;
- a move towards the more effective use of human resources, and especially 'knowledge workers';
- capitalizing on workforce diversity as part of new human resource management initiatives; and
- the adoption of new technology to reduce costs, improve the control of operational processes and increase output.

These trends often imply change towards an upskilling of work through the development of multi-skilled, 'empowered' team players; the redefinition of supervision from a policing to a coaching role; greater flexibility and choice (for example, in enabling employees to choose non-standard employment to meet family needs); and a general movement from an 'adversarial' to a 'collaborative' system of employee relations as staff negotiate their conditions of work directly with their employer (or management representative) rather than through a union representative. In practice, however, these changes have not resulted in a simple upskilling of work, a straightforward change in the role of the supervisor, a simple life-enhancing choice for workers of the type of job they require, or the general emergence of a new, enlightened, harmonious workplace. On the contrary, the context of decreasing job security through downsizing strategies (Littler and Bramble, 1995: 47–8), the decline in union membership (*Australian*, 1995: 24; Tingle, 1995: 17), the growth in part-time and casual employment (Bradley et al., 2000: 54) and the sudden demise of companies or the closing of divisional or branch operations does not present an environment conducive to an improved working experience. As *The Economist* (1996: 28) reported, in a context whereby 'the life expectancy of the average Fortune 500 company is 40 years (and shrinking), and in which giants such as AT&T celebrate a new year by sacking 40,000 people, employees might find a better focus than companies for their feelings of loyalty'.

This rapid shift in the fortunes of companies has continued in the twentieth and twenty-first centuries (as witnessed by the rise and fall of dot.com companies) and has led many organizations to search for new ways to improve their flexibility and adaptability to changing market conditions. It is perhaps not unreasonable to state that flexibility is a central driver of company change in the twenty-first century. Typically, the language of flexibility is tied to notions of goodness, adaptability and open-mindedness, while inflexibility is associated with old ideas of traditional thinking, rigidity and recalcitrant employees. It is assumed that organizations must be malleable and quick to adapt to global markets that are characterized by fast-flowing change and innovation (Jaffee, 2001: 151). This assumed need for flexibility and change defines as unreasonable any attempts by employees to resist such initiatives. In such a landscape, the supporters of change are generally cast as the 'good guys' and those who resist are often viewed as 'bad' or obstinate, even when the outcomes of change result in an overall deterioration of employees' experience of work. Although the constituent elements of much of the work restructuring currently underway are seen to represent a movement towards the development of multi-skilled, self-regulatory work groups that liaise with teamwork supervisors and facilitators on the shop floor (Clark, 1995a), empirical evidence also highlights how the pursuit of 'flexibility' may bring about an increase in both job insecurity and the intensity of work (Baldry et al., 1998; Burchell, 2000; Turnbull, 1988). As a report on the experience of an aircraft dispatcher captured in a newspaper article spotlights, the demands of flexible work arrangements can severely disrupt the work–life balance:

> The biggest problem is the shifts, which change at a moment's notice. There are early shifts (from 6 a.m. to 2 p.m.) and lates (2 p.m. to 10 p.m.) but those times alter according to flight patterns. . . . Basically this is a job where you're given no flexibility but expected to give plenty yourself. It's impossible to plan any private life because of the shifts. We're constantly reminded we're expendable. (Spence, 2001: 28)

In replacing neo-Taylorist or Fordist-type work structures (such as the machine-paced manufacturing assembly line) with a more flexible model of management practice (see, for example, Storey, 1994; Thompson and Warhurst, 1998), the rhetoric of this new method of work organization emphasizes the importance of worker involvement, multi-skilling and a team approach to production and process work tasks (Oliver and Wilkinson, 1988; Procter and Mueller, 2000). The team approach involves shop floor employees in elements of industrial engineering which, in turn, influences worker involvement through placing greater emphasis on the quality rather than simply the quantity of output (Dawson and Palmer, 1995). In conjunction with other changes, such as the push for quality management, cellular work arrangements, business process re-engineering, best practice management and lean manufacturing (see Harrison and Samson, 1997), these changes raise serious questions about teamwork, supervision and management control (Garraham and Stewart, 1991, 1992). In the US (Womack et al., 1990), the UK (Oliver and Wilkinson, 1988) and Australia (Dawson, 1994), the adoption of these management concepts has been ongoing during the last two decades, but whether they result in 'greater empowerment for workers' (Hammer and Champy, 1993: 53) or in a 'deterioration in the quality of work' remains contentious (see, for example, Thompson and Warhurst, 1998). As Knights and Willmott (2000: 11) have suggested:

> the kind of empowerment envisioned by BPR [Business Process Re-engineering] is seen to involve a form of false charity: 'charity' because it seeks to bestow the gift of greater discretion and involvement upon employees; and 'false' because it is motivated less by any concern to reduce the hierarchical relations of authority than it is by a calculation that such a change will engender enhanced performance and profitability. The employee is expected, in a self-disciplined manner, to respond enthusiastically to new responsibilities.

In the management literature, flexibility has been a central concept and has been used in a number of ways (see, for example, Atkinson, 1984; Atkinson and Meager, 1986; Clutterbuck, 1985; NEDO, 1986). Handy (1984, 1994) has used the term 'shamrock organization' to refer to three broad groups of workers (corresponding to the three leaves of a shamrock). He uses the term 'core worker' to refer to those who carry out key activities and who readily adapt to change. 'Peripheral worker' refers to those who generally carry out less central tasks and are employed on contracts which allow for the rapid adjustment of numbers. The third category, 'external worker', refers to those who are employed on a part-time basis as required. A key feature of shamrock organizations is their small size in relation to productive output; this is achieved by investment in labour-saving technologies and the use of outsourcing strategies. Under such conditions, the management of human resources is far simpler as the contractual fringe is no longer directly employed on standard contracts. It is argued that the well-paid core with good benefits and operating conditions supports rapid adjustment, whereas,

> the rest are all scattered in different organizations or their own homes, often linked through sophisticated communication systems. Such organizations, with their flexibility and skills, are well suited to the provision of high-performance products and services to demanding and rapidly changing markets. The beauty of it all, as Handy argues, is that they do not have to employ all of the people all of the time or even in the same place to get the work done. (Burnes, 2000: 112)

In examining an agenda of issues for flexible labour and non-standard employment, Felstead and Jewson (1999: 7) note how opinions are divided about whether flexible labour practices are simply supporting poorly-paid unsocial forms of work, or whether these human resource strategies offer desirable forms of employment for those who want to fit work around family commitments. As will be discussed in Chapter 4, the push for change initiatives in the name of competitive survival may sometimes do little to improve the position of the company and can prove damaging to employees' experience of work. Consequently, careful thought should be given to change initiatives that have the potential to worsen employee relations. Some studies have also shown how, in situations where flexibility is valued more highly than commitment and loyalty (Brannen et al., 2000), employees are likely to resist any further attempts to introduce change. In the case of teamworking, Procter and Mueller (2000) suggest that employees may feel an 'abuse of flexibility' if change is accompanied by some form of downsizing that intensifies work. Employees know that although flexibility suits the company, it may render staff more interchangeable and leave them in a weaker position in terms of job security while also increasing their work responsibilities. Under such circumstances, employee resistance to change is understandable, but what is less clear is why change per se is deemed a good thing.

CONCLUSION

This chapter has provided a basic introduction to organizational change. A simple definition of new ways of organizing and working was put forward and the way theoretical perspectives influence how we view change was also addressed. The structural (rational decision-making), bureaucratic (technical) and cultural (symbolic) perspectives on management were each shown to provide a different lens through which we may view organizational change. A more processually informed and reflective approach is advocated, one that takes into account the political and contradictory nature of change, and the contextual and historical traditions from which change emerges. On the issue of triggers to organizational change, it was argued that, while there is general agreement that a number of internal and external factors drive change, their relative importance remains open to debate. In the process of characterizing different types of change initiative, four common dimensions in the literature were identified: the temporal transition from a present state of organization to some future state, the scale of change, acceptability of change (politics), and the substantive element of change. In developing change models, various elements of these dimensions have been combined and there remains considerable disagreement over the importance of various factors in understanding change (some of these are discussed in more detail in Chapter 3).

In addressing the issue of why people resist change, a number of possible causes were outlined. The common tendency to view employee resistance as a 'problem' was questioned because it assumes that change is by itself a good thing. In practice, there may be very good reasons why a company should not introduce change. However, employees who supported any form of change were generally viewed positively (as innovative and forward looking) while the motives of those who resisted change were often questioned and viewed negatively (behind the times thinkers who need replacing). These everyday assumptions can misdirect and blinker the way we approach and make sense of change; it is therefore important to reflect critically on our own position when evaluating how we interpret change.

The final section of this chapter drew attention to the notion of 'flexibility' as a central concept to understanding the experience of change in the twenty-first century. Flexibility has been used in a number of different ways, including flexible operational arrangements (rapid adjustment to new product or service demands); flexible multi-skilled employees (rapidly re-deployed and/or retrained staff); and contract flexibility (quick adjustment to the number of temporary staff, and the use of contract and part-time employees). Whether these new forms of flexibility simply service the new business economy or whether the growth in non-standard employment offers desirable alternatives to people who wish to fit work around family commit-ments remains a contentious issue, although a number of studies have highlighted the trend towards greater job insecurity and more intensive forms of work. Whatever position one takes, it is clear that significant changes are occurring in the world of work and employment, and that flexibility is often a central element of this change.

3

A historical overview of theoretical perspectives and change frameworks

A limestone pyramid built by Khufu (Cheops) in *c*.2580 BC provides the evidence of early developments and innovations in work practices utilized in the construction of a 480-foot stone tomb in Egypt. These Egyptian workers were not slaves but engaged in sacred employment (being free to farm at other times). They believed that such work would ensure the continuance of social order and peace after the death of their Pharaoh (who would accompany the Sun God in a new life). The dominant values and norms that governed behaviour in this early society help us to speculate about worker involvement in pyramid construction by providing important contextual clues about the nature of Egyptian society at this time. Similarly, in charting a brief history of organizations since the Industrial Revolution (*c*.1730–1850) and the transition from a mainly agricultural society to an industrial economy (late nineteenth and twentieth centuries), to what Bell (1973) has termed post-industrialism (late twentieth and early twenty-first centuries), contextual elements are crucial in helping us to understand processes of change. From early systems of sub-contracting, to the establishment of textile factories and steel works, to the more recent developments in computer and information technologies, change has been central to the employee experience of working in organizations. This historical period (*c*.1750 to the present) has also been marked by major political and social changes in the relationships among nations, in our attitudes to work and the family, in culture and the way we make sense of the world. In this chapter, a number of frameworks for understanding change are discussed and the key dimensions to the processual approach adopted in this book are outlined.

CHANGE AND THE INDUSTRIAL REVOLUTION

During the early phases of industrialization considerable emphasis was placed on the structure of organizations and on the effective utilization of machinery. The new industrial entrepreneurs decided the type, speed and direction of change, and were often authoritarian in their approach. Many were inventors and industrialists, such as Richard Arkwright who established a mill in Nottingham that used his water-powered spinning frame. Steam was the basic source of power for mechanization (Thomas Newcombe built the first usable steam engine in 1712, then considerably improved in 1781 by James Watt). The harnessing of steam power to newly invented machines enabled rapid improvements in productive output. The abundance of rich mineral resources, particularly coal and iron ore, led to the construction of bridges and canals, the building of ships and the development of railways. George Stephenson built the first practical railroad locomotive in 1829 and his famous *Rocket* could travel at 36 mph. New industrial towns developed around Glasgow, Newcastle, Manchester and Birmingham, and new forms of industrial organization were imposed on workers in these growing urban centres. In its infancy, the Industrial Revolution offered wealth to the new industrial owners and hardship to working families who often suffered long hours and poor working conditions for little pay. Rapid urbanization brought with it many social problems. Prior to the Factory Act 1833, many – including children – suffered under the abuses of workplace factory regimes. During this time, employees had little say in the changes imposed on them by owner-managers except through forms of resistance, such as industrial sabotage.

Throughout the nineteenth century workshop relations were dominated by a system of internal contracts of three main types (Littler, 1982: 64–79). First, the familial system where, for example, skilled spinners in the cotton industry were put in charge of machines and required to recruit their own assistants, who were generally their own children. Second, the master craftsman system, where a skilled craftsman recruited workers, organized production, determined hours and rates of pay and forms of discipline. Third, the gang boss system, associated with the docks and coal mines, where the 'ganger' had responsibilities similar to the master craftsmen, although his position was far more precarious because it was based on the employer–ganger personal relationship rather than on craft skill. Typically, the internal contractor or piece-master would undertake a certain project at a given price, receiving the difference between the stipulated rate and the costs in the form of a profit or loss (Hobsbawm, 1964: 298). The leading hand or master craftsman was normally responsible for the pace of work and the behaviour of the workers (Melling, 1980: 183–221). These 'overseers' were regarded as 'undisputed masters' and had the authority to hire and fire, set wages and plan the allocation of work (Child, 1975: 72).

By the 1870s the use of sub-contractors was in sharp decline and, by the turn of the century the directly employed foremen and forewomen had largely replaced the internal contractor (Littler, 1982: 86). In most work-places, with the possible exception of those employing large groups of craftsmen, such as in the male-dominated printing and building trades, the traditional supervisor held an 'undisputed' position of power and authority over shop floor workers. The major difference between the internal contractors and the traditional supervisors was that the supervisors did not employ their own labour; their main source of income was in the form of wages. The role of the supervisor was carried out internally within the organization rather than externally through sub-contractors. The change in the duties of the supervisor was complex. Essentially, contractors either became integrated within the organizational structure as directly employed foremen or forewomen, or they became leading hands (the next level down in the formal hierarchy) answerable to supervisors, or they became 'submerged workgroup leaders' (Littler, 1982: 86–8).

SCIENTIFIC MANAGEMENT AND CHANGE

With the growth of factories, new methods for organizing work were adopted which followed the early division of labour principles put forward by Adam Smith (1776) in *The Wealth of Nations*. Smith used the well-known example of pin-making to demonstrate how by allocating tasks (an employee would constantly perform one simple task rather than doing all the tasks required to make a pin), output could be significantly increased. These ideas were taken up by pioneering factory owners such as James Watt, Matthew Boulton and Josiah Wedgewood (Burnes, 1992: 8). Smith's ideas were further developed by Babbage (1835) and Taylor (1911). The latter was to have the most significant influence on approaches to the organization and control of work. Taylor championed the application of the scientific method to the study, analysis and solution of organizational problems. He believed that through systematic time and motion studies it would be possible to identify the most efficient way of performing a task. He took into account the tools used, physical characteristics of workers, physical motions employed, time taken and the type of material or machine being used. As Taylor states:

> Under scientific management absolutely every element in the work of every man in your establishment, sooner or later, becomes the subject of exact, precise, scientific investigation and knowledge to replace the old 'I believe so', and 'I guess so'. Every motion, every small fact becomes the subject of careful, scientific investigation. (Taylor, quoted in Pugh, 1990: 210)

Taylor argued that this information could be used to redesign organizational structures to ensure that employees worked to their full capacity. By so doing, it was believed that inefficiencies could be remedied and the greater prosperity of increased production could benefit both the employer (through increased profits) and the employee (through increased wages). Although there is considerable debate as to the extent and uptake of scientific management, Taylorist forms of work organization can still be found in various guises throughout the industrialized world, and his principles have further influenced the development of change theories. For example, some of the problems associated with Taylorist forms of work organization have been tackled by human relations theory and the more participative change strategies advocated by the field of organizational development (French and Bell,

1995). In other cases, some change initiatives such as BPR (Hammer and Champy, 1993) have been accused of simply re-introducing a technology-mediated form of Taylorism based on the enabling characteristics of new information and communication technologies. In the words of Hugh Willmott (1995: 96): 'the silicon chip plays an equivalent role in BPR to that performed by the stop watch in Scientific Management'.

THE HUMAN DIMENSION TO CHANGE

After the Second World War, with the growth in size of the industrial enterprise, economic prosperity and unionization, the 'problem' of dissatisfaction, alienation and industrial unrest became an organizational concern. Essentially it was argued that with the advent of relatively full employment since the late 1940s, people were able to find employment and switch jobs (the job mobility of labour increased) and consequently workers felt less compelled to submit to the authority of management (Roethlisberger, 1945). Changes in the functional organization of work, the substantial growth in the collective organization of employees and the power of the shop steward had shifted attention towards leadership and the management of human relations. The classic study by Roethlisberger and Dickson (1950) into the Hawthorne Works of the Western Electric Company in Chicago is well documented in the organizational behaviour texts (see, for example, Buchanan and Huczynski, 1997: 178–87). Their studies were used to show the benefits of 'democratic' leadership which encouraged employee participation in decision-making. The importance of consulting and listening to employees prior to embarking on change and the need to provide open and accurate information are central tenets of this approach. In viewing industrial organization as a complex social system, the study draws attention to the problems of employee resistance resulting from technical change initiatives that ignore social dimensions.

> Distrust and resistance to change . . . was expressed whenever changes were introduced too rapidly or without sufficient consideration of their social implications; in other words, whenever the workers were being asked to adjust themselves to new methods or systems which seemed to them to deprive their work of its customary social significance. In such situations it was evident that the social codes, customs, and routines of the workers could not be accommodated to the technical innovations introduced as quickly as the innovations themselves, in the form of new machines and processes, could be made. . . . Not only is any alteration of the existing social organization to which the worker has grown accustomed likely to produce sentiments of resistance to the change, but too rapid interference is likely to lead to feelings of frustration and an irrational exasperation with technical change in any form. (Roethlisberger and Dickson, 1950: 567–8)

Although resistance to change is not peculiar to workplace employees (it can happen at all levels within an organization), Elton Mayo and his team (see

Rose, 1988; Smith, 1987) at Harvard identified strongly with management and largely ignored other groups and individuals who might influence the change process (including the unions).

THE ORGANIZATIONAL DEVELOPMENT MODEL OF CHANGE

The change aspects of the human relations approach were further taken up and developed by what is now known as the Organizational Development (OD) model of change. A founding figure of this approach is Kurt Lewin whose work on inter-group dynamics and planned change has proven to be particularly influential (see Kreitner and Kinicki, 1992: 723–61). Lewin argued that for change to be managed successfully three general steps must be followed (Hellriegel et al., 1995: 667–9). The three general steps identified by Lewin (1951) are:

- unfreezing;
- changing; and
- refreezing.

Unfreezing is the stage in which there is a recognized need for change and action is taken to unfreeze existing attitudes and behaviour. This preparatory stage is deemed essential to the generation of employee support and the minimization of employee resistance. For example, in his pioneering research (some of which was published after his death in 1947), Lewin found that in order to minimize worker resistance, employees should be actively encouraged to participate in the planning process (see Clutterbuck and Crainer, 1990: 105).

Managing change through reducing the forces that prevent change, rather than through increasing the forces that are pushing for change, is central to Lewin's approach and his technique of force-field analysis (1947: 5–42). He maintained that within any social system there are driving and restraining forces that maintain the status quo and within which organizations generally exist in a state of quasi-stationary equilibrium. Thus, in order to create conditions conducive to change it is necessary to identify the restraining and driving forces, and to change one or other of these in order to create an imbalance.

In the management of organizational change, the focus of OD specialists has been on providing data that would unfreeze the system through reducing the restraining forces rather than increasing the driving forces (Gray and Starke, 1988: 596–629; Weisbord, 1988: 94). Once an imbalance has been created the system can be altered and a new set of driving and restraining forces put into place. A planned change programme is implemented and only when the desired state has been achieved will the change agent set about 'refreezing' the organization. The new state of balance is then appraised and, where appropriate, methods of positive reinforcement are used to ensure that employees 'internalize' attitudes and behaviours consistent with new work regimes.

Although there are many different OD models, the general approach has been described by Huse (1982: 555) as 'the application of behavioural science knowledge in a long-range effort to improve an organization's ability to cope with changes in its external environment and increase its internal problem-solving capabilities'. It is based on a human relations perspective which stresses the importance of collaborative management and, according to French and Bell (1983: 15), can be defined as 'a long-range effort to improve an organization's problem-solving and renewal processes . . . with the assistance of a change agent or catalyst and the use of the theory and technology of applied behavioural science, including action research'.

Typically, the OD approach is planned. It attempts to consider and include all members of an organization; the proposed change is supported by top management; the objectives of change are to improve working conditions and organizational effectiveness; and an emphasis is placed on behavioural science techniques that facilitate communication and problem-solving among members (Beckhard, 1969). The most common distinguishing characteristics of modern OD approaches are (French and Bell, 1983, 1995):

- the goal is to improve an organization's health and effectiveness;
- the focus of the change effort is on the whole system (whether an organization or a divisional department);
- the change programme involves planned interventions that are introduced systematically;
- top-down strategies are applied: that is, change begins at the top and is gradually applied downward throughout the organization;
- employees at all levels must be committed to the change (in other words, change must never be forced);
- change is made slowly, allowing for the continual assessment of change strategies;
- specialist change agents should be used to guide OD programmes;
- the approach should be interdisciplinary, drawing on behavioural science knowledge;
- OD programmes are based on data, so that choices are made on the basis of objective information, rather than on assumptions, about what the real issues are;
- the objective is to achieve lasting rather than temporary change; and
- the OD approach can be used with both 'healthy' and 'unhealthy' organizations.

Generally, the OD approach involves a number of steps beginning with the appointment of a change agent (usually an individual outside the organization) who intervenes to start the change process. The six major steps in an OD programme are (Aldag and Stearns, 1991: 724–8):

1 Identifying a need for change.
2 Selecting an intervention technique.
3 Gaining top management support.
4 Planning the change process.
5 Overcoming resistance to change.
6 Evaluating the change process.

However, the main problem with this approach is that it adopts a normative framework and assumes that there is one best way to manage change that will increase both organizational effectiveness and employee well-being. The professional consultants engaged in OD are generally not concerned with the development of theory or with the design of systematic programmes of research, but with a set of normative prescriptions which guide their practice in managing change (Ledford et al., 1990: 4–6). Nevertheless, this planned model of change remains an integral part of the conventional orthodoxy taught in university business departments and management schools around the world. Although academics have generally been slow to criticize the relevance of this model and continue to teach the Lewinian view of change management to their students, there is now a growing recognition both of the need for alternative strategies (Dunphy and Stace, 1990) and of the political processes involved in the successful management of change (Buchanan and Badham, 1999).

CHANGE AND SOCIO-TECHNICAL SYSTEMS THEORY

The influence of human relations in Europe is evident in the work carried out by the Tavistock Institute of Human Relations which was established in the late 1940s. Over the years, this consulting and research organization has produced a considerable body of research on the design of work structures that accommodate both the social and technical requirements of production. During the 1940s and 1950s, the main aim of the Tavistock group was to develop ways of simultaneously improving worker satisfaction and employee productivity (Trist and Murray, 1993). A study of coal mining showed how work could be restructured around technology so that the social and technical components could be jointly designed both to yield higher levels of job satisfaction and produce a high-performance work organization (Dunphy and Griffiths, 1998: 49). On the basis of these studies, it is argued that change initiatives that focus on either the purely technical or the purely social aspects of work are likely to have limited 'success' as they create a situation where the whole is sub-optimized for developments in one dimension. In Sweden, for example, the success of the work redesign programme at Volvo's Kalmar automotive plant in the 1970s provided a practical example of Social Technical Systems (STS) theory, which was further supported by car production at Uddevalla in the 1980s (prior to the closure of the plant in the 1990s).

The plant was reopened for a short period during the 1990s to manufacture the C70 coupé model, but production ceased when the plant was sold to Ford in 1999 (Buchanan, 2000: 32). Since these early achievements, one major criticism of the STS approach has been that while it purports to view organizations as organic open systems, key proponents have tended to look inwards and have consequently ignored the external business market environment (or, as some of the critical commentators cynically note, moving the chairs on the Titanic does not improve the chances of survival). In spite of these criticisms, activity has continued and, with the growing uptake of team-based manufacturing, many of these original STS ideas have been further developed (Dunphy and Griffiths, 1998; Willcocks and Mason, 1987).

In Australia, the work of Richard Badham has rekindled interest in modern socio-technical approaches by claiming that it is necessary to address not only the interdependent and interpenetrating nature of the technical and the social, but also the change process through which these elements are reconfigured (Badham, 1995: 81). He proposes a configurational process model in which technology is viewed as malleable and socially shaped. In this model, there are three configurations:

- technological (the technical and non-human elements);
- operator (the social and human elements), and
- intrepreneurial ('intrepreneur' is the term used for people involved in the change process who configure emerging forms through championing certain developments and/or obstructing others).

Unlike the traditional STS approach, Badham's model is more contextual and negotiated, one in which individuals and groups may shape processes and outcomes of change (Badham, 1995). This shift in emphasis moves attention from a concern with resolving the tensions between human needs and the technical system of operation towards the contextual process by which these systems come to be designed and implemented. However, this perspective maintains a prescriptive intent and action agenda towards both under-standing and managing the process in a particular direction (the researcher becomes an active change agent and consultant). There can be a tendency towards less theoretical and more prescriptive models, which may prevent a rigorous analysis of the contextual shaping process and limit theoretical insight (Knights and Murray, 1994: 12).

A SITUATIONAL APPROACH TO CHANGE

A theory that looks beyond the organization to accommodate the need for companies to adapt to changing business environments is the contingency approach. Originating in the 1960s from the classical studies of Burns and Stalker (1961), Thompson (1967) and Lawrence and Lorsch (1967), this influential approach advocates that the best way to organize depends on the circumstances. The basic theoretical tenet is that, while there is no one best way of organizing, it is possible to identify the most appropriate organizational form to fit the context in which a business has to operate (Wood, 1979: 335). The emphasis of a number of contingency models is on regaining strategic fit in the new organizational order. The contingent factors which are deemed to be of primary significance include single variables, such as technology (Perrow, 1970; Thompson, 1967; Woodward, 1980) or the environment (Burns and Stalker, 1961; Lawrence and Lorsch, 1967), or a range of variables, such as in the ambitious study by Pugh and his colleagues (Pugh and Hickson, 1976) which examines the relationship between contextual factors and structural variables (for a critique, see Wood, 1979). In short, contingency theorists reject the search for a universal model (a single best way approach) and aim to develop useful generalizations about appropriate strategies and structures under different typical conditions.

In Australia, an influential model of organizational change which adopts this situational (contingency) approach was developed in the late 1980s and early 1990s by Dexter Dunphy and Doug Stace (1990; Stace and Dunphy, 1994). They identified two key dimensions. First, the scale of change, seen to lie along a continuum from small- to large-scale; and second, the style of leadership required to bring about change, which covers both participative and autocratic leadership styles. On each dimension they identify four gradations. The scale ranges from 'fine tuning' and 'incremental adjustment' to 'modular transformation' and 'corporate transformation'. Fine tuning refers to small-scale changes ranging from the refining and clarification of existing procedures through to the actual adjustment of organizational structures. Modular transformation refers to large-scale changes from divisional restructuring to revolutionary change throughout the whole organization. On the style of leadership dimension, the authors identify 'collaborative', 'consultative', 'directive' and 'coercive'. Using these dimensions, Dunphy and Stace identify four types of change strategies: participative evolution, forced evolution, charismatic transformation and dictatorial transformation. 'Participative evolution' refers to incremental change through collaboration and 'forced evolution' refers to directive change. 'Charismatic transformation' is a large-scale discontinuous change achieved by collaboration. 'Dictatorial transformation' refers to major coercive change programmes. Dunphy and Stace argue that the model provides a framework for planned change strategies that challenges the personal value preferences of managers and consultants. They suggest that 'appropriate' change strategies are generally determined by the change agent and not by the needs of the organization. For example, they point out that organizational development practitioners have tended to focus on collaborative models, whereas corporate strategy consultants have tended to select dictatorial transformation as the appropriate strategy for managing large-scale discontinuous change. The authors argue that, while there is a place for each strategy, the choice should be made on the basis of dominant contingencies.

The model developed by Dunphy and Stace is clearly influenced by Lewin's work and while it attempts to tackle some of the problems associated with the universality of OD, as David Wilson (1992: 31) notes, 'the addition of an extra variable – whether or not the organization is out of fit with its environment – merely adds to the list of driving and restraining forces'. Perhaps one of the major failings of this model is the way change is characterized as an apolitical process. There is a surprising lack of reference to notions of power (Pfeffer, 1981) and the political nature of workplace change (see, for example, Mangham, 1979; Pettigrew, 1973). As Dunford (1990) points out, 'managers are portrayed as neutral conduits' who ignore their own self-interest in making rational decisions that seek to promote organizational effectiveness and survival. On this count, Buchanan and Badham (1999: 189) suggest that, while there are no simple strategies for effective change management, paradoxically change programmes are often presented to others (such as the public and other commercial organizations) as rational programmes even though they are far less tidy in practice. Consequently, an essential problem with this type of contingency model of change centres on its aprocessual and apolitical character. As Wood (1979: 337–8) indicates:

> The contingency theorist neither ignores nor is unable to deal with change . . . but rather treats it as largely unproblematic. . . . In effect the contingency theory places the social scientist above the organization's participants and assumes that he can simply impose the 'correct design' on an organization. . . . Thus despite its applied orientation, contingency theory remains abstract and scholastic and, in effect, views organization change as essentially an intellectual and techno-cratic exercise.

CELEBRITY PROFESSORS AND CONSULTANTS

In conjunction with the persistence of organizational development, socio-technical systems and contingency approaches to change, a range of consultant-led approaches to managing change has also been developed. Following the publication of Peters and Waterman's (1982) best-selling book *In Search of Excellence: Lessons from America's Best Run Companies*, a plethora of recipe books on how to successfully manage change have been published. Some of the more popular ones have been written by what Huczynski (1993) terms the 'management gurus' and 'celebrity professors', such as Handy (1996), Kanter (1990), Kotter (1995) and Peters (1997), as well as those associated with particular movements, such as Crosby (1980), Deming (1981) and Juran (1988) with Quality Management, and Shonberger (1982) with JIT. Although it is not possible to detail all these developments here, it is worth highlighting some of the main themes and approaches that have been promoted by some of the more popular management gurus.

In Search of Excellence was a landmark text. It captured the imagina-tion of American managers who were quick to digest proposals that offered a western route to competitive success, particularly in the light of articles in the *Harvard Business Review* during the 1970s which drew attention to the productivity gap between American and Japanese workers (see Burnes, 2000: 75–81) and the success of Japanese manufacturing in the uptake of JIT techniques and quality management (Mitroff and Mohrman, 1987). In using the well-known McKinsey Seven S Framework (strategy, structure, systems, staff, style, shared values, skills), Peters and Waterman argue against too much analysis and planning (although recognizing that some planning is needed) as this can serve simply to block action. They identify eight major determinants of organizational excellence:

1   Organizations should have a bias for action through encouraging innovation and through active response to problem situations.
2   Organizations should develop closer relationships with their customers.
3   Organizations should foster and support an entrepreneurial spirit among their staff and aim to increase the level of responsible autonomy among their employees.
4   Employees should be treated with respect and dignity in order to ensure productivity through people.
5   All employees should be driven by the values of the organization.
6   Companies should do what they know best and should restrict diversification.
7   Flat organization structures and slimmed-down bureaucracies enable greater flexibility and provide for more rapid communication.
8   Simultaneous loose–tight properties should be established through high levels of self-supervision and the development of a common cohesive organizational culture.

As Peters and Waterman conclude (1982: 322): 'We find that autonomy is a product of discipline. The discipline (a few shared values) provides the framework. It gives people confidence (to experiment, for instance) stemming from stable expectations about what really counts.'

This work, by putting forward a simple recipe for achieving organizational excellence, has been very influential. In a similar vein to other prescriptive texts published during this period, high-trust cultures, productivity through people and closer relationships with customers were all identified as key ingredients to competitive advantage. Little attention was given to the potential diversity of organizational forms and there was an assumption that blueprints for success could be created, identified, implemented and sustained, thus ensuring company survival in turbulent and competitive business environments. In practice, however, these simple management recipes have not stood the test of time and have been criticized for trying to present simple prescriptions of a 'one best way' for modern organizations to follow (Guest, 1992; Shapiro, 1995). Their inability to deliver practical long-term solutions highlights the problem of management books that identify and codify supposedly best practice strategies for achieving organizational effectiveness based on commonsense interpretations of organizational life (see Abrahamson, 1996; Huczynski, 1993; Pascale, 1990).

During the 1990s, the codified blueprints for implementing particular techniques, such as World Class Manufacturing, TQM and best practice management, largely replaced the broader 'excellence recipes' of the 1980s. But once again, the complexities of managing large-scale transitions that incorporate cultural as well as structural change are largely downplayed. It seems that the lessons of the past are forgotten under the dazzling banners of new methods and techniques. For example, Tom Peters has continued to promote action for success in books such as *Thriving on Chaos* (1989), *Liberation Management* (1993) and *The Circle of Innovation* (1997). A theme running through them and much of the guru management literature is the need for managers to act as leaders of change and to be proactive in the search for strategies that will make organizations more competitive (Ulrich and Lake, 1991; Vesey, 1991). This new bias towards organizational action is based on the premise that companies that cannot manage ongoing change will cease to exist (Peters, 1989: 401; Gray and Smeltzer, 1990: 615–16). Typically, what is advocated is a revolution in the world of management through the adoption of policies that discard traditional hierarchical structures, rigid bureaucratic systems and inflexible work practices (Dunphy and Stace, 1990: 11–12). For example, Rosabeth Moss Kanter (1990: 344), in her popular book *When Giants Learn to Dance*, claims that competitive corporations of the future must develop a strategic business action agenda towards 'flatter, more focused organizations stressing synergies; entrepreneurial enclaves pushing new stream businesses for the future; and strategic alliances or stakeholder partnerships stretching capacity by combining the strength of several organizations'.

The new bias towards organizational action rests with an emergent breed of manager whose job involves successfully managing strategic change in work structures, process and product technologies, employment relations and organizational culture. These managers are expected to compete in the new 'corporate Olympics' and to balance the apparent contradictions between, first, centralizing resources while creating autonomous business units and, second, replacing staff through 'lean' restructuring programmes while at the same time maintaining employee-centred personnel policies (Kanter, 1990: 17–31). According to Kanter, the seven managerial skills required of these new business athletes are an ability to achieve results without relying on organizational status; to be self-confident and humble; to maintain high ethical standards; to attain cooperative competitiveness; to gain satisfaction from results rather than financial rewards; to be able to work across functions and find new synergies; and to be aware of the process, as well as the outcomes, of change (1990: 359–65).

The intention behind these managerial competencies is to help managers become 'masters' rather than 'victims' of change. However, due to an over-reliance on metaphors, Kanter presents little of any real use to the discerning manager. As Gabor and Petersen (1991: 98) note: 'clichés and banalities depicted by chapter headings . . . detract measurably from Ms Kanter's fervent and sincere hope that America's business community will be energized to change direction to compete and succeed in the current and future global business climate'.

The call for action is also evident in the work of John Kotter (1995) who provides a recipe for successful change and suggests that failure to be proactive in these areas is likely to result in business failure. He claims (1996: 185) that it is important to push people out of their comfort zones in promoting the significance of change and that it is often complacency and fear of the future that inhibit successful company transformation. As he states:

> For a lot of reasons, many people are still embracing the twentieth-century career and growth model. Sometimes complacency is the problem. They have been successful, so why change? Sometimes they have no clear vision of the twenty-first century and so they don't know how they should change. But often fear is a key issue. They see jobs seeming to disappear all around them. They hear horror stories about people who have been downsized or reengineered out of work . . . they cling defensively to what they currently have. In effect, they embrace the past, not the future.

After identifying eight major reasons why transformation efforts fail, Kotter (1996) then turns this around and offers eight key steps to ensuring successful change. These are:

1   Establish a sense of urgency.
2   Form a powerful guiding coalition.
3   Create a vision.
4   Communicate that vision.
5   Empower others to act on the vision.
6   Plan and create short-term wins.
7   Consolidate change improvements.
8   Institutionalize new approaches.

For Kotter successful change is marked by a clear vision which is relentlessly communicated to everyone; people are rewarded throughout the change process; any change obstacles are removed; and change outcomes are anchored in the corporation's culture. The focus is on embracing the future rather than living on past success. Similarly, Hamel and Prahalad (1994) argue that the downfall of companies often arises from the unsupported belief by senior management that past strategies (which proved successful) can and should be sustained into the future. They suggest that the seeds of company failure are often sown during the years of company success and point out that the top companies today are often not those who were the top companies 10 or 20 years ago. They identify two key elements in competing for the future. First, the counter-intuitive claim that the need for continuity is embedded in change. In other words that, due to the ongoing nature of change (regulatory change, product and competitor change, and so forth), continuity of the company will necessitate change. Second, that companies require foresight to influence the future world of business. This may be through creating new markets, services or products, or simply by changing the rules of the game.

In looking towards the future, all these commentators emphasize the need to question cherished assumptions and to reflect critically on current practice. As Ridderstrale and Nordstrom (2000: 245) suggest, irrelevancy may become a much greater problem than inefficiency; they signal the need to break away from the straitjacket of traditional ways of thinking. They highlight the place of imagination and emotion, and stress the importance of knowledge. These authors draw our attention to the need for change for competitive survival and emphasize how assumptions based on past experience may limit our vision of the future (Ridderstrale and Nordstrom, 2000: 30).

A TIME TO QUESTION SIMPLE CHANGE PRODUCTS AND ACCOUNTS

Although there clearly remains a market for logical sequential models of change (Abrahamson and Fairchild, 1999), these are increasingly being called into question by both popular management writers (Kanter et al., 1992: 10) and academics (Burnes, 2000; Collins, 1998). And yet, for all the criticisms levelled at past prescriptions, manuals that provide simple solutions to complex problems remain an attractive management commodity (Jackson, 2001). Consequently, many of the pitfalls and failures associated with implementing pre-planned packages for organizational success reassert themselves with amazing regularity, only under different titles and names. The continual push for newly labelled change packages and techniques has resulted in a proliferation of management fads (see Collins, 2000; Mitroff and Bennis, 1989) and an increased tendency for companies to imitate other organizations (DiMaggio and Powell, 1983, 1991). Furthermore, while Eric Abrahamson (1991: 609) has argued that 'fads and fashions may constitute vital processes that animate random variations from which increasingly efficient innovation can evolve', some of the simple recipes associated with new management initiatives may contribute more to the wealth of consultants than to the performance of organizations. As Jackson (2001: 13) describes in quoting Shapiro (1995: xiii):

> New programs and initiatives that seize the corporate imagination on a wide-scale basis are regularly derided as 'fads', 'buzzwords', 'flavors-of-the-month', 'quick fixes' and 'silver bullets'. This tendency has perhaps been most succinctly captured in the term 'fad surfing' or 'the practice of riding the crest of the latest management panacea and then paddling out again just in time to ride the next one, always absorbing for managers and lucrative for consultants; frequently disastrous for organizations'.

Jackson argues that for too long academics have failed to examine the phenomenon of management fashions and calls for a greater dialogue between academics and practitioners. He claims that many of these fads can have deleterious effects on our contemporary experience of work and as such, 'popular movements in management like re-engineering, TQM and Excellence, while essentially transitory and superficial in nature, are nevertheless important areas of research' (2001: 178). In the empirical chapters that follow, company uptake of a number of these types of initiatives is examined and the consequences of change for employees' experience of work are analysed. These changes have real effects for people and, as Jackson rightly points out, should not be dismissed as mere rhetoric and vacuous consultant-speak. There is a need to research these phenomena and to engage in critical processual studies to further our understanding of the appeal of management fashions and their effect on the quality of working life.

These change products are often combined with change accounts or n-step guides (do this, then this, then this) on how best to bring about change. Once again, research and critical analysis are required to draw attention to the problems of the recipe and linear planned approach, especially as a conceptual map for understanding change. As indicated at the outset, one of the major arguments of this book is that it is inappropriate to treat change as a discrete series of stages since organizational change is an ongoing complex process with twists, turns and restarts. Although this alternative position is gathering support, because it provides no simple solution but draws attention to complexity, it is of little surface appeal to the practising manager. Practitioners need to be educated about the value of the more critically-informed processual approach which rejects the short-termism of 'fad surfing' and provides a more detailed and longer term view of change.

Since the 1980s, there has been a theoretical and empirical movement towards these more fluid, dynamic and processual accounts of change (see Clark et al., 1988; Dawson, 1994; Pettigrew, 1985; Preece et al., 1999). For example, Hatch (1997: 350) argues that this movement away from more stability-oriented frameworks to change-centred perspectives that emphasize the dynamic and processual aspects of organizing is necessary to make sense of contemporary change. Collins (1998: 193) argues for more reflective approaches to the study of change, approaches that are able to accommodate contradiction and complexity rather than focus on consensus and stability. Support has been growing for studies that are both critical and processual, where the 'established priorities and values are not assumed to be legitimate' (Alvesson and Willmott, 1996: 31) and where power, status and political struggles are not simply viewed as disruptive to the 'rational' management of an organization (Knights and Murray, 1994: 3). Although disagreement remains over what should comprise a critical processual perspective, the need to go beyond snapshot models and unreflective accounts is far more widely accepted today than it was in the 1980s and 1990s.

One such framework, which I developed to carry out longitudinal research on change, is outlined in the following section. This processual approach has also been adopted and adapted in a number of collaborative empirical case study programmes on change (see, for example, Dawson and Palmer, 1995; Harrison and Samson, 1997). It views change as an ongoing dynamic process and promotes the position that change should be studied 'as-it-happens'. It also seeks to give equal attention to all perspectives on change, as well as being concerned with underlying power relations and the politics of change in order to explain the process by which certain rational accounts are orchestrated and maintained over others. This approach – as a perspective for making sense of change – is briefly outlined below.

MAKING SENSE OF CHANGE: A PROCESSUAL PERSPECTIVE

The push to identify and define strategies to aid change management under prevailing contextual conditions has, in the past, tended to downplay the processual and ongoing nature of organizational change. However, there are a growing number of academics in Europe and, more recently, North America and Australia, who are starting to recognize the importance of processual research for understanding the dynamics of organizational change (Ropo et al., 1997a, 1997b; Van de Ven and Huber, 1990). For example, the early work of Pettigrew (1985) charted the unfolding and non-linear aspects of change at Imperial Chemical Industries. He has criticized the aprocessual character of much of the material on change management in its advocacy of the need for the adoption of a particular type of research strategy and methodology (Pettigrew, 1990). In contrast to the dominant approach which emphasizes the importance of sophisticated quantitative analyses (Ledford et al., 1990: 6–8), the processual approach is concerned with the collection of longitudinal qualitative data which facilitates a more detailed understanding of the complex and dynamic processes of change (Dawson, 1994). As Pettigrew (1997: 338) reflects: 'human conduct is perpetually in a process of becoming. The overriding aim of the process analyst therefore is to catch this reality in flight.'

The processual framework I have developed is based on the assumption that companies continuously move in and out of many different states, often concurrently, during the history of one or a number of organizational change initiatives (see also Dawson, 1994, 1996). Although for analytical purposes it may prove useful to identify and group a number of tasks and decision-making activities, such as the search for and assessment of options or implementation, these should not be treated as representing a series of sequential stages in the process of change (as with conventional stage models). The approach taken here is that since organizations undergoing change comprise a number of dynamic states which interlock and overlap, the processes associated with change should be analysed 'as-they-happen' so that their emergent character can be understood within the context in which they take place.

In developing an alternative framework for analysing change, attention has been given to the potential conflict of designing an approach that is both flexible and yet clearly defined, and that is able to deal with the complexity of change while remaining uncluttered and of practical use. With these objectives in mind, it is suggested that the timeframe of before, during and after change can be used to break down the complex change process for analytical purposes. This framework mirrors the work of Beckhard and Harris (1987) who characterize organizational transition as a movement from a present state of organization to some future state (the process of getting from position A to position B). The three general categories advocated here are:

- the initial conception of a need to change;
- the process of organizational change; and
- operation of new work practices and procedures.

Initial conception

The initial awareness of a need to change may be either in response to external or internal pressures for change (reactive), or through a belief in the need for change to meet future competitive demands (proactive). The latter has stimulated a wealth of research into the adoption of management fads (Abrahamson, 1996; Jackson, 2001; Lawler and Mohrman, 1985) that promise a painless solution to rising international competitiveness (Mitroff and Mohrman, 1987: 69). The increased complexity and uncertainty of international business markets have led some organizations to base change on imitation (which organizations are successful and what changes have they introduced), rather than on any conception of a need to adopt untried technologies or techniques (see, for example, DiMaggio and Powell, 1983; Thompson, 1967). Whether fads and fashions generate vital processes towards the evolvement and adoption of efficient innovations or promote organizational inefficiency and actually damage organizations (see Collins, 2000, 2001) is not our major concern here. What is important is how the conception of a need to change can be influenced by factors within the organization such as operational inefficiencies and employee disputes, and by factors that emanate from outside an organization – for example, through business press and media reports on the success of other organizations, and the direct or indirect promotion of various management fads and fashions (see also Jackson, 2001).

The process

Once a need for change has been identified, the complex non-linear and 'black box' process of organizational change begins. As already indicated, this period will comprise a number of different tasks, activities and decisions for individuals and groups both within and outside the organization. To clarify this statement, let us take the example of a firm where senior management have identified a need to change to meet competitive pressures and a fall in profitability. Once a decision to change has been made, management then have to decide on the type of change they wish to introduce. This may be a change in human resources, products or services (task), technology or administration (Daft, 1986: 269–86). In the case of new technology, a number of strategic objectives have been identified that influence management's decision to embark on a programme of change. These include business market objectives, operating cost objectives, product quality objectives and operating control objectives (see, for example, Boddy and Buchanan, 1986).

A change in technology may offer several possibilities for increasing an organization's ability to adapt to changing market conditions. For example, the flexibility of state-of-the-art equipment may permit the modification and redesign of production without necessitating any major structural alterations to the operating system. Alternatively, the new technology may enable a more effective use of existing resources and increased operating efficiency while reducing overall operating costs, thereby improving an organization's business market position. Such an objective is achievable in cases where modern technology is introduced for the purpose of providing rapid access to accurate, up-to-date information on the disposition of material resources (see, for example, McLoughlin, 1999).

Apart from improving a firm's market position and reducing operating costs through the more efficient use of resources, savings could also be made by reducing the total number of jobs required. Alternatively, the introduction of new technology could be used to eliminate management's dependence on in-house labour by transferring from an employment to a contracting-out basis. The third objective, improving the quality of products or services produced, may be particularly important in service industries where there is little to differentiate competing services. Finally, advanced technology may improve operational control by providing rapid access to information and integrating previously diverse areas of operation.

The strategic decision to adopt new technology, to introduce new products or services, or to change administrative structures is generally taken at senior management level. However, the formulation of strategic objectives is not always as clearly defined as the example of a change in technology may suggest. For example, the research of James Quinn (1980) demonstrates how strategic decisions are often not highly formalized and may take the form of what he terms 'logical incrementalism'. This involves the blending of behavioural techniques, power politics and formal analysis in a logical and incremental movement towards ends that are broadly conceived and constantly revised in the light of new information. Quinn's findings illustrate how strategies can often be implemented prior to their final formulation (that is, during the conceptualization phase). This lends support to the need for a processual model that is able to accommodate the non-linear nature of complex processes of change in modern organizations.

When a decision has been made on the general theme or content of change, then the task of research and assessment may follow, where members of an organization set out to find the best option for achieving a particular change objective. In our example, the research task would involve identifying the technology required and the assessment task would involve the analysis of available products. In practice, many of these decisions may have been made during the conception stage and may undergo revision as more information is collected on what is available, what the costs are and what the payback is likely to be. The timeframe may be relatively short, involving a quick analysis of options, or it may instigate a major evaluation exercise requiring a team to visit other organizations and suppliers operating in different states and countries. After assessing possible options, a decision will be made on the system and its design. In the case of technology, while the choice of a piece of equipment may be made by senior management, the actual design of the system will often reflect the values and assumptions of design engineers (Luff et al., 2000).

System selection is also likely to influence the process of planning for the task of implementing change. For example, the logistics of managing the change (what equipment, where, in what order) and of ensuring that staff can use the new equipment (how much training is going to be required) will be partly determined by the type of system selected. Moreover, in planning for change, decisions have to be made about the design of the organizational operating system – that is, on the organization of work in the daily operation of the new equipment. In the case of technology, a number of studies show how these decisions reflect social choices such as whether to use technology to enhance the existing skills and experience of employees, or to use technology as a means of degrading jobs and enabling the remote electronic surveillance of work (see Preece et al., 2000).

The task of implementing change has been well documented in the literature (see, for example, Preece, 1995; Preece et al., 1999) and has been identified as a period that requires considerable political skill on the part of the change agent (Buchanan and Badham, 1999). It is during the implementation of change programmes that occupational and employee concerns normally begin to influence the transition process (Dawson, 1994). For example, Edwards (1979) has argued that employee resistance to the imposition of management's implementation strategies can transform the workplace into a battleground of political dissension and control. However, these internal conflicts may not simply be a manifestation of workers' resistance to management, but may represent a complex political struggle between various occupational groups (managerial, supervisory and operative) with differing vested interests (see also Clausen et al., 2000).

Operation of new work practices

The final general timeframe refers to the period when, following the implementation of change, new organizational arrangements and systems of operation begin to emerge. During this period, a number of novel developments or contingencies may compromise the change outcomes. For example, unanticipated technical or social problems may undermine the usefulness of the system in its replacement of traditional methods. This may cause conflict and confusion among staff and management, and threaten the establishment of new working relationships. The early stages of operating under new systems may be characterized by uncertainty, conflict and misunderstanding among employees, who may variously adapt, modify, reassert or redefine their positions under the new operating procedures and working relationships set up during the implementation of change. This is also the period in which a relatively stable system of operation may emerge with new patterns of relationships and new forms of working practices. It is during this timeframe, therefore, that the outcomes of change can be examined and contrasted with the operating system prior to change. Although in reality it is often unrealistic to talk of an 'endpoint' of change (since the process continues *ad infinitum*), it does make sense to talk of the 'effects' of a particular type of change. In the case of large-scale or radical change initiatives, it is possible to identify a period after implementation when the daily work routines become part of the operating system (which is no longer regarded as 'new'). While the ongoing process of change will continue, this is the period that can be used to identify the outcomes of change on organizational structures and traditional operating practices.

FRAMEWORK FOR DATA ANALYSIS

These three general timeframes – initial conception, process and operation of new work practices – provide a useful framework from which to begin a detailed examination of the process of organizational change. However, although every major change programme will have an organizationally-defined beginning, middle and end, in practice it is not only difficult to identify the start and completion of change programmes (for example, there is often more than one organizational history of change and these may be reconstructed over time), but also to explain the complex pathways and routes in establishing new operational processes. Therefore, in examining the complex and 'black box' process of change, considerable returns are to be gained from developing a framework for data analysis. It is argued here that a useful way of tackling the problem of analysing complex change data is to construct data categories either around themes or around the various activities and tasks associated with organizational change. For example, data categories for the activities associated with the establishment of new organizational arrangements may include system selection, identification of type of change, implementation, preparation and planning, and research and assessment. These tasks are unlikely to occur in a tidy linear fashion, but will normally overlap, occur simultaneously, stop and start, and be part of both the initial and later phases of major change programmes. Nevertheless, the tasks are useful for locating and sorting data on change that might otherwise be too complex to deal with systematically. Although at a more general level there can be no definitive list of appropriate data categories (they should be modified or revised to fit particular case examples and the characteristics of different change programmes), task-oriented or thematic categories can provide a useful starting point for locating and analysing change data.

In accommodating the temporal aspects of change the processual perspective aims to examine change 'as-it-happens' and is concerned with three groups of determinants that shape this process:

- the politics of change;
- the context of change; and
- the substance of change.

Politics of change

The politics of change refers to the political activity of consultation, negotiation, conflict and resistance, which occurs at various levels within and outside an organization during the process of managing change. Examples of political activity outside an organization are governmental pressure, competitor alliances and the influence of overseas divisions of large corporations. Internal political activity can be in the form of shop floor negotiations between trade union representatives and management, between consultants (working within the organization) and various organizational groups, and between managerial, supervisory and operative personnel. These individuals or groups can influence decision-making and the setting of agendas at critical junctures. On the issue of political process, management writers such as Stace and Dunphy (1994) can be criticized for ignoring trade union and employee actions in response to management's decision to introduce change; whereas political writers, such as Braverman (1974), can be criticized for treating management as a homogeneous political group. My position is that an understanding of organizational politics should be central to any approach that seeks to explain the contemporary experience of change. As Buchanan and Badham (1999: 231) conclude:

> In the domain of practical action, as we noted earlier, management is a contact sport. If you don't want to get bruised, don't play. There is little to be gained by complaining about the turf game, its players, its tricks, its strategies, its tactics and its potential damage. Criticism of the existence of organizational politics is likely to have as much impact as criticism of British weather. . . . The main argument of this book is that the change agent who is not politically skilled will fail.

Context of change

The second major concern of a processual approach is the context in which change takes place. A historical perspective on both the internal and external organizational contexts is central to understanding the opportunities, constraints and organizationally-defined routes to change (Kelly and Amburgey, 1991: 610). As already noted, the coexistence of a number of competing histories of change can significantly shape ongoing change programmes. In this sense, the contextual and historical dimensions can both promote certain options and devalue others. Under this framework, the contextual dimension refers to both the past and the present external and internal operating environments, as well as to the influence of future projections and expectations on current operating practice.

External contextual factors include changes in competitors' strategies, level of international competition, government legislation, changing social expectations, technological innovations and changes in the level of business activity. Internal contextual factors include Leavitt's (1964) fourfold classification: human resources, administrative structures, technology and product or service, as well as an additional category labelled the history and culture of an organization. This last category incorporates both a historical perspective that takes account of the multiple histories of the context in which change is taking place and an understanding of organizational culture. In this way, the framework is able to accommodate the existence of a number of competing change histories (that may be further refined, replaced and developed over time) and recognizes that the dominant or 'official version' of change may often reflect the political positioning of certain key individuals or groups, rather than serving as a true representation of the actual process of chang. These change stories may in turn shape, constrain and promote the direction and content of future change programmes.

Substance of change

The third and final area of concern relates to the substance of change. The four main dimensions of the concept of substance used in the processual framework developed here are:

1 *Scale and scope*: which may range along a continuum from small-scale discrete change to a more 'radical' large-scale transformation. A distinction can also be made between change at the level of the unit, plant, branch, division or corporation.
2 *Defining characteristics*: refers both to the labels attached to change projects and to the actual content of the change. In other words, content is never assumed to correspond to the label attached to a particular change programme.
3 *Timeframe*: at it simplest this refers to the period over which change occurs from the conception of the need to change through to routine operation. It is also concerned with the starting and stopping of change and the way certain tasks and decision-making activities may overlap and interlock. Some programmes may evolve incrementally over a number of years only to be followed by a fairly rapid and specified period of

implementation, in contrast to others that may be triggered by a sudden shift in business market activity (as illustrated by some of the commercial consequences of September 11).

4 *Perceived centrality*: whether change is seen to be critical to the survival of the organization. For example, if change is viewed as central to the competitive position of the company, then it can have major implications for the timescale, resource support and overall employee commitment.

Finally, it should be stressed that the substance of change is not static but is itself subject to change. It both influences and is influenced by contextual and political elements. For example, it is not uncommon for definitional confusion to surround the introduction of new management techniques and for the content of change to be redefined during the process of implementation. Moreover, knowledge of the substance of change and clarification of what the change means for a particular organization can themselves become a political process, influenced by external contextual views and the setting of internal agendas. In this sense, there is a continual interplay between the politics, context and substance of change.

The processual framework (see Figure 3.1) is concerned with understanding the political arenas in which decisions are made, histories recreated and strategies rationalized (politics); the enabling and constraining characteristics of change, and the scale and type of change (substance); and the conditions under which change takes place in relation to external elements such as the market environment, and internal elements including the history and culture of an organization (context). Although this processual perspective is deemed the most appropriate for studying change and is the one adopted in this book, it is important to remember that it does represent a particular frame or lens through which change can be examined. As indicated in Chapter 2, the perspective adopted influences what we study, the data we collect, our analysis and ultimately our explanation of change. Under a processual perspective, our main concern is with how people variously experience the change process and how this dynamic non-linear process is shaped over time.

CONCLUSION

This chapter has set out to provide a historical overview of the development of change frameworks from the early phases of industrialization to the present day. This review has necessarily been brief and selective, and many students of management will have already covered much of this material in courses on management, organization theory and organizational behaviour. However, some areas, such as the contribution of socio-technical systems thinking and the processual approach, may be less familiar. Consequently, this chapter has attempted to contextualize these theoretical developments

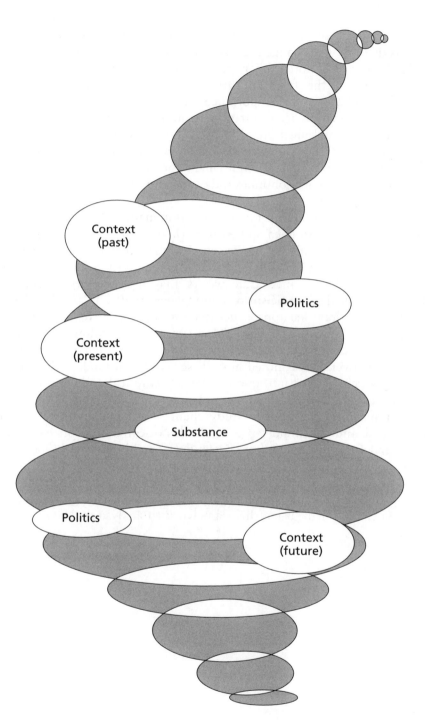

FIGURE 3.1
The process of
organizational
change

Context
(past)

Politics

Context
(present)

Substance

Politics

Context
(future)

and clarify their contribution to understanding change. From an early concern with the division of labour and the structure of organizations (Scientific Management), attention focused on the human aspects of organizing work to improve employee morale and motivation (human relations theory). The change aspects of this approach were further taken up and developed (most noticeably in North America) as a change perspective in its own right in the form of Organizational Development (OD). This approach emphasizes the importance of collaborative management and employee participation in an attempt to minimize employee resistance. In Europe, the Tavistock Institute of Human Relations proved influential in the research on the design of work structures which sought to accommodate both the social and technical requirements of production (interest in socio-technical systems theory continues today and is part of an ongoing debate on change management).

In turning our attention towards the dominance of contingency theory (especially in North America and Australia), an influential Australian model was described and critically appraised. I argued that context needs to be treated as an ongoing dynamic and that it is therefore necessary to develop more processually-informed frameworks that are able to accommodate political process. This criticism of contingency models is also levelled at a number of consultant-led approaches that put forward n-step recipes on how to 'successfully' manage change. These simple prescriptions for managing change fail to acknowledge the murky, unforeseen and dynamic character of change. Moreover, it was noted how these sequential models of change are increasingly being called into question by a theoretical and empirical movement towards more fluid, dynamic and processual accounts. In developing such a framework, the need to study change 'in-flight' and 'as-it-happens' was stressed and the importance of the historical dimension emphasized. Finally, under the processual framework developed in this book, the politics, substance and the unfolding context of change were all identified as being central to an adequate explanation of the change process. The remainder of the book focuses on the contemporary experience of change for people in work and employment, using this framework to analyse the data.

Flexibility, workplace change and non-standard employment

In this chapter, the views of a number of workers from a range of industries with contrasting cultures and traditions are used to explore how those on the receiving end of change make sense of their working lives. One intention is to balance the tendency in the literature to concentrate on management and the management of change from a managerialist perspective without giving due attention to the way the shop floor worker or office clerk experiences change. As Thompson and Ackroyd (1995) note, it has been rather quiet on the workplace front as research moves away from interviews with workers to a focus on management (although there has been a lively and extensive debate on the labour participation rates of women and the growth in part-time work; see, for example, Crompton, 1997; Drew et al., 1998; Walby, 1997). Another aim is to examine workers' views from a range of workplace environments rather than to present the view of an 'ideal employee' which misrepresents the variety of worker experience. For example, it is often claimed that the growth in casual, part-time and temporary employment benefits both employers (in linking jobs to market demands) and employees (the independent portfolio worker who develops a range of skills and engages in a number of jobs). It is argued here that, while some workers approved of part-time work (enabling them to accommodate other demands, such as child care), for others the shift away from standard full-time employment (as experienced by a number of those interviewed) has been marked by a deterioration in the conditions of work with the added burden of job insecurity (see Itzin and Newman, 1995). For example, Itzin and Phillipson (1995) have highlighted how the combined effects of ageism and sexism have left many older women in low status, low-paid, sex-segregated part-time work. Similarly, Newman and Williams (1995: 111) draw attention to the role of gender in making sense of the growth in part-time work and in explaining differing employee experiences of these shifts in employment practice. They caution against simple generalizations of employee experience that assume a gender neutrality by universalizing 'a white, male experience' of manufacturing work.

This problem of work myths – developed by academics and consultants, and then popularized in the media – is taken up by Bradley et al. (2000). They point out how the myth of globalization has been used to explain the growth in part-time work, the feminization of work and the decline of manufacturing in the West (see also Chapter 8). In examining issues such as technology, lean production and non-standard employment, the authors investigate work myths to uncover those elements that are credible and those that are not. They stress that while myths capture some of the changes that are occurring (that is, they are not synonymous with 'falsehoods'), they also present misinformation that can mislead and result in unfounded generalizations. These generalizations in turn influence strategic decision-making, such as the need to adopt flexible employment structures to meet the competitive demands of global competition (Bradley et al., 2000: 3). Similarly in this chapter, our concern is with unpacking some of the 'honeymoon' accounts of change reported in the literature by paying attention to the views of employees which are often missing or hidden in the reports of 'successful' change programmes.

SHIFTING EMPLOYMENT STRATEGIES IN THE DRIVE FOR PROFITS AND FLEXIBILITY

> Part-time and casual work is increasing and that's just the end of the story. People do part-time work because that is what is being offered. Different people, different needs. I don't ever want to work full-time. I enjoy doing part-time work and always have done. And probably for most of my working life I've done casual work. (Part-Time Worker)

Over the last two decades, there has been an ongoing change in types of employment signalled by the growth in part-time and casual work in the service sector and a decline in standard employment in manufacturing. In the UK, North America and Australia, changes in government legislation, business market restructuring and developments in technology are just some of the factors that have contributed to programmes of work reorganization and accompanying shifts in the nature and availability of jobs and career path opportunities. These changes have not been restricted to national boundaries, but are occurring on a global scale. For example, outsourcing (certain products and services are contracted out to another company) has rapidly increased in Europe, North America, Asia and Australia (Hunter and Gates, 1998: 133). This increase is contributing to a shift away from full-time employment as these new product and service providers adopt non-standard employment policies. The use of outsourcing in the public and private sectors has been questioned by some commentators who advocate that the main management motivation behind such decisions rests on ideological belief rather than empirical knowledge that outsourcing will improve their competitive position by reducing costs while maintaining quality (Domberger and Hensher, 1993). As Hunter and Gates (1998: 143) conclude in their discussion of outsourcing, 'outsourcing is functionally questionable, certainly fashionable, and the existence of considerable evidence to suggest that its current, unquestioning application is foolish'.

A rapidly expanding area that has been identified with non-traditional forms of work activity – outsourcing of service operations and the growth in part-time labour – is teleworking (Daniels et al., 2000; Jackson and Van der Wielen, 1998; Lamond et al., 1998). By the mid-1990s there were already around nine million teleworkers in the US and this upward trend continues on a worldwide scale. The growth in teleworking and the creation of, for example, call centres is not only bringing about change in the working environment and employment (see Taylor and Bain, 1999; Venkatraman and Henderson, 1998) but also increasing the job vulnerability of workers in the UK and Australia as companies view this type of work as being more 'profitably' serviced by employees outside of the domestic labour market. For example, a news item on BBC Radio 4 in November 2000 drew attention to the 'explosive demand' for young Indian graduates to work in call centres. Located in Delhi, these workers earn only one-half or one-third of their counterparts in Britain and have proven to be competent and efficient. They are trained in the use of small talk, are encouraged to cultivate an American or British accent, often adopt western names, and additional information (such as the weather conditions at the caller location) is automatically provided to aid conversation. Workers are able to establish a rapport with the customers who may be unaware that their service provider is located in India. The option for companies to use geographically remote employees to service domestic operations is an increasing concern for local employees who may find their bargaining position weakened and job security reduced. (It is also a concern for trade unions; see Chapter 9.)

The general shift towards non-standard employment has been summarized by Hutton (1995) as creating a '30–30–40' society. He argues that in Britain 30 per cent of the working population are employed in non-standard work (part-time and temporary work with few associated benefits), 30 per cent are unemployed and 40 per cent hold secure jobs (in full-time work, but they may be experiencing greater demands to work longer hours). According to Atkinson and Meager (1986), these changes have been associated with a general movement towards an ideal 'flexible firm'. The employment strategies of these companies centre on dividing their workforce into 'core' employees, who have standard employment contracts with a number of additional benefits to maintain their loyalty, and 'peripheral' employees, who are employed on a part-time or temporary basis. Peripheral employees are not necessarily low skilled. They may be self-employed professional workers who are hired for a particular contract; they are taken on by the company only when necessary and their numbers can be easily adjusted to meet changing market demands. This ability to rapidly increase or decrease the number of employees is generally referred to as numerical flexibility. As discussed in Chapter 2, Handy (1984, 1996) has used the term 'shamrock organization' to refer to three broad groups of core, peripheral and external workers (to correspond to the three leaves of a shamrock), and argues that such labour strategies provide organizations with three key advantages: numerical flexibility, functional flexibility and distancing. First, it allows for numerical flexibility – companies are able to adjust employee numbers by using part-time, temporary contracts, overtime and flexitime. Second, 'functional flexibility' can be achieved through a more adaptable core workforce. In other words, multi-skilling, job enlargement and the breaking down of job boundaries increase a 'firm's ability to adjust and deploy the skills of its employees to match the tasks required by its changing workload, production methods and technology' (Atkinson and Meager, 1986: 4). Third, 'distancing' can be achieved by allowing companies to sidestep job design problems by matching employment contracts to commercial contracts. These concepts have been used in the literature to explain the emergence of a model of the flexible firm where a core multi-skilled and functionally flexible workforce is combined with contract staff and temporary employees (Clutterbuck, 1985: 19). However, Pollert (1988) has found little evidence to suggest the widespread take-up of the flexible model and Gallie (1998) has noted that while there has been a 25 per cent rise in part-time employment in the UK (between 1984 and 1995), these jobs have largely been permanent. Nevertheless, as we shall see later, the use of part-time labour linked to weekend and shift work rosters have in some companies become the main form of employment contract (see also Beynon, 1997).

In examining worker experience of change, it is important not to lose sight of the experience of many full-time workers in more traditional and often declining industries. For example, the views of longstanding automotive workers, who may have spent their entire working lives in full-time jobs with a single company (such as Ford or General Motors), provide useful insights and are not as dissimilar as one might expect. As shown in the section that follows, workers who have a standard form of employment contract are also living with changes that undermine traditional behaviours, intensify work and threaten job security. Many of the traditional manufacturing areas where standard employment has been common are undergoing radical change. Employees have typically experienced an overall reduction in the number of jobs and significant changes in workplace arrangements (Beynon, 1984; Garraham and Stewart, 1992). They do not romanticize full-time work, but they do feel threatened by the changes being introduced both for their own job security, the changing methods of work and their own working experience. The worker views that follow demonstrate how the experience of work is not simply determined by the nature of the employment contract, but by a range of social, political and economic factors.

Under certain circumstances, a movement away from traditional full-time employment could be viewed as a good thing if people are in a position where they are able to make that choice and still maintain a reasonable standard of living. In other words, a context in which households are able to choose types of employment to meet their current needs could be viewed as a beneficial social development towards a more egalitarian society. In practice, however, it is usually the poorest sections of society who have the least choice, are employed in the worst working environments and have few, if any, options to improve their working life experience. It is understandable that for many of them the threat of unemployment is a major concern. Moreover, in the context of job vulnerability, whether actual or believed, management are able to pursue flexible labour strategies with industrial impunity and with little regard for the effects of change on worker experience. In the following section, the experience of change for workers in more standard forms of employment is examined prior to a discussion of outsourcing and employee experience of part-time and casual work.

MANAGEMENT OF CHANGE AND EMPLOYEE EXPERIENCE OF WORK

In all of the studies of change I have carried out from 1980 to 2002, it is possible to identify 'casualties' of change, that is, people who view change negatively and talk of a deterioration of their working environment. Unlike the popular consultant literature which views problems of employee commitment and acceptance as a problem of management implementation, the lived experience of employees draws attention to the diversity and variety of employee experience, and to how large-scale change is unlikely to be readily accepted by all employees. As one shop floor automotive worker said when asked to explain the good things about his job following a programme of work restructuring:

> The good things? That's difficult to say. I suppose basically it's a steady job and it brings you in your money at the end of the week. But as for really good, I can't say that there is much really good because there's not much prospect for promotion and you know that every week you're going to be doing the same thing over and over again. There's not much on the good side, I'm afraid.

Although this interviewee stressed the importance of money, other employees highlighted a wide range of different motivations to work, including camaraderie, family expectations, respect, personal identity, social status, responsibility for others and enjoyment. From economic instrumentalism to social expectations and personal choice, there was a surprisingly wide range of positions on work and on the effects of change on work experience. Involvement in change also varied. For example, some employees actively supported change initiatives, others resisted any attempts to change traditional work practices, and some remained on the sidelines monitoring change processes. What is noticeable is the range of worker responses to management change initiatives. For example, in a study of workplace change at Central Linen Services in South Australia, it was found that change in one area of the factory (which had been positively appraised by workers) had implications for the work of those in another section. In this case, the company had invested in the latest technology for their laundry facility and for many employees this had significantly improved their working conditions. The work environment was cleaner, safety standards had improved and injuries were reduced. But for some employees there had been a deterioration in their working environment. As one worker commented:

> Oh, yes. I can go back 10 years ago. Some guys have been here nearly on 25 or 30 years. But then – oh, it was good. See, we had a lot of room and it was a lot easier to work. Even then, when I walked in and saw the machinery I looked and thought: 'This stuff's out of the ark, it has to be.' Well, it was pretty old even then, worn out or whatever. But no, it was good. It was impressive, even then. When you told people what – from an outsider's point of view, if they'd never seen a laundry and you try to explain what it's like, they go in and they don't believe it. They think: 'You've got to be joking.' It's the same with the new machinery there now. We said, 'Oh, we've put in some new washers', and they said, 'Oh, yeah'. I said, 'They're about as long as your building and about ten feet high and eight feet wide'. They look at you and they don't believe it. . . . From my point of view, I suppose it's difficult, because it all looks to you beauty and great; but it hasn't affected my end of it except made it harder. Because they've taken up so much space that it's cramped our working area there and made it harder. So it's all great and all that, and they're putting out tons more linen. Well, as far as I'm concerned – that's not my job, you see – that's the figures and the people who collect the money. They think that's great because we're doing a whole lot more work. But then, by doing that, they've made it harder at the other end where we are. I suppose in a lot of areas they feel the same, too. In the dry fold area and that sort of thing, they're pressed for space, too, because there's a big monster in there that pumps out so much stuff that at times we get a bit snowed under.

The empirical evidence does not support the notion that change brings improvements for all. For many workers, it means working harder with fewer resources and more responsibilities. As one shop steward said when referring to change initiatives and employees' experience of work:

> God they've worked harder, they've worked smarter, they've worked faster, and they've worked with less. I mean they're doing everything that's been asked of them. And still they [management] keep coming back saying: 'We need more, we need more.'

In a South Australian automotive component manufacturing plant, lean production was introduced in order to cut down on work inefficiencies and enable employees to 'work smarter rather than harder'. In practice, many of the natural rest pauses and movements within the job – which allowed for social interaction – were eliminated and employees generally experienced an increase in on-the-job work demands and associated stress. From the perspective of management, these new production strategies were deemed central to ensuring the competitive future of the business. This myth was promoted internally and supported by external media coverage, and there was a tendency among employees to accept these changes as necessary to the survival of the company. In other words, although they did not appreciate work intensification they believed that these new techniques combined with hard work would ensure long-term employment security. As it turned out, some 18 months later a decision from corporate headquarters in Melbourne resulted in a reduction in the number of jobs at the plant. Staff morale plummeted, and anxiety over future job prospects became a major employee concern. In New Zealand, Fortex successfully introduced a number of changes into their Silverstream plant which considerably improved productivity. The plant at Mosgiel was able to track the quality of sheep products from the farm through meat processing to final shipment and distribution. The plant employed around 900 people and operated 22 hours a day on a shift work system that ran from 6 a.m. Monday until 6 a.m. Sunday morning. The major upturn in productivity was applauded in the local news media, and the workers – who lived in the expanding town of Mosgiel – understandably assumed that their jobs were secure. However, poor financial management and decision-making elsewhere in the corporation led the company to announce an overall loss of over NZ$45 million. Under these circumstances, the successful management of change at plant level did not offset corporate problems which ultimately resulted in closure of the Silverstream plant and the company going into receivership. From being named by *Management Magazine* as the top company of the year, Fortex declined under the free-market competition where it had initially flourished. Employees lost their jobs and many owned property in areas that no longer had any work to offer. Another blow came when former Fortex workers, who had taken out mortgage protection insurance against possible unemployment, found that they could lose their right to social welfare benefits. The fact that the plant had developed a new model of employment relations, was using advanced technology and was actively involved in TQM did not prevent the loss of nearly 900 jobs.

In a final illustration of 'successful change' – where the introduction of cellular manufacturing was generally accepted by employees and trade union officials as a good development – casualties of change can be identified. In this case, some workers at the General Motors plant who preferred operating a single machine rejected the shift to new teamwork arrangements. These workers (many of whom had previously been model employees) were expected to change their behaviours and adapt to the new form of work organization implemented by the local management team. Since the union had been involved in and supported the change – with many members preferring the changed work environment – support for their position was not forthcoming from either their union or other work colleagues. During this longitudinal study of change (which involved regular visits to the plant) employee groups in the work cells developed a new set of social rules to regulate 'appropriate' employee behaviour. Over time, the enforcement of these rules became less visible to 'insiders' who continuously reinforced the values and beliefs of their group. These new social rules resulted in resistors to change being labelled as 'outsiders'. Although these established workers did not accept the redefined social rules that were being used to judge their actions (and thereby viewed their evaluators as 'outsiders'), in practice they moved from being the rule-enforcers (based on tradition) to being rule-breakers (under the new consensus). The extent of their 'outsiderness' may be a reflection of how they view their own position and of those who label them 'deviant' (perhaps in using stereotypes, such as 'older workers find it difficult to change their behaviours'; see Chapter 6). In this sense, the deviant worker becomes the person who has been successfully labelled deviant by others (Becker, 1973), a social process that combines with the structural changes to bring about a marked deterioration in the experience of work for these particular employees.

Each of these short examples highlights the variety of worker experience. They draw attention to the popular myth that change benefits all, to the view that new forms of work organization are better than older forms of work (and that teamwork is a good thing per se), and to the importance of social processes in shaping worker experience of change. They also draw attention to the mistaken belief that successful workplace change (in terms of productivity improvement, cost reduction, and so forth) equates with long-term job security. It is of little value to know that you were part of a particularly successful change initiative if you no longer have a job. This is the lived experience of many workers who find themselves at the sharp end of decisions made elsewhere and over which they have no control. Job security remains a key issue for many workers and it is to their views on this issue and their experience of non-standard employment that our attention now turns.

FULL-TIME EMPLOYMENT AND THE PUSH FOR FLEXIBILITY: OUTSOURCING AND PART-TIME WORK

Many organizations have sought to introduce new forms of employment in the expectation that this will provide greater flexibility in accommodating fluctuations in business activity. One organization that pushed for this shift was Ansett Australia (an airline that ceased operations from midnight on Monday 4 March 2002, leaving Qantas as the major Australian airline). In the case of Adelaide airport, one employee explained:

> We never ever had anything but full-time employment at the airport. They pushed and pushed and pushed and pushed and pushed part-time. We were the last people in the nation here to agree to part-time. Now they use two part-timers to do what one full-timer could do. Part-time is a totally useless facility at the airport. Their maximum hours has got to be 30 and they can do that just like that, it doesn't take any time. Most of them sit on 29.6 hours per week, and then they go onto overtime. So most part-timers would work up to their maximum part-time hours then they would probably work between 15 and 20 hours a week overtime. So why don't they put on full-time employment?

It was argued that the general manager was convinced of the benefits of part-time work because of what was happening in businesses elsewhere. There was no attempt to look at the particular context of operations at Adelaide airport; rather, it was assumed that benefits would result:

> The last General Manager . . . was sold the bill of goods about part-time contracts and they convinced him that part-time was the only way to go. So he insisted that everyone has part-time employees. At a lot of the other bases they won't allow part-timers to work overtime, but we can't operate without the part-timers doing overtime. There's just too much work for us to do.

In negotiating with the union over the introduction of part-time work, it was agreed that there would be no more than 12 part-time positions. These new posts were created in the late 1990s. At this time, management anticipated that this new group of employees would be paid a flat rate of pay. In practice, however, they consistently worked overtime and typically doubled their weekly income. In other words, the employer was paying a higher rate for the part-timers to do overtime to meet normal work demands. Initially, these new posts created some conflict among existing staff at the airport, as one interviewee recalls:

> It took a long time for the full-timers to accept them. But probably now we wouldn't give them back. But they're people that you know now, you've worked with them for the last three years. Once you get the familiarity thing going you know, nobody can do things to anybody once they know who you are. They can do it to strangers but they can't do it to someone that they know. So we've got the part-timers, they do provide bulk and it's good now. But I'm just terrified of the casual situation and I think a lot of the full-timers are very nervous about the loss of full-time employment. Outsourcing and all these sort of things may come.

A union shop steward was particularly concerned over the growing tendency for business organizations to outsource operations and the implications of this for full-time employment:

> The outsourcing thing is the biggest thing. I think that's the biggest worry with our full-time employment. I mean if they outsource customer service then we're stuffed. I mean there's no way you are going to be able to unionise an outsourcing company – well I suppose you can if everyone wants to join in. But they're not going to be entitled to anything like they're getting with an airline company. That's one of the main worries; outsourcing is really big on the agenda. Full-time employment and security of that employment is probably the biggest thing. Now if the shit was to hit the fan tomorrow and these people were forced into a position that said like, 'We had to walk'. And the company said, 'If you guys walk the decision is out of our hands and we'll outsource customer service'. I would not get them out of the door. They wouldn't go. I mean, I probably wouldn't go either. So everyone is so insecure because they're selling it off piecemeal, a little bit here, a department closing down there, door-to-door freight is going to go . . . everywhere you turn they seem to be getting rid of bits and pieces. Of course it's making people very nervous and you're looking at a workforce, the average years of working at the airport, in my environment, is

something like 17 or 18 years and that's just average. The rest of us are since Adam first trotted down to have a bite of the apple.

It has been argued that with the growing trend to outsourcing, a climate of uncertainty can be created in which the power of employees and trade unions may be significantly weakened. In discussing the effects of this change on employee behaviour a number of workers indicated that there was a growing tendency to accept what they were told by management. This was reinforced by their labour market position and fear of job loss. As one interviewee at Savings & Loans Credit Union reflected:

> They're happy that they've got a job, so let's not rock the boat because I don't want to lose my job. So there's that fear there because you hear it all the time now, nobody's job is secure now. There is no job security. That works well from the employers' point of view because they can just use that. So the employee doesn't rock the boat, doesn't make noise because they could lose their job.

In this example, the spectre of unemployment is a factor that weakens the position of employees and lends support to the creation of a more compliant workforce. In the case of Mitsubishi Motors, the possibility of further job losses was also a major concern among employees. In this instance, employees claimed that worker numbers had been reduced and yet the management hierarchy remained. As two employees from the company noted:

> A: We've always said that there's too many chiefs and not enough Indians.
> B: That's the whole punch of the story. There's just too bloody many managers and bloody people down there like that.
> A: It's always been frustrating hasn't it? We're never going to get them to move that because they're going to protect their asses. They build their own little castles then they put moats around them. Well, companies are starting to come to the realisation that maybe we are a little bit top heavy . . . but those people are still going to fight as hard as us. I mean, shit I don't want to be out there. I've got to pay the same butcher's bill, I've got to pay for the same grocery bill. I'm going to hang on to my job and if the Indians have to go, well, bad luck as long as I've not got to do their work.

This transcript spotlights employee recognition of how different groups are likely to react to a change that threatens their position within the organization. There is a clear realization that there is neither a simple common culture nor a new collaborative system of employment relations where everyone is on the same team. Power and class are recognized as central to the political processes of change. However, the solidarity of workers at Mitsubishi is once again undermined by the threat of redundancy. Within this context, attempts by management to divide and rule were noted on a number of occasions. As one employee recounted when he attempted to get management to let them finish earlier prior to Christmas:

> 'We don't want to finish on Christmas Eve, we want to finish two days before Christmas.' They're all going 'Go on do something about it'. Okay. So I go to

the boss and I say to him, 'All the [people] out there are unhappy. They don't want to finish on Christmas Eve. They've got families, they want to finish two days before.' And he goes, 'Who's that?'. And I go, 'I can't give you names but it's all those out there'. He says, 'Okay I'll get all the managers together and we'll ask them individually'. What's the response? [all laugh] The manager goes, 'When do you want to finish? Are you not happy with Christmas Eve?'. 'Oh no, Christmas Eve's fine.' So he says, 'You seem to be the only one who's got a problem with Christmas Eve'. So I'm not going to do that again.

The reluctance of employees to question management and stand firm on a particular position was not uncommon. Many employees were cynical about management change strategies. This tongue-in-cheek cynicism was especially noticeable when discussing change initiatives that sought to develop harmonious work relations. It was argued that many of these changes were not about improving the working environment but about eroding full-time employment opportunities and intensifying work.

Although outsourcing strategies are generally employer-driven, the demand for part-time work can be employee-driven and have social and familial origins. For example, in the case of Mitsubishi, there was a problem for some employees who wanted part-time employment rather than the full-time jobs they held. In one instance, an employee who had a 2-year-old child wanted to go part-time, but under the regulations the only way this person could go part-time was under the maternity arrangements (but the child had been born two years earlier) or if the person had a physical disability. However, immediately following the birth of her child she had returned to full-time employment because her husband had been off work as the result of an industrial injury. Recently he had returned to full-time employment and now the Mitsubishi employee was seeking to go part-time. Although this clearly raises a question over the regulations, the flexibility in working arrangements has largely been introduced to benefit the company rather than employees. For the union, there was concern about the growth in part-time employment which might reduce the number of full-time positions, and yet there is a potential conflict with securing the job requirements of members. Once again, there are many things going on in this example. Not only does it raise questions about power relations between the union and employer, but also about the culture of trade unionism in the automotive industry. Historically, women have exercised little formal bargaining power in this traditionally male bastion and, consequently, their views are interpreted by others who may consciously or unconsciously marginalize women. As noted elsewhere, it is by looking through a 'gender lens' (Williams and Macalpine, 1995) that 'it is possible to bring into focus patterns in women's experience of organizational life'. This lens also enables us to make sense of how the world is viewed by certain social groups in particular contexts. In this example, four union representatives and an industrial officer (all male) talked around the issue at some length. (I spent the whole day with this group, including an informal lunch at a local hotel.)

A short extract from this discussion follows:

A: Let me read you the part-time clause and see what you think. You know what the principles of the union is – well it's certainly ours – we've got 65 to 70 per cent of our membership is female, not that that's reflected around here at the moment – sorry guys. So we've got to take that into consideration. This is where we're still back to the Chrysler days when it was more male-orientated when they were bringing these Awards together. I know that the intention of the part-time clause was to make sure that employers don't have the position of being able to put a pile of part-time people on. It was really about giving people the ability to have a full-time job. That was the first cab off the rank, and then part-time was by agreement down the track.
[discussion]
B: Didn't we put a percentage on that? . . .
A: No, no, that's to do with temporary. This is the Award provision for part-time employees: 'where an employer is willing to employ a person full-time but such person because of some physical disability can only accept work for a limited number of hours each week, then such person may be employed as a part-time employee and be paid at an hourly basis of the weekly rate prescribed for the classification involved'. So if you're a Lord Nelson and you've got one eye, one arm and one asshole, you'll take part-time but if you haven't you can't.
B: Well would a physical disability include having a child that you have to look after?
A: No, no. A physical disability is . . .
B: Well it is physical, it depends on which way . . .

Clearly a male-oriented perception of the issues dominates the conversation, even to the extent of questioning whether having a child could be considered to be equivalent to a physical disability (even though tongue-in-cheek, the notion was nevertheless raised just in case others might take this point more seriously). Over the next 20 minutes the discussion continued around the issue of part-time employment and the restrictive nature of the clause. It was noted that while management would like greater opportunities to employ part-time people at the site, the union was concerned about losing permanent full-time positions. For some, job-sharing was a good option (you maintained a full-time position which was carried out by two people, possibly with both being union members). However, management were reluctant to go down this particular route and opposed this development. Again, this highlights the different interests of the groups and individuals, the importance of the 'gender lens' in helping us to make sense of what is going on, and how power relations and political processes shape employee experiences of change. As it turned out, the employee was able to take up a part-time position, but union concern over job loss remains.

THE CASUALIZATION OF WORK, JOB INSECURITY AND EMPLOYEE REPRESENTATION

The casualization of work is another area that is changing employee experience of work. For Bradley et al. (2000: 58–9), the increasing use of casual labour by companies has been ideologically driven. As they state: 'Behind the rhetoric of enterprise, individualism and flexibility, the reality for many workers is employment that is casualized: characterised by low pay, insecurity and poor working conditions'.

Savings & Loans Credit Union provides a good example of a company that has increased its use of casual labour. In this organization there is no upper limit set on the number of casuals employed (approximately half of the 300 employees were casual), as one workplace representative explained:

> You are either full-time or you're casual. We've got a dilemma where at the moment we are trying to get the casuals recognised as a form of permanent part-time. . . . They have regular hours, they're given rosters – so it's not like you're being called in willy nilly – it's like you've got a fixed roster to work from and you tend to have that roster for a few months. Our argument is that they're really permanent part-time, so we're trying to get that sorted out now. And when I talk to casuals I try and mention that the union is trying to get something for you casuals, to get you some form of stability or some security. But if we've got the numbers it does help to negotiate a fairer deal and stuff like that. So I tend to use that. So I guess that casuals have the lower number of union members because they always bring it down to cost, or they have this mentality that they're only here for a short while, or they're casual and they don't have any rights. . . . If you're a casual you don't have to give them any notice. I mean they can resign on the spot because they're casual but management can also terminate their job on the spot. I mean, we'd argue the point. If we could prove that this person had been working three years, I'm sure they'd have a good case to argue for permanent part-time and get some sort of back pay. But nobody has actually ever done that.

There were also a number of issues concerning the employment status of women who return to work after maternity leave. Essentially, if you are a full-time member of staff and you take maternity leave, when you return you have a choice between permanent full-time and casual employment status. At the time of the study, there was no provision for permanent part-time or any job-sharing options at Savings & Loans. Consequently, women returning from maternity leave who did not want to work full-time found themselves downgraded to lower skilled casual work:

> There's also a problem with women going on maternity leave. Savings & Loans hasn't got, what I call, a good history with that. . . . If you're spending all this money training somebody and they've got years of experience, why suddenly lose them because you're not prepared to be a little bit more flexible, or a little bit more open-minded to get somebody to come back to work and use that knowledge. I mean they might only want to be part-time for a few years and then go back to full-time. If management bring them back as casuals they go back to the bottom of the ladder. So you've got this person with all this experience and knowledge, but suddenly they're not using it anymore because you've got them at the bottom. And you've just wasted all that, you know, if they could come back into a similar position as before but in a job-share situation part-time, they could use that knowledge. I mean you spend all this time and money, why not use it?

The tendency to provide lower graded work in the part-time and casual category was found in a number of organizations. As an employee at Mitsubishi in South Australia explained:

> Unfortunately with part-time and casual employment. It's 80 to 90 per cent of the jobs done by part-time and casual employees are at the bottom rung, the bottom end of the scale for want of a better phrase. And all of the more demanding jobs are up on a full-time basis which a lot of people still want to do.

Another issue at Savings & Loans is the absence of child care facilities. The majority of employees are women and yet there is little understanding of the problems faced by casuals with child care responsibilities who may be suddenly called in for extra work. The organization is not developing more flexible arrangements for those who have child care responsibilities, or for those who, having taken maternity or paternity leave, would like to return to a permanent part-time job. Once again, these arrangements have been developed for the benefit of the company rather than for the mutual benefit of employees and employer.

At TAB (an Australian betting organization) casual work is the major form of employment. Apart from supervisors, all other workers (just over 150) are employed on a casual basis. The business operates six days a week from 9.30 a.m. until the last race each evening, with a growing number of Sunday meetings. The telephone betting operations take place in one building over two floors. On quieter days (such as Sundays and Fridays) it is mainly the second floor that is used, while on busier days the third floor is used as well. In this way, the organization is able to adjust to fluctuations in demand, cancellation of races and the running of additional race meetings. Unlike conventional forms of work organization, there is no scheduled collective break for workers; rather, small groups of employees take their break on a rotation basis.

> We tend to have 15-minute and 10-minute breaks and so you're not really structured in a way that you might be in a normal workplace, where everybody has that half-hour break. You know, five people will go on a 15-minute break, then another five will go on another 15-minute break, then another five will go on a 15-minute break and that. Because it's all timed in with the races. The whole business runs around the races. We do have a very good work environment but there's a lot of room for improvement. We do have a lot of misinformation that goes around as far as what people are entitled to and that seems to come from this middle management structure.

The rotation break arrangement limits social interaction and undermines collective forms of representation. Although some of the workforce is unionized, joining a union is no longer compulsory (as it was at the beginning of the 1990s).

> Within the TAB there was a noticeable drop in union membership when you had freedom of choice. And that was for any number of reasons. There were a few

people who simply didn't agree with unions so they dropped out and that's fine. And then you just had people who were ambivalent. They just didn't care. And then there's natural attrition where people have just left, so that also lowered it over the years. In telephone betting the membership is in a minority now and that's partly because it's very difficult to get in touch with the people.

In this organization, being casual simply means being paid for the hours that you work. The rate of pay for casual employees is higher than that for permanent staff as it includes penalty rates to cover holidays and sick pay. However, contracts can be terminated and the hours of work cut back without formal notice. If management deem it necessary, they can roster a casual employee for only two hours a day (the minimum). Typically, employees work four- to six-hour sessions over a six-day period:

> The way they operate in telephone betting because you can be there from any time from 9.30 to last start time which is usually 6.45 at night. Two to three weeks in advance you get what we call a roster. And that just basically says on Monday you're working at 5 o'clock, on Wednesday you're working at 11, on Friday you might be starting work at 2 and on Saturday you're starting work at 10. And most shifts during the day will go five to five and a half hours. On Saturday they can go from four hours if you've got a night shift to six hours. So that varies and that may change because it depends on when the races start. The industry does revolve around when the actual races are.

Although job insecurity was an issue, jobs were viewed as more secure than many other types of casual employment. This was explained in terms of the demand for betting (viewed as unlikely to fall in the immediate future) and by the interest of the government in keeping the organization going (to provide government revenue). Although these jobs were relatively secure, if a manager took a dislike to an employee then that person could end up unemployed. In this respect, casual employees are far more vulnerable than permanent workers (whether part-time or full-time) and, as a consequence, there is a tendency for workers to keep a low profile and not to 'rock the boat'. As one interviewee explained when talking about the reluctance of some employees to join a trade union:

> Unionism isn't something that's really ever talked about. You don't hear it as a conversation because the women don't want to make waves. It's because of a genuine fear that they might lose their jobs. You know, if I upset the person higher up then I might get less shifts and I can't afford to work less shifts, so if I get less shifts I might as well leave. And that's a very real attitude here, especially with people who've been here a long time. And I think that attitude could get a little bit stronger too with the new boss we've got.

The insecurity of working in this type of environment does shape employee behaviour and serves to weaken the bargaining position of workers. The rostering arrangement also constrains the development of a collective identity among employees and thereby strengthens the power relations of management. This shift in power in favour of management is reflected in the following transcript:

> The woman in charge of rostering who allocates the shifts doesn't have to give you any amount of set hours. . . . You could say, 'I'm available to work four shifts a week', but they might only give you two. So they don't have to give you what you would like as far as shifts go. And again that's because you're casual – there's no set hours that you have to work and there's no set hours that they have to allocate you.

Since it is important to maintain a good relationship with their supervisor, employees are generally reluctant to complain about decisions or changes that affect their jobs:

> A lot of people they just want to go in, do their jobs, get paid and go home. Which is fine, I mean that's what I want to do too. But I mean, if I'm being asked to try and flog a type of bet, then excuse me, I expect to get some sort of reward for that. You're asking me to do something that's not really in the description of this job when I first started here. But people don't view it that way.

For some employees this form of casual work offered some real advantages over standard full-time employment. For example, it was stressed that men and women who have child care responsibilities can find this form of employment beneficial. (This finding has also been supported by the research of Mauthner et al. [2001] on work and family life in rural communities.) In our case, Joan gave the example of her own situation where the care of their children is shared between her and her partner. John finishes work at 4 p.m. and Joan starts work at 5 p.m., so between them, there is usually one who is working and the other who is at home looking after the children.

> When he does overtime, which means that he finishes at twenty-to-six and I'm due to start work at five, we just take the child around to his mother. And that's not straining the friendship there because it's only for two hours. And it's only a couple of times a week and not necessarily every week. I mean [John] is not working on Saturday so I go off to work during the day on Saturday. So sometimes with casual jobs, you've got children and a husband, then you can fit in with the hours. But then there is a woman at work whose husband's a taxi driver. She has to come in to work at 4.30 and he has to finish at 4 and he complains because he's missing out on two hours' pay. It's a mixed bag, it really is. . . . For as many different combinations of people that you've got, you're going to have as many different outcomes, really.

Students are another group who have increasingly taken up casual positions at TAB. The job provides income to help them finance their time at university. University students are mostly in evidence on the weekends, but many also make themselves available on certain afternoons when they have no lectures. Casual employment does provide some benefits to employees who seek to schedule other activities (child care, study and so forth) around a casual job that provides a higher rate of pay and more flexibility than permanent forms of employment. On the other hand, their bargaining position is often weakened and an attitude of conformity is more likely to prevail. Employees see themselves as being in a weak bargaining position and, in so doing, contribute to the unequal power relations between managers and workers. This is also demonstrated by the reluctance of employees to engage in behaviours that may conflict with management and may attract attention. The rostering of breaks and the organization of work also act to limit any sense of collective solidarity, which is further frustrated by the different backgrounds and expectations of employees. In addition, legislative change that makes union membership no longer compulsory has also contributed to a deterioration in employee power and a strengthening of management (although access to union representation is still available, there has been a noticeable fall in union members). Under this casual form of employment, workers do not get paid sick leave and holiday entitlements, yet this form of employment also offers opportunities for people to coordinate work and family lives to suit their changing requirements. These new patterns of work do not provide any kind of enhanced working experience, but they do enable some flexibility in combining paid employment with other life activities (see Mauthner et al., 2001).

CONCLUSION

This chapter set out to examine employees' experience of changes in work and employment. Drawing on interview data collected over the last ten years, a small number of case illustrations demonstrated the variety of worker experience. In particular, attention was given to change programmes that have generally been supported by employees and union officials to show that even under such circumstances, it is possible to identify casualties of change. Workers who reject new working arrangements and attempt to hold on to traditional work practices may not only suffer the discomfort of local management pressure to change, but they may also become isolated from other workers and their union. Furthermore, as a new set of rules and social consensus emerge in the work group, those unwilling to change may become labelled as 'outsiders'. For these workers, behaviour that was previously praised and supported by the local culture has now become defined as inappropriate, outmoded and deviant. In other examples, it was shown how change that may be positive for one section of a factory may have implications for work elsewhere, and how in a number of cases the implementation of change resulted in an intensification of work (work was not smarter but harder).

Two case companies were used to illustrate how, even when change is successful, problems created by management elsewhere in the company or decisions to rationalize operations at corporate headquarters can result in the loss of jobs. These brief accounts break open some of the myths of workplace change, such as the myth that successful change equates with long-term survival for the company and job security for workers. Too frequently, the view that companies have to change to survive in the competitive business world is used to promote change initiatives that are unnecessary and damaging. Blind change stimulated by unfounded beliefs popularized in the media is no better than a no-change approach that either dwells on past commercial success or is stifled by tradition and ignores the need for change. Similarly, it is not the case that all employees will readily accept or reject workplace change initiatives, or view the growth in part-time and casual labour as simply a good or bad thing. Worker views are far more varied and complex. For example, in the case of part-time work, some workers wanted this type of work and could never see themselves returning to full-time permanent employment. However, many of these new employment policies were a consequence of an uncritical belief by management in the competitive advantage of having part-time and casual workers. The assumption of competitive flexibility (being able to reduce or increase the number of employees in response to market demands) was not supported by the airline example (where part-time employees worked overtime as a matter of course).

Taken as a whole, change in employment policies in addition to company outsourcing strategies were identified as weakening the position of employees by undermining the development of any collective form of employee representation. The concomitant growth in job insecurity and fears of unemployment created a more compliant (yet dissatisfied) workforce and strengthened the position of management. It is not part-time work per se that workers view as an issue; rather, it is the political consequence of holding a weak labour market position. In other words, the precarious employment position of workers creates a context in which employees are more likely to remain silent. Although quelling the voice of workers may suit some companies, it also suggests a general deterioration in the work experience of many employees who feel powerless to question the decisions of management. In a climate where the future of jobs is increasingly uncertain, where factories or branches can be closed through corporate decisions or management failure, where jobs for life and company career progression are a thing of the past, where collective representation is in decline, and where company outsourcing and the use of part-time and casual labour are on the increase, it is no wonder that some employees have become disappointed, fatigued and cynical about company change initiatives.

New technology and power relations

5

This chapter illustrates how a company (Dalebake Bakeries) developed a strategy to meet changing market conditions only to experience unanticipated changes in the business environment that threatened the commercial viability of its operations. A heavy investment in technology to produce large quantities of standard loaves at low cost was met by an unforeseen shift in public demand for different types of bread that was not simply determined by price. The demand for greater customer choice was further reinforced by the purchasing policies of the powerful supermarkets who acted to limit the strategic options open to Dalebake Bakeries. This case study is an example of a major change initiative that almost locked the company onto a trajectory doomed to failure even though the initial planning made commercial sense at the time. The case analysis examines the need to reinterpret the strategic direction of the company and reconfigure what appeared as fixed technical–structural arrangements. The next section provides a brief overview of some of the debates surrounding technology and change at work.

TECHNOLOGY AND CHANGE AT WORK: AN OVERVIEW OF CONCEPTUAL DEBATES

Understanding technology and change at work has stimulated a large body of research (see Preece et al., 2000). Early studies were concerned with developments in production technology and the effects of different levels of mechanization on the structure of jobs and the experience of work (Dawson et al., 2000). In these studies, structures appropriate for organizations working in different environments are identified (Burns and Stalker, 1961) and some classifications of the relationships between technology, organization structure and operating performance are developed (Woodward, 1980). For example, the importance of technology in configuring the work situation and the alienating consequences for employees were prominent in the work of Blauner (1964). Under his typology, workers in the 'modern' factory had regained control over technology – a control lost under mass production –

and had greater opportunities (freedom) to engage in meaningful work experiences. (Interestingly, Woodward's work on production systems reached similar conclusions.) Against this kind of reasoning grew the labour process debate, which was stimulated by the work of Braverman (1974). It was argued that the dominant organizational form of mass production (which was closely aligned with Taylorism) was responsible for 'the degradation of work in the twentieth century'. In taking a strong structural–theoretical position, the labour process and the general societal situation were seen to largely reflect each other (the class divide was replicated in the workplace). This concept of management as a united group exploiting a compliant workforce was later refined and criticized by other commentators (Burawoy, 1979; Friedman, 1977; Piore and Sabel, 1984).

In promoting the concept of 'strategic choice', Child (1972) drew attention away from the technical by emphasizing the importance of social choice and negotiation in shaping work and organization. Studies that took a technological–determinist stance – where technology was seen to determine organizational forms and change outcomes – were heavily criticized during the 1980s and 1990s (see McLoughlin, 1999). A principal contribution from the sociology of technology has been its persistent critique of technological determinism and its development of analytical approaches that can handle the socio-technical construction of technology. Technology is seen to be the result of negotiations, involving a multiplicity of diverse actors cutting across established organizational borders. Where the social shaping of technology tradition has pointed to the role of established players and their diverse interests, the social constructivist perspective has pointed to the parallel and mutual construction of actor interests and the notion of weaving the 'seamless web of socio-technical ensembles' (Clausen and Koch, 1999; Williams and Edge, 1996). This Social Construction of Technology (SCOT) approach takes the view that what technology is, and what it can be, are not structurally determined or influenced by independent technical variables; rather, they are socially constructed and therefore cannot be understood independently of human interpretation (Grint and Woolgar, 1997: 10).

In analysing the development of the bicycle, Pinch and Bijker (1987: 40) show how the 'political situation of a social group shapes its norms and values, which in turn influence the meaning given to an artifact'. According to this approach, there is 'interpretative flexibility' both in the way people view technology and in the way new technologies are developed and designed. In drawing on the example of the controversial pneumatic tyre during the late nineteenth century, the authors illustrate how by redefining the innovation from a vibration solution (it was considered an aesthetically unsavoury accessory) to a solution to the problem of speed (it was success-fully mounted on a racing bicycle) the sporting cyclists and general public were convinced of its feasibility – which resulted in the 'closure' and 'stabilisation' of the technology through the 'disappearance' of 'problems' (Pinch and Bijker, 1987). Although, as the authors illustrate in quoting from a section of the Stanley Exhibition of Cycles in 1890, some engineers viewed the air tyre as 'an ugly looking way of making the low-wheeler even less safe' (Pinch and Bijker, 2000: 709):

> The most conspicuous innovation in the cycle construction is the use of pneumatic tires. These tires are hollow, about 2 in. diameter, and are inflated by the use of a small air pump. They are said to afford most luxurious riding, the roughest macadam and cobbles being reduced to the smoothest asphalt. Not having had the opportunity of testing these tires, we are unable to speak of them from practical experience: but looking at them from a theoretical point of view, we opine that considerable difficulty will be experienced in keeping the tires thoroughly inflated. Air under pressure is a troublesome thing to deal with. From the reports of those who have used these tires, it seems that they are prone to slip on muddy roads. If this is so, we fear their use on rear-driving safeties – which are all more or less addicted to side-slipping – is out of the question, as any improvement in this line should be to prevent side slop and not to increase it. Apart from these defects, the appearance of the tires destroys the symmetry and graceful appearance of a cycle, and this alone is, we think, sufficient to prevent their coming into general use.

Grint and Woolgar (1997: 164) take this argument further in their onion model of the sociology of technology, in which they argue that the capacities and representations of machines are not objective reflections but social constructions (the machine always 'appears cooked and never raw') and that 'even at the very centre of the onion, then, we would argue that there is no residual technical core which is in principle impervious to social analysis'.

From a related perspective, Actor Network Theory (ANT) points to the radical indeterminacy of the actor in allowing entities to define and construct one another (Callon, 1999). Latour (1991) draws attention to the importance of non-human actants in which he posits the view that technology is society made durable. Moser and Law (1999) usefully illustrate this weaving of non-humans into the social fabric of society in their exploration of the subjectivities and materialities of a person who is physically disabled. Studies that seek to highlight the subjective indeterminacy of technological arrangements, the interpretative flexibility of the design and use of technology, or the material constraints of artifacts and systems on the political process of choice and decision-making in organizations all form part of a lively and, it would seem, expanding debate on political process and technology. A special issue of the journal *Technology Analysis and Strategic Management* (Clausen et al., 2000) captured some of these concerns. For example, in drawing on three Australian case studies, McLoughlin et al. (2000) are critical of those who treat technology as simply something that is designed elsewhere without an understanding of the way technologies are shaped within the local context of the adopting firm. They use the term 'configurational' to refer to the way change agents ('intrepreneurs') manage the interpretations and understandings of others in gaining legitimacy for the establishment of new operational configurations, and to highlight the importance of studying technological change 'as-it-happens' on the shop floor. In addition, studies by Luff et al. (2000) on how technology is used in everyday work activities draw attention to the need to examine the methods and resources used by individuals in their place of work. Heath and Luff (2000) argue that technologies do not simply function outside of their use and that we often mistakenly assume that we know how others use them in the coordination of workplace tasks and activities. This again demonstrates the problem with studies that assume how technology will be used in practice without any detailed examination of actual use in context.

The case study that follows illustrates how people are able to accommodate the limitations and constraints of a technology designed for the production of a mass product that is no longer in demand. In dealing with practical issues, innovative solutions and new ways of working emerged in both the use and reconfiguration of the technology. Interestingly, it shows how a technology designed to dominate the way work was organized soon became outmoded following a market shift, and how it was the knowledge of traditional tools and the use of conventional methods that became critical to the workplace accommodation of this change. The resilience and abilities of people in the face of technology echo some of the findings evident in the studies described above. However, the data collected in this case study not only draw attention to the issue of technology and workplace reconfiguration, but also illustrate how the unequal power relationship between this company and their customers (the large supermarkets) shaped outcomes.

NEW TECHNOLOGY AT DALEBAKE BAKERIES

During the early 1980s, Dalebake Bakeries (part of the parent company Yorkshire Foods) operated a number of individual bakeries in the York area (Leeds, Bradford, Dewsbury and Whitby). In these factories a lot of manual operations were associated with the process of bread-making. Employees would manually load and unload the bread tins as they moved from the prover to the oven and were finally depanned from the baking tins and placed on a series of racks to cool, prior to packaging, loading and distribution to the customer. The typical output at these sites was approximately 2000 standard loaves per hour. These bakeries serviced the main retail outlets in the York area.

In seeking to reduce costs and improve productive output, a new state-of-the-art bakery was opened in 1991 at Mossdale in South Yorkshire. The new highly automated operation used computer technology to control process operations. The computerized system regulates the flow of raw materials into mixers where the ingredients are combined to produce up to 650 kg of dough every six minutes. The dough is automatically divided, rounded and moulded and then machine-placed into tins which travel along machine-paced conveyors into the computer-regulated ovens. The baked bread then continues its journey and is automatically depanned and placed on cooling racks prior to packaging. Under this new automated system (which represented an investment of some £16 million in new machinery and equipment), the bakery can produce 13,000 loaves per hour. The other four sites have been closed, labour reduced and York operations consolidated into the Dalebake Bakery at Mossdale.

CONSUMER DEMAND AND CUSTOMER POWER: A CHANGING MARKET

Since the early 1990s, there has been a shift in consumer demand from the standard loaf towards a higher quality and more diverse product range. This trend has combined with an expansion in the size and market position of the supermarkets. In the South Yorkshire market the two main players are Asco and Tesda. These two powerful customers have pushed the price of bread down and actively shaped the nature of the market. As the factory manager noted:

> In a ten-year history we've gone from our proprietary brands, our stock standard bread which ten years ago was very popular, household names I suppose and less variety. There was one-sized bread, white, you may have got a grain and a wholemeal and that was what the market was happy with, and it was generally proprietary brands. Then the supermarkets came along and they obviously wanted to try and squeeze prices down – the supermarkets see bread as part of the staple diet – so if bread is at a good price that gets customers in the turnstiles and you can make it on other stuff. . . . That's fine for them, but for us, we only make bread and a few other things. But generally, that's our business so it makes it a bit tougher for us.

The other major player in the South Yorkshire market is Breadcoop, a group of independent store owners who have come together to compete with the larger supermarkets. There is a Breadcoop Board, which being made up of owner-operators is far more entrepreneurial. Unlike store managers in Asco and Tesda, Breadcoop operators tend not to be driven by some specific global strategy and are less likely to follow any rigid party line. Because managers have greater discretion and independence, there is more room for negotiation and discussion between Dalebake and the Breadcoop outlets. For example, in discussing the value of having representatives in the field, it was explained that with the big supermarkets local managers might have very little room to manoeuvre:

> If we have a sales rep out at the market place and he has a good rapport with local managers, sometimes that isn't a real value. You know I might say, 'Patrick, you know, can I get an end here with bread?'. And you go, 'Ah yeah, that is unlikely mate because our policy now is that we don't allow that'.

Over the last ten years the big supermarkets have implemented a range of new initiatives. For example, one wide-scale change in the early 1990s was the introduction of in-store bakeries. However, the cost and efficiency of running these bakeries were soon called into question and today they are largely used to make just a few runs in order to create the so-called 'baked-fresh' smell in the supermarket. As one interviewee explained:

> Then the supermarkets realised that it [in-store bakeries] was quite expensive. You needed to have a baker, and bakers have good penalty rates and good conditions through their award. Then you had to have knowledge and know-how, you had to have the ingredients and equipment, and all this sort of stuff. So it got a bit too hard for them. So you saw an era of home-brand products. So what they did was to bring out these products but get their normal suppliers to make it under their bag wrap, but of course at a reduced rate. So on a shelf you might have our proprietary stuff, ten years ago at say 80 per cent and 20 at home-brand, then as the price was cheaper the proprietary stuff would squeeze as people started to buy the straight white bread under the home-brand banner, and the consumer perceived little difference. On day one they'd be right but on day three you'd be chucking one out. So the market went to cheap bread and the supermarkets have tried to get the consumer to buy on price.

In discussing the in-house bakeries it was noted that while they still have them, they do not bake much in them anymore. They may do a run of hot rolls to get the aroma in the air and to give the perception/image that they are producing. In practice, most of their bread is supplied in plain wrap so that it looks like an in-house product. As a Dalebake employee explained:

> Today, we provide their plain wrap bread at a cheap price with their labels on it, we deliver it and we pack it at the shelf. We've got a team of 56 merchandisers that all they do is pack bread all day. They don't actually work for Asco but they spend all their time in Asco and Tesda. So they've lost the wages factor of it as well. Summary, your costs are going up but you are not getting any more margins on it. So it's a little bit more difficult.

Another strategic trend has been a movement away from the standard loaf towards a greater variety of options and a higher quality loaf. Increasingly, new loaves are developed and marketed to meet the needs of a specific segment of the market (such as iron supplements for women). These initiatives have combined with changing consumer demand to create a bread market that is significantly different from that in place during the design, development and building of the then state-of-the-art bakery at Mossdale. As the factory manager highlighted:

> Factories like this rely on economies of scale. We have to have volume to meet our direct fixed costs. We can't really survive if we lose 200,000 units a week. Because capacity is the key, mate. Our capacity is still not wonderful but it's good enough I suppose.

Consequently, this has necessitated workplace change in the design, use and operation of technology; product development and the making of bread; and the organization and control of work. Moreover, these changes go beyond the boundaries of the factory to include new initiatives in the management of

customer–supplier relations and in delivery, sales and marketing. The importance of power in managing these shifting relations was identified by
Emerson (1962) who highlighted the close relationship between power and
dependence (see also Clegg and Dunkerley, 1980: 380–5). In this case study,
there is an unequal power relationship between Dalebake Bakeries and the
supermarkets (Aldrich and Mindlin, 1978). As Pfeffer and Salancik (1978)
point out in their resource dependence perspective, customers, suppliers,
competitors (for both customers and materials) and regulatory groups (such
as governments) are all important in making sense of the proactive strategies
that companies pursue in relation to changes in their task environment. In
our case, the supermarkets are critical, and therefore Dalebake are spending
time and money developing strategies for the mutual construction and
redefinition of ongoing customer–supplier relations (what Weick [1969]
refers to as an 'enacted environment'; see also Blau, 1964). With the
increasing importance of managing these negotiations and of maintaining
good customer–supplier relations (which are now weighted in favour of the
supermarkets), Dalebake Bakeries have recently introduced the position of
National Category Managers (NCM). Each NCM deals solely with one
particular client, such as Asco or Tesda, to negotiate bread contracts.

The need to diversify and accommodate changing market demand while
developing new products, and working within and negotiating operational
parameters with the large supermarkets, has placed considerable strain on
the Mossdale operation. Dalebake strategy has centred on the development
of their own proprietary range with the intention of gaining differentiated
consumer 'loyalty' to their wider range of products.

> Our strategy has been, let's grow our proprietary range and make our bread
> something they would want to buy. Our range has diversified more, you've seen
> 700 size bread compared to the 680 size bread. Then the one at the end, the high
> bake that has a perceived bake-and-home look, country look, and a lot of health
> benefits. That one has an iron-fibre plus, then all the things like wholemeal
> grains and stuff like that. But the basic bottom line is that we've had to diversify
> our range to keep people thinking that they would like to buy our products and
> it has worked.

However, one problem is that if a new product is successful the supermarkets
put considerable pressure on Dalebake Bakeries for a plain wrap version.
These plain wrap versions are sold at a lower price, reducing Dakebake
margins and ultimately killing demand for the proprietary product. Dalebake's aim is to increase the range of breads perceived as 'healthy' in a way
that focuses attention on the nutritional benefits of the bread rather than
simply on the price. As one employee explained: 'The strategy is to try and
grow the category but not butcher the price. But unfortunately price is a very
hard mindset and the cold hard reality is that people buy on price.' On
discussing other competitor developments, such as Bonne Baguette (a
gourmet bread franchise chain), Dalebake management argued that these
developments have been good in refocusing consumer attention back onto
the value rather than the price of bread. Consumers are now willing to pay

extra for something a little different but which tastes good. (Furthermore, Yorkshire Foods supply the ingredients to Bonne Baguette, so they are also a customer.)

THE MOSSDALE FACILITY: A FACTORY AFTER ITS TIME

The facility at Mossdale was built in 1991 to service a market characterized by low product range and high volume. Millions were invested in state-of-the-art technology to meet market place demands and to consolidate operations within one site. As already noted, prior to building this factory operations were spread over four sites which serviced their local areas. Total operating costs were high and there was considerable duplication across the four factories. Furthermore, the facilities were operating with old and outdated technology and were in need of attention. Thus, rather than invest in upgrading existing sites, the decision was made to build a highly automated factory at Mossdale which would be able to service the whole of Yorkshire.

> Now we go to Sheffield every day and we've got trucks running from there. We go to Leeds every day and we go to Bradford every day, then we've got trucks running to Lincoln and right around the county. You see, these supermarkets are very powerful in the country. You know, Asco at Leeds is a fantastic big giant store. But we've got to supply them from here. So the thing that has really grown in the last ten years is logistics. I think it was £180 million sales last year nationally and £50 million it cost us to deliver it. So it's extremely expensive. About a third of the cost is logistics just getting it to the customer. And of course the time window is very short, because everybody wants their bread at the same time.

Although the factory produces bread for the entire county market (as intended), the nature of that market has significantly changed. The strategic purpose behind the heavy investment in technology was to build an operation with quick run rates for high volume products and thereby reduce wages and overall operating costs. The set-up could handle high volume white, grain and wholemeal loaves of standard size. Profit margins would improve and further investments could be made to sustain the competitive position of Dalebake Bakeries. As it turned out, shortly after the opening of the site, shifts in market demand necessitated a rethink of the strategic direction of Mossdale operations. Today, the technology is being used in a way not originally anticipated by the factory design team. For example, in accommodating a more diverse product range the number of machinery set-ups in any 24-hour period (the factory operates a two-shift system over 18 to 20 hours) has increased significantly. As a result of this stop–start with the set-ups for the various breads, there is more wear and tear on the equipment, more machinery breakdowns have to be dealt with and the run rate goes down as changeovers increase. Furthermore, quality issues arise from the regular changing of product runs. For example, every time you produce a different type of bread you have to clean the system out (the divider) before you can put new dough on top of it to start a new range. If this is not done properly, you can get a 'swirl loaf' (a mixture of two different types). Moreover, different breads are processed in different ways, such as the requirement for different oven temperatures. In short, one of the main operational problems facing Mossdale today is that in order to get the run rate they require to be productive (in the efficient use of labour and equipment), they need to do the longest run possible. For 80 per cent of their total output this is not a problem – it comprises 20 varieties of bread. However, they have to produce 130 varieties of bread to service customer demand and it is these small runs that cut efficiency rates and increase costs of production per unit produced. As one interviewee reflected:

> Ninety-five per cent of bread sales is generated by 47 varieties out of 130, and 95 per cent of roll sales is generated by 59 varieties out of 115. The problem is that if you don't produce the little stuff you don't get the big stuff. That's how the supermarkets treat you. So if you don't make this range of rubbish then you don't get the big fish. You've got to be in it to stay in it.

If a particular type of bread is put on special offer and demand increases, then the rise in output volume makes life at the plant far easier for employees. As one interviewee explained, 'As soon as you get around 120,000 units a day with straight white this place lights up like a Christmas tree'.

Normally on the morning run they do the diverse range and on the afternoon run they go back to the core range. In the metropolitan area they operate a system of fresh returns whereby a customer can indicate on delivery that he does not want as many units as ordered. However, once the units are taken then there are no cash returns for unsold bread. In the case of Bacup (which is just over the border in Lancashire), Dalebake York operates a return of sale (that is, any bread that they don't sell they can send back). In other words, customers only pay for what they sell:

> We waste 30,000 units a week just on fresh returns. The other big constraint is because the local managers are judged on what they call shrinkage or waste in their own stores. They don't want to place the order until the latest possible trading time. So we won't receive tomorrow's order until 5.30 tonight, but we'll be baking all day. So we're basically forecasting all day, we're baking on our knowledge of what we are used to, and then we do a top-up. Really what I am saying is that there are three bakes. There is the spec' a.m. bake, the top-up a.m. bake and there is the p.m. bake.

These changes in the market highlight how a factory that was set up with the latest technology to produce long runs of a small variety of loaves is no longer well suited to the more diverse demands of the modern bread market. For example, if you have to produce a greater variety of loaves and reduce the run rate, then output will decrease, inventory will increase (with the greater range of raw ingredients required), more equipment maintenance is likely to be required (greater down-time), set-up times increase as you switch from one variety to another and finally, in accommodating a more diverse range of products, manual handling increases with a corresponding increase in the number of manual handling faults.

In this case, the strategic decision to invest in advanced technology to improve Dalebake's competitive position made sense at the end of the 1980s, but in less than a decade a shift in market forces necessitated the redesign of work arrangements to accommodate these new customer demands. A major driving force has been the powerful supermarket chains. As a basic food, specials on bread can get customers into the store, and in the development of in-store bakeries (which also provide a pleasant aroma for the shopper) there is both heightened competition and increased variety which have given the buyer far more choice over a more comprehensive range of products. Dalebake Bakeries offer over 400 varieties of bread and rolls (with 95 per cent of sales coming from only 106 varieties out of 245 lines).

In servicing the demands for a more diversified product, Dalebake Bakeries Mossdale have become more flexible by re-introducing a range of manual operations around new products and by using equipment which can be 'bolted on' to the automated plant. Mossdale now produces a diverse range of small run products, whereas the significant investment in automated plant and equipment was to be price competitive in long efficient runs of a small number of standard loaves. A good example of this change was the decision by Dalebake Bakeries to launch a new type of bread, 'the Bergen loaf', in 1998. The bread used soy and linseed grain and was shown to be beneficial to women during menopause. However, the automatic bread mixers could not be used because the dough needed to be made in two stages. In addition, the grains required a longer soaking period and could not be automatically loaded, nor could the dough undergo existing automatic processes (the product needed to be extruded into baking tins). In modifying work arrangements, new 'bolt on' equipment was purchased (at a cost of £100,000) and more manual operations were used. In this case, Bergen tins were placed within a frame that would allow them to be used within the existing system and the grains (soy and linseed) were soaked manually rather than through the automatically-fed grain soaker.

> This is a new Bergen bread that we have brought out. And we've had to make a frame around it to make it the same size as what the system's used to. Just little things like that. So what we've done is kept our same technology – which is a massive investment – but we've bolted on equipment. We've got a 5000 plant and an 8000 plant and we call the 5000 plant the gourmet plant because there are that many bolt-ons and extras and bits and pieces and stop–starts, to try and produce the different breads you need to produce to stay in the market.

The technology is not static, but is constantly being adapted and reconfigured to meet current operating needs and changing market demands. Innovative solutions are required to cope with the unforeseen problems arising from the investment of large sums of money in a highly automated plant that was designed for volume runs but that must now accommodate a diverse product range.

THE POWER OF THE RETAILING GIANTS AND THE FUTURE OF MOSSDALE

Throughout the study the power of the supermarkets was continually referred to as a major challenge and potential problem for the future development of Dalebake. It was recognized that these powerful customers could potentially destroy a company like Dalebake and, in their drive to reduce costs, it was getting harder for bread producers to stay in business. Moreover, with the decline in profits (in 1999 it was 0.4 per cent) and narrower margins, it was becoming increasingly difficult for the company to invest in new technology. From the perspective of Dalebake York, they were operating fairly new machinery and they knew that their major competitors were going to face problems in operating with old plant and equipment which were going to need replacing over the next few years. In a number of ways, it was not the market that influenced management action but the actions of the powerful retailing giants. As the manufacturing manager explained:

> What we are basically saying is that we are over-servicing our customer. We're delivering and killing ourselves with kindness for the customer's sake. You see, I could go to Asco today – just say for example it's a Thursday. I could go for an a.m. delivery, come back here and then go and do a p.m. delivery, and then do three extra deliveries by run-outs that day. So we've serviced them five times that day. Now realistically that's just ridiculous, at some point they've got to wear that they've got to order properly. So the challenge will be – we can't get any more out of the business as far as costs go, every year you've got a rise in wages and every year you'll put the price up to match that, and the same with ingredients, costs going up or anything like that. Any costs which go up will be reflected in price. But it's what you're giving away is the thing. Since March 1996, the price has gone from 50p to £1, so in four years it's risen 50p, which is a considerable amount. But in real terms we only got out of that 20p. The supermarkets get the rest in case deals, discounts, you know, all these things. Now the effect on our bottom line is that if we had that 17.4p which we should have got, that we've given back to them, that's worth £2.25 million to us a year. So you know, that's the big thing. So if you do that scenario in every county, I think you'll find that's where you've lost your money. . . . The biggest issue this company faces is how to convince or influence supermarkets. If I was the CEO, tomorrow I would hire a bloke for two million quid or whatever it took, because that's what you're losing hand over fist. I'd hire some bloke to just go and get the price back off the supermarkets. . . . The name of the game is to turn the supermarkets around.

As Mintz and Schwartz (1985) point out, powerful customers can severely limit the ability of a company to make relatively independent strategic decisions and this case certainly draws attention to the unequal relationship between the supermarkets and Dalebake Bakeries. The two forms of constraint that Mintz and Schwartz (1985) identify are mutual deterrence and hegemony. It is hegemony that is most in evidence in our case, where the supermarkets hold a far more powerful and less dependent position than Dalebake. These small groups of large retailers are the prime customers for the output of the smaller and less powerful bakery. Dalebake is thus in a highly dependent position with only limited opportunity to influence this relationship. The creation of the new position of NCM is an attempt to help manage this important relationship, as part of the process whereby differing parties come to make sense of their related environments. These 'active' subjects seek to shape the environment and improve the position of Dalebake Bakeries, rather than accept a more passive and reactive position within these unequal customer–supplier arrangements. Furthermore, in contemplating the future of Dalebake, the production manager felt that the company would always be strong in South Yorkshire because of the nature of the market.

> York is a stagnant ageing market. I think as we get on finding units will be harder. But we're going wider and wider to find them. We now do a hundred pallets a week for Newcastle/Durham. It's those sort of things you've got to do to keep the wheels turning. But with margins like they are no-one's going to come in and invest say £8 million which is turning an ROI [return on investment] on the margins that we're getting. The other thing is that our competitors have got the old factories, they haven't done this. So, I wouldn't like to be in their shoes, because they've actually got to improve their factories. Another year and a half or two years our equipment has depreciated to nothing. So straightaway to the bottom line, you know, straight trading bottom line, we've got all this equipment's depreciation costs back. So you may start to bear the fruits for holding on for ten years I suppose. As long as we don't get our sales folk giving it away.

CONCLUSION

The case study outlined in this chapter could be used to highlight a 'technical fix' approach to corporate strategy where the inevitability of technological change as an external force is tied up with notions of rational decision-making and a competitive advantage/cost-efficient conception of technology. From this technological determinist perspective, we could view the creation of a new highly automated plant as the result of external market developments (in technology and competition) which necessitated organizational adaptation – you 'automate or you liquidate' (for a critique of this approach, see McLoughlin and Clark, 1994). As Thomas (1994: 208) has noted, the view that automation is cost-efficient as a labour-saving device can become institutionalized. In his case studies of American companies, he claims that the 'benefits' of automation are taken for granted by managers and engineers, and it is common to view technology as providing the solution for organizational problems. He concludes that rather than see technology as determinant it would be more appropriate to view as determinant 'the ideal of technology as the only legitimate alternative'.

By taking another perspective, the case could be used to illustrate the value of the strategic choice approach. The importance of external developments is clearly demonstrated and yet the selection and implementation of technology can be viewed as the outcome of choice among a powerful dominant coalition (Cyert and March, 1963). As Child (1972: 13) argues, such an approach would

> direct our attention towards those who possess the power to decide upon an organization's structural rationale, towards the limits upon that power imposed by the operational context, and towards the process of assessing constraints and opportunities against values in deciding organizational strategies.

In adopting the concept of 'dominant coalition', Child makes clear that this does not refer simply to the designated holders of authority but rather to those who collectively hold most power over a given period of time. The group will make strategic decisions and, by so doing, highlight the role of choice. In other words, organizations do not merely respond to contingent circumstance, they make active strategic choices on the future direction of the company (Child, 1972, 1997).

However, it is argued in this book that it is not enough to view change as some form of external force or the outcome of strategic choice but, rather, that there is a need to investigate why technology is viewed as the only legitimate alternative while certain other options are never considered, and to study the way choices are framed and narratives crafted during the political process of change. Our analysis of how previous decisions on technology influence actors' current interpretations of change options draws attention to the processual nature of change. In other words, how technology affects organizations is not a one-off event. The conception of the need to change (and of what is possible and preferable) is part of a political process in which options and conflicting views compete. A number of narratives may be constructed in the formulation of compelling rationales. These alternatives may reflect different worldviews of multiple actors or groups and may constrain the range of possibilities considered (Thomas, 1994: 203). The history and culture of the organization will further influence the emergent character of these processes, act as levers and shapers of change and serve to maintain, reconstitute and legitimize existing orders. What is excluded from consideration and the formulation of choice are both central to understanding the process and outcomes of change (see Kamp, 2000).

The multi-dimensional and dynamic relationship between technology and organization is also highlighted in the local configuration and reconfiguration of technology. Employee innovations and developments were instrumental in making technology work. They were both creative and accommodating in finding new ways of doing things that were able to circumvent the limitations imposed by the design and implementation of the 'new' technology. During the course of employee engagement in using the technology, elements of the technology previously viewed as hard technical or structural constraints gradually became open to change. In other words, operations that had previously been seen as technologically determined became redefined through a social process that enabled a far greater degree of 'interpretative flexibility' (see Bijker, 1995). The meanings of technology were thereby reconstituted in the formulation and translation of new ideas for future possible change options. This case study spotlights the temporal process of company transition and the complex interplay between politics, context and substance in the social shaping and use of technology.

The experience of supervisors and older employees under conditions of change

6

The consequence of change for older employees is not an area that has stimulated a wide-ranging debate or extensive empirical research, yet there are widely held beliefs about how older employees are likely to respond to new ideas and patterns of work organization. The popular notion that the older you are the less likely you are to accommodate and adapt to change is a long-standing workplace myth. As noted in Chapter 4, the concept of myth is not used in the sense of being unreal or wholly fictitious; rather, a myth is seen to provide a generally accepted explanation that while limited, misleading and partial, nevertheless influences the change process. As Bradley et al. (2000: 3) note, 'myths inform strategic choices made within workplaces, which then affect the lives of all within them'. Although the myth of the older worker is not one they explore, they argue for a theoretical perspective that would enable us to capture the way older workers and supervisors make sense of their working lives. In examining age and the supervisor as change 'problems', it is also important to identify and clarify the assumptions that support and sustain these misconceptions, in order to more fully understand how these myths influence and shape the process of change. After a brief examination of some of the commonly held myths about supervisors and an analysis of data on the supervisory experience of change, the chapter examines the issue of age more broadly. Particular attention is given to the dissimilar experiences of different groups of older workers under conditions of change. It is shown how older employees in senior management can have a very different experience to those occupying more junior positions in an organization. The chapter concludes by calling for further research to unpack the myth of the older worker and the role of the supervisor as an organizational change 'problem'.

THE 'PROBLEM' OF THE SUPERVISOR AND WORKPLACE CHANGE

The traditional career route for supervisors – working their way up through the ranks – means that a significant proportion of these employees are older.

As an older worker, their extensive knowledge and experience of the work process can be an important resource in the planning of implementation strategies and yet their contribution is rarely sought. More often, these older workers are cast as being 'fixed in their ways' and their occupational position associated with traditional practice (which might mark a final step in their career progression) is commonly viewed as a barrier to future development and change.

The older supervisor has long been cast as a 'problem' that the change agent has to overcome. For example, following the Second World War, with the growth in the size of the industrial enterprise and unionization, the role of the supervisor became the focus of criticism and concern (Child, 1975: 73–4). Essentially it was argued that with the advent of relatively full employment since the late 1940s, the mobility of labour had increased and consequently workers felt less compelled to submit to the authority of the supervisor (Roethlisberger, 1945). The supervisor became the 'man in the middle', required to satisfy the needs of both management and workforce (Gardener and Whyte, 1945). In addition, it was argued that changes in the functional organization of work, the substantial growth in the collective organization of employees and the power of the shop steward had aggravated the supervisory 'problem' of conflicting demands and created the 'problem' of marginality. As Wray (1949: 301) concluded:

> In short, the position of foreman has some of the characteristics of management positions but lacks other crucial ones. . . . With respect to management the foreman's position is peripheral rather than in the middle. The poor fellow is in the middle of course, in the sense that . . . he gets it from both sides.

Throughout the twentieth century articles have been written on the problem of supervisory resistance to change and work reorganization schemes (for example, Child and Partridge, 1982; Littler, 1982: 143–81). A long-standing argument is that the supervisor is becoming increasingly peripheral to the system of control and that there is no longer a need for traditional supervision within modern organizations. For example, Edwards (1979: 124–5) argues that with advances in technology the traditional labour control function of supervision will be increasingly incorporated into the technology of production. He concludes that the ability of modern computer systems to monitor and evaluate work performance will bring about an erosion of the supervisory tasks of detection, inspection and evaluation. Edwards' conclusion that traditional supervision is becoming increasingly peripheral to organizations rests on the claim that impersonal control mechanisms have replaced supervisors as the main instrument for controlling staff. It is argued that developments in systems of bureaucratic control have relieved the supervisor of the task of disciplining staff, and developments in technical control have incorporated the element of direction (Edwards, 1979; see also Sewell, 1998). However, a central problem with this analysis is the way that the supervisor is equated with a traditional labour control function, with no account being taken of the range of different supervisory tasks and roles that exist within organizations. Despite early research into the job of the super-visor – which highlighted how supervisors were no longer primarily con-cerned with the supervision of labour activities but were involved in a much wider range of tasks (see, for example, Thurley and Hamblin, 1963; Walker et al., 1956) – the tendency to equate supervision with labour control has continued. As Thurley and Wirdenius (1973: 53) note:

> The idea of the supervisor in charge of his group of men, which was a very accurate picture at earlier stages of industrialisation, has lingered on, and is highly misrepresentative of many situations in modern technology, where super-visors are extremely dependent on each other and working together with other supervisors and functional specialists.

The tendency to question the need and place of the supervisor continues into the twenty-first century and reflects a series of unfounded assumptions concerning the role of the supervisor and the nature of supervision. It is also assumed that older employees who hold supervisory positions are likely to resist change (a combination of age and position) and, within the more recent literature, the emphasis has been on the 'problem' of managing the change from the so-called 'policeman' to 'coach' supervisory role. This misunder-standing of the job of the supervisor has served to perpetuate the myth of the supervisory 'problem' and has often resulted in inappropriate change strat-egies which can create the very 'problem' that is assumed to exist.

In practice, changes in supervisory jobs are far more complex than indicated by current debates, reflecting a historical and ongoing shift in emphasis with changes in responsibilities and tasks being variously eroded, enhanced, replaced, created and redefined. While the nature of some of these changes remains unclear, it is argued here that today's supervisor is neither an 'industrial dinosaur' nor a 'lost manager', but a key organizational player in both the successful management of change and in the management of routine operations under new and changing organizational arrangements (Dawson, 1991). Thus, the outcomes of change on supervision are far more complex than indicated by a simple erosion thesis or transition from policeman to coach. The 'problem' is not with supervisors, but with the fact that their jobs have evolved and developed often in ways unknown or misunderstood by management. To put it another way, the 'problem' of supervision is not of the supervisors' making but a consequence of management inaction and reluc-tance to tackle the issue of supervisory change and the contribution of older employees to the management of change.

THE OLDER SUPERVISOR AND WORKPLACE CHANGE

Management often view their older supervisory staff as a potential obstacle to new ways of working. It is assumed that any supervisory criticism or reluctance to adapt to new change initiatives simply reflects traditional thinking and a commitment to the status quo. As such, older supervisors are generally seen as being set in their ways and reluctant to change. As a senior manager at Pirelli Cables commented, 'The foreman who has been making cable for 20 years and thinks he makes the best cable in the world is very hard to convince that he needs to change'.

In re-examining data from a series of case studies on change, numerous examples were identified where older supervisors had been asked whether they would consider early retirement (older employees are taken to refer to those who are 50 or older). Significant pressure was often applied in order to reduce staffing levels through policies of so-called 'natural attrition'. In addition, the shifting nature of supervision and the precarious position of the older supervisor frequently stood out as a major supervisory concern and organizational issue. For example, in an Australian automotive company that was restructuring work and introducing teams on the shop floor, the role of the supervisor was changed from trouble-shooter and problem-solver to facilitator and administrator. The traditional control responsibilities of the supervisor were devolved to team leaders (who held a supervisory relationship to other members of their group). For the most part, the new team leaders were far younger than the plant supervisors, who had tended to work their way up through the ranks and had attained their positions on the basis of the large stock of knowledge and experience they had gained in shop floor operations. In this sense, the authority of the supervisor was based on their ability to deal with unforeseen events and to fire fight in the case of a wide variety of production emergencies, such as machine breakdowns. Today, the emphasis has shifted towards the management of people in coordinating the smooth operation of the plant. As one management interviewee recounted:

> Supervisors have to be more people-oriented than they have ever been in their entire careers, bear in mind that their training initially is task-oriented not people-oriented. Now we are trying to get a balance between the two, with perhaps a little more emphasis on people-oriented than task-oriented.

From the perspective of the supervisors interviewed, the content of their jobs prior to change had never been fully understood by management, who they claimed tended to downplay the people managing skills required of the position. They explained that apart from technical contingencies, there have always been regular human contingencies which supervisors were expected to deal with on a day-to-day basis. In this case, the supervisors (who were also older workers) felt that they were often falsely portrayed as anti-change merchants, when in fact a central part of their job had always involved dealing with unexpected change situations. In other words, over time, supervisors had adapted their role to meet the changing expectations of other employees and the changing conditions of work. From a management viewpoint, this redefinition of supervision had largely gone unnoticed. Typically, managers talked about a clear, yet somewhat mythical, contrast between the traditional labour control function of supervision (the policeman) and the newly emerging coordinating role of enlightened supervision (the coach). Consequently, these supervisors would often find themselves ignored during programmes of change. Moreover, due to their age and long-standing attachment to traditional ways of working, they would often be cast as a major source of resistance to new initiatives. As indicated by Dawson (1994: 177):

> In many of the cases, the job of the supervisor was being redefined and the number of supervisory staff was being reduced. These changes threatened the position of supervisors and resulted in conflict and resistance to 'imposed' implementation strategies. Change was also impeded by the general failure to recognise the central function of supervision under changed systems of opera-tion and the role of the supervisor as a potential change catalyst.

Typically, a major obstacle to change occurred in cases where supervisors, or those holding a supervisory relationship to production, were not taken into account in designing training programmes and implementing change. For example, in the case of Pirelli Cables management encountered considerable resistance from supervisory staff to the implementation of a TQM pro-gramme. In part, resistance to TQM derived from supervisory concern over the threat to their jobs of a programme that offered to take away the 'problem' of fire fighting, which they viewed as a central task. The resistance of supervisory personnel to the TQM project could also be explained by a failure to integrate supervisors into the implementation programme. For example, the TQM manager argued that, if he was to introduce TQM from scratch, he would first win over his supervisory staff by running a two- or three-day supervisory training session. In retrospect, one of the major lessons learned from the programme was the importance of supervisory personnel to the successful management of change.

In contrast, in another company studied, senior management took a very different view. In this case, which involved the introduction of new technol-ogy, senior management decided that the older traditional supervisor needed to be replaced by younger staff. Supervisors were relocated to shop floor positions and were encouraged to leave the organization with 'dignity'. No attempt was made to accommodate the older supervisor. Instead it was assumed that the long-serving supervisor would be better off leaving the organization rather than trying to 'cope' with the new tasks and responsibili-ties associated with the change.

In many of the companies studied, the number of older supervisors was reduced with a concomitant increase in the control responsibilities of newly emerging supervisory positions. In other words, a decrease in numbers was combined with an increase in the control responsibility of 'new' supervisory staff. Voluntary redundancy and early retirement were the most common route to staff adjustments, particularly in cases where work restructuring occurred from major change initiatives that were not linked to any broader strategy of downsizing or delayering:

> If any supervisors have to move out of the system it would be done by the normal method which we have been able to do in the past. That is, by agreed

early retirement and to date we've been able to manage this all the way through the change. We haven't had to retrench any supervisor as a result of the introduction of new technology. (Management Interviews)

With a general reduction in the number and level of supervisors and an increase in supervisory control responsibilities to cover a broader range of operations, some supervisors indicated that they found themselves caught in the middle between management and the shop floor. As already discussed, issues concerning organizational change and the 'middle' or 'marginal' position of the supervisor are not new (see Gardener and Whyte, 1945; Wray, 1949). These early findings mirror a number of contemporary concerns. Three main questions commonly raised by management are:

1 What are the changing qualities required of individuals in supervisory positions? (It is often assumed that stern old-fashioned supervisors need to be replaced by younger more people-oriented shop floor facilitators.)
2 How can supervisory resistance be overcome? (This of course rests on managements' assumption that older supervisors will be a barrier to change due to their position and age.)
3 Is there a need for supervisors under new forms of work organization? (This rests on the view that supervisors are becoming increasingly 'marginal' to manufacturing and service operations.)

In the research I conducted, management frequently misunderstood the nature of the supervisor's job and viewed the longer-serving supervisor as an industrial dinosaur that needed to be replaced with a younger and more people-oriented team leader. This lack of understanding of the job of the supervisor often resulted in poor decisions and inappropriate strategies which jeopardized the smooth transition that management were seeking to achieve. When ignored and threatened, it is understandable that supervisors will question and respond to management change initiatives. However, their knowledge, advice and experience were rarely used and often bluntly scorned if they were critical of the management plans. Consequently, any questioning of the need to change or suggested alternatives was inappropriately labelled as 'the resistance to change' that was to be expected among older and more backward-looking supervisors. Although many of the qualities and tacit skills required of the changing role of the supervisor were already present among existing supervisory staff, this valuable human resource was too quickly rejected and displaced by management. Ironically, commonly held workplace myths perpetuate the traditional thinking of management which drives decision-making during the process of organizational change. Consequently, the position of the supervisor continues to remain open to misunderstanding. Most notably, the views of management and their change agents often reflect a number of crude assumptions about supervisors and misconceptions about supervision. For example, the traditional conception of the supervisor as a labour controller has continued to influence the response of management to the 'problem' of supervision during modern programmes of workplace change. Although others have recognized the 'peculiarly middle' and difficult position that a supervisor holds, higher levels of management have not readily done so. As a technician explained in describing the position of the supervisor in the organization in which he worked:

> It's certainly not easy to be a . . . supervisor. I mean, I wouldn't want to be. Sure, the pay might be better but I don't know, you certainly lose friends. They've tried out quite a few chaps in the labs for supervisory sort of positions, but the same thing always happens. You know, they were one of the boys and now they've got to start giving a few orders and directions, and it never goes down too well. It ends up with them just getting totally frustrated and chucking it in, and getting back to being one of the boys again. You can't seem to be a supervisor and be a nice guy as well.

In being viewed by management as an 'obstacle' to change, there is often little appreciation of supervisors' contribution to understanding potential problems or issues that might be part of proposed change programmes. For example, in a case study of the implementation of TQM at Sydbank (an Australian bank), Allan and Dawson (1995) illustrate how resistance from older supervisors, who were intimately acquainted with traditional work procedures, resulted in their immediate dismissal. Their experience and knowledge of the work process and their claim that the new job designs would be largely unworkable were viewed as a 'rational response' of older workers to the 'threat' of workplace innovation and change. As a potential barrier to the speed and direction of change, the decision to remove them was deemed as both a necessary and appropriate action in the pursuit of 'successful' implementation. Interestingly, attention was given neither to the substance of their claims, nor to the consequences of their displacement on the morale of other staff. As it turned out, general staff quickly became disillusioned about the project. Job security also became an issue, with a number of employees indicating their distrust of senior management who were willing to remove long-serving, highly respected staff simply because they disagreed. As one branch employee commented: 'You know, even us, we're sort of thinking: "Well, I've been with the bank for fifteen years and look what they did to Gary. They weren't very kind to him. How are they going to be with me?" ' In this case, the response to older workers (who had built up considerable respect among their staff) had implications beyond the individual to the morale of the staff as a whole. The autocratic top-down approach neither mobilized supervisory commitment nor stimulated staff enthusiasm, but rather promoted employee scepticism about the change programme and ultimately created further obstacles to the successful implementation of change. The end result was a failed attempt to introduce TQM into a medium-sized Australian bank.

OLDER EMPLOYEES AND WORKPLACE CHANGE

These commonly held assumptions about supervisors are also more broadly evident among older shop floor and branch level employees. It is assumed that older workers are likely to be far more reticent than their younger counterparts about changing established ways of working and adapting to new forms of work organization. However, Chapter 7 demonstrates that groups of workers can respond very differently to attempts by management to introduce change on the shop floor. Workers' behaviour and their response to change will be influenced by a range of factors including culture and group customs, and not by a single factor such as age. Although instances can be found where older workers variously resist, support or are largely indifferent to change, the belief that older workers find change difficult often directs management to strategies that enable them to displace older workers, for example through early retirement schemes. But how do these policies align with governmental initiatives and legislative change on ageism at work?

In Australia, age discrimination is 'generally defined as the less favourable treatment of a person compared to one or more others on the basis of their chronological age' (Bennington and Calvert, 1998: 137) and is illegal (Encel, 1998: 43). Evidence from countries that have legislation (such as Canada, the United States and Australia) indicates that the law does have some influence on age discrimination at work (although research in this area remains limited). In the US, the Age Discrimination and Employment Act was passed by the US congress in 1967, whereas the UK government only began to consider the issue of legislation following a European Commission Directive on Equal Treatment in August 2000 (Homstein, 2001). Article 13 of the EC Treaty requires all EU member states to introduce legislation prohibiting age discrimination. As a response to this directive, the UK government has set up a website to promote their 'age positive campaign' at [http://www.agepositive.gov.uk]. The site encourages employers to have their say and provides information on what other companies are doing, events and publications, as well as putting forward a voluntary code of practice. Although the government has indicated an intention to introduce age discrimination legislation by 2006, they state that:

> There are a number of complex and sensitive issues which need to be addressed and resolved so that the eventual legislation is practical and helpful to employers and employees. For example, the Directive recognises that differences of treatment on grounds of age can sometimes be justified. The challenge for implementation is to identify which types of differences of treatment are acceptable and which are not. For example, might it sometimes be necessary to make special provisions for younger or older workers in order to protect their safety and welfare? (http://www.agepositive.gov.uk)

Since the 1970s, European concerns over unemployment have led to a range of governmental initiatives that promote incentives for older workers to retire. As Encel (1998: 41) reports, the labour force participation rate of older workers in the Organization for Economic Co-operation and Development (OECD) fell from 88 per cent to 75 per cent among men (aged 55–59) between 1970 and 1994. Although there is now a commitment by the UK government to combat age discrimination at work, early retirement schemes remain a common vehicle for reducing staff during change. In a study of company employment strategies, Bennington and Tharenou (1996) argue that age is often a critical factor in management decision-making. They claim that age-based decisions are often dependent upon stereotypes and that, given the introduction of legislation to prevent age discrimination at work, the status of the older worker is likely to be an ongoing issue for both employers and older employees (see also Encel, 1998; Steinberg et al., 1998). They state that:

> The research indicated that older workers are interested and satisfied in their work, that they fit in with young workers, and that their memory and intelligence do not present problems. However, older employees may be less creative and, with existing management and methods, they take longer to train, especially in relation to new technology, and have lower training performance. Overall, though, there is little justification for age discrimination because older employees are as useful to organizations as younger employees. (Bennington and Tharenou, 1996: 72–3)

Their research suggests that while age may affect the training requirements of older workers, it does not represent a change management 'problem'. Far from being threatened by change, older workers can prove instrumental in allaying the fears of their younger colleagues. Moreover, in analysing age differences and employee well-being, Birdi and Warr (1995: 369) conclude that differences in occupational well-being are not caused by age itself but rather by the influence of age as an indicator for a range of psychological, social and physiological factors. Kaemar and Ferris (1989) suggest that analysing well-being in relation to an individual's career stage or life stage, may prove fruitful in explaining general trends in the levels of job satisfaction, job stress and job boredom (Birdi and Warr, 1995).

In the case of older women in the retail sector, Patrickson and Hartmann (1996) illustrate how a sizeable group was willing to work beyond 65 (they generally had few financial benefits in the form of superannuation or separation packages) and that many of the women interviewed enjoyed their jobs and had little interest in leaving the workforce. However, they also found that downsizing within the retailing sector had resulted in the loss of casual jobs and that these women were not financially secure from generous 'voluntary' separation packages. They conclude that:

> Our research would tend to confirm that older women are a largely untapped labour resource. Rather than targeting older workers in downsizing attempts, an alternative strategy might be to make a more deliberate effort to restructure so part-time opportunities arise, and to seek to employ a higher proportion of older staff, especially women. (Patrickson and Hartmann, 1996: 97)

Older women working as part of a casualized labour force are increasingly finding their positions under threat during programmes of work restructuring (Patrickson and Hartmann, 1998). Job insecurity is a more significant issue facing older female workers than it is for their male counterparts who are likely to have experienced a more stable pattern of employment. For example, Itzin and Phillipson (1995) have shown how the organization of work is generally structured to fit the male-based chronology of continuous employment and not the discontinuous character of female employment. They conclude that gendered ageism is a double jeopardy for women in organizations undergoing change as little, if any, account is given to the 'ways that age and gender intersect and interact to the disadvantage of women' in the design and implementation of change strategies (Itzin and Phillipson, 1995: 89).

In a broader discussion of older workers, Patrickson and Hartmann (1998: 23) argue that while there is irrefutable evidence that the workforce is ageing, this issue has largely been ignored by organizations.

> The ageing of the workforce is a reality but the extent to which older workers will maintain a consistent share of the workforce in the near future is uncertain. . . . It will be argued in later chapters that the present lack of attention given to older workers may be strategically disadvantageous for organizations if predictions of workforce change prove accurate. In future years it may well be in the interests of organizations to help older workers.

Research on employment strategies and age suggests that change initiatives aimed at reducing employee numbers disproportionately threaten the job security of older workers, for example through the promotion of early retirement schemes and the social pressure to leave jobs available for younger colleagues. Under such a climate, the health of older employees can suffer and it has even been shown how those who feel forced to take early retirement exhibit far lower levels of well-being (Warr, 1997). Consequently, the assumption that older workers are more likely to be a change management 'problem' can have significant implications both for the job security of older workers and for their future well-being after 'forced' or pressured retirement. This highlights the need to critically reflect on how we interpret and act upon popularized myths, especially when many of the underlying assumptions are questionable. It also leaves open a number of questions in need of further empirical investigation, for example:

- is the 'problem' of the older worker a consequence of false assumptions about the position of older employees?
- can legislation be used to break open the myth of older employees and change?
- are reasons not to change more easily ignored when they originate from older workers?
- to what extent do older employees actively resist or support change?
- how far are the views and experience of older employees underutilized in company change initiatives?

These and a host of other questions need to be addressed in studies on age and employment. The tendency to ignore (both in change initiatives and in academic studies of change) the place and contribution of older workers reflects an inclination to focus on innovation and change as a process in which the 'new' replaces the 'old'.

CHANGE INITIATIVES AND OLDER EMPLOYEES: A QUESTION OF HIERARCHY AND POSITION

The contributions that older workers can make to programmes of change generally remain untapped. Although they may appear to be unimportant to 'successful' implementation, they can often be an integral element in shaping employee experiences and expectations of change. Older workers, who have developed long-standing relationships within the company and who are respected by other employees, may represent continuity and security for younger employees who are seeking to work their way up the organizational ladder. They may also have a historical understanding of the place of the company, in addition to considerable knowledge and experience of the organization and its daily operating procedures and activities. Moreover, the tacit knowledge held by older workers is not always recognized and is often not easily translated into formal training guidelines. For these reasons, the human resource assets tied up with more experienced older workers may only become evident after the employees have been relocated, taken early retirement or been retrenched.

From an analysis of empirical data collected over two decades of research, negative experiences of change were most noticeable among older workers occupying operative and supervisory positions. For example, in a study of group technology at General Motors, the adoption of cellular manufacture brought about an increase in the demands placed on individual operators to conform to teamwork practices. Traditional operating practices that enabled employees to 'distance' themselves from the work were no longer deemed 'acceptable'. In contrast to conventional functional layouts that were criticized for their alienating properties in constraining social interaction and task engagement, the new teamwork structures demanded group work and collaborative employee involvement. Management also set clear parameters on what was to be regarded as acceptable employee behaviour under these new production arrangements. Paradoxically, traditional model employees who continued to distance themselves from process involvement were now engaging in behaviour defined as 'inappropriate' by management. Typically, these operatives were older employees, had been employees at the plant for most of their working lives, and in some cases were reluctant to adapt to the new methods of working. Furthermore, organizational evaluation of their behaviour took no account of personal choice; it explained their resistance to new ways of working in terms of an inability to adapt to change. The main 'solution' put forward by management was to encourage these individuals to take an early retirement package (failure to do so resulted in job transfer). Consequently, the new working principles under which appropriate employee behaviour is evaluated do not even attempt to accommodate the work preferences of older 'model' employees.

In contrast, older employees in senior management positions were often used as champions of change in directing and coordinating large-scale change initiatives. Although younger, enthusiastic and career hungry employees often formed a critical element during the implementation of change, the senior project leader was typically an older employee. Even in cases where the position of the older senior manager was called into question, their experience of the process was often markedly different from the shop floor operative or supervisory employee. An example of this was illustrated in the case of Telecom Australia which displaced a number of senior staff during a restructuring programme in the 1990s. The main thrust of the change centred on the creation of a single region that would cover South Australia, Northern Territory and Western Australia. The senior managers in both South Australia and Western Australia indicated a reluctance to move, and a decision had to be made on whether to locate the headquarters in Perth or Adelaide. As it turned out, Perth was chosen and although the reasons for this decision were never fully documented, there was an informal view that Perth had a time-zone advantage in being able to support the east coast in the early hours of the evening (that is, without having to run with overtime costs and so forth). For the regional manager in South Australia, the generous redundancy conditions made the decision to leave the company and stay in Adelaide an easy one. While only in his early fifties, the thought of moving to Melbourne or Sydney – with the possibility that his new job could be made redundant within six to 18 months – did not prove an attractive option:

> They offered me the opportunity to try and place me in Sydney or Melbourne, but the restructuring, the continuous churn in the place is such that – I've never been that interested in going to Sydney or Melbourne, anyway, and the churn is such that I just said, 'Look, there's a high risk in doing that'. In fact, in this current restructure, which not only limits my job – there were 12 regional general managers carrying two divisions and they merged two divisions and restructured to five, so seven jobs got abolished at that layer. So the risk of going to Sydney or Melbourne with the company – there are not particularly good relocation conditions anyway and there's absolutely no guarantee of any job security. (Senior Management Interview)

After talking to senior management in Sydney, he decided to take the generous financial package and remain in Adelaide. In this case, the financial incentive made the outcome not only palatable for the individual involved but also provided a sense of optimism. In contrast, other employees were far more threatened by the change, while at the same time being further removed from management decision-making. This was particularly noticeable among older staff in country towns. As one senior manager commented:

> So the issue with country is more one of (a) workload, because if you do take one of three out, there are workload issues for the remainder; and (b) grief, which tends to be greater when you're cutting a small team. In metro you take one person out of 50 or something in a big depot, and it sort of self-heals. In a country town there may be two or three guys who've worked together for years, drunk together, lived together – you know, their wives know each other and the kids went to school together and all the rest of it. That's more difficult to manage.

Although reductions in staff were being made on a voluntary basis, there were more volunteers in the central metropolitan districts than in the country areas. In one country area in South Australia, there was considerable resistance to the voluntary redundancy scheme. The local team was eventually instructed to identify five staff to leave the company or the regional general manager, without further consultation, would make the decision. As recounted in an interview:

> In the end, in a very directive way with the whole group, we got the numbers right. But no, some people in the country take redundancy and come to town; many buy businesses. There are heaps of older Telecom people running caravan parks, pubs and all sorts of funny things. It's very common. We did some work in the Northern Territory and found I think it was something like 70 per cent of all our ex-employees had gone into business on their own.

Employee perception of future opportunities influenced their views on the company programme of voluntary redundancy. In the more isolated country areas, where there were fewer alternative jobs or career options, unemployment posed a threat both to the individual and to the community. In this context, limited employment opportunities meant that younger workers were more likely to move to other parts of Australia than were older workers who had greater family ties and local community commitments. One option for older workers was setting up a small local business rather than uproot and move to larger towns and cities in search of company employment. Over time, the development of long-standing relations within a local community acted as an inhibitor to the option of relocation and constrained the mobility of older workers. Other factors, such as the cost of housing in metropolitan areas and the more social aspects, such as lifestyle changes, all influenced household decisions to remain in country areas. Although the findings from this limited data must be treated with caution, it would appear that while there are common experiences for older workers being made redundant, there are also likely to be significant differences depending on their position within the company hierarchy and the local context.

CONCLUSION

Many common interpretations about the attitudes and beliefs of older workers are not generally based on empirical evidence, but rest on everyday assumptions about the way older employees are likely to respond to change initiatives and on myths about the reaction of old minds to new ideas. Although change programmes are often tied up with political agendas and career aspirations, the more distant and impartial views of those who may have less at stake are generally ignored (or even scorned) rather than welcomed by agents of change. Typically, change and new ideas are seen to be the preserve of the young and as traditional forms of work organization are replaced with new methods, the place of the older worker is called into question. It is often assumed that older employees have little to offer in a world of rapid change where dynamism and youthful initiatives go hand-in-hand. Although there is legislation in Australia, Canada and the United States to prevent age discrimination at work, it appears that employment decisions are still often made on the basis of age and the assumed characteristics of older workers.

In examining change initiatives and the place of the older worker, the long-serving supervisor was identified as an area where the workplace myth of a supervisory 'problem' has been perpetuated. It was argued that many of the changes being introduced into organizations, particularly in the manufacturing sector, were bringing about both a redefinition of the role of the supervisor and an overall reduction in the number of supervisory positions. In many cases, the older supervisor was portrayed by management as an obstacle to change when, in practice, supervisory resistance often stemmed from the tendency of change agents to ignore the potential contribution that supervisors could make in facilitating change. For example, it was commonly assumed that the new methods of working would require the displacement of 'old' supervisors by 'new' younger recruits. Such views were not founded on empirical evidence but reflected stereotypical assumptions about the inability of older workers to adapt to change.

In the case of older employees in senior management positions, it was found that in contrast to operative and supervisory staff, they would often be involved as key decision-makers or leaders of major change initiatives. In cases where their jobs were under threat, the provision of generous redundancy packages often made leaving the company a comparatively easy decision to make. However, for the older employee working on the shop floor or in the branch office, financial concerns and the threat of long-term unemployment made forced retirement not an option to be so easily embraced. It was also shown that in the case of Telecom Australia, there was a greater reluctance among employees in the country area (as opposed to the metropolitan area) to accept redundancy packages. This illustrates the importance of context and how employees' perception of future opportunities will influence their response to company redundancy schemes.

Although the conclusions drawn from this analysis should be treated with caution, they do highlight the need to unpack the common misconceptions about older workers, supervisors and managers that influence management decision-making during programmes of change. The analysis also illustrates the need for more detailed critical research on supervision, work-place change and the older worker. Without further study, the assumed 'problem' of these employees may persist in the minds of management and promote company change strategies that fail to utilize the knowledge and expertise of their older employees.

7
Cellular manufacture and the politics of change

This chapter examines how plant-level management set about overcoming shop floor resistance to a change initiative to restructure individual work regimes into new team-based cellular arrangements. Electronic surveillance techniques were used to monitor night shift operations in order to confirm management suspicions that employees were engaged in 'inappropriate' operating practices that had remained hidden for years. Through a combination of participative and manipulative methods (involving both employees and their union) management secured their turf in the implementation of cellular work arrangements and the dismissal or relocation of dissenting employees.

In charting employee resistance to management change strategies, the case of Washdale Manufacturing spotlights some of the darker sides to change initiatives, and the importance of power and politics in understanding change outcomes. Employee attempts to block change resulted in a hard-line response by plant management. A number of employees lost their jobs, night shift operations were shut down and targeted individuals were relocated to more mundane and less 'rewarding' positions. However, before embarking on an analysis of this case, the section that follows provides an explanation of the term 'cellular manufacture' and a discussion of teamworking.

CELLULAR MANUFACTURE

Cellular manufacture (CM) simplifies material flow, reduces machine set-up time and enables the formation of team-based work groups (Alford, 1994). Since the 1980s, the commercial benefits of adopting CM have been highlighted (Ang and Willey, 1984; Ashton and Cook, 1989; Knight and Wall, 1989; Shtub, 1989), with manufacturers increasingly looking towards alternative methods to improve their competitive position without having to rely on large capital investment (Gallagher and Knight, 1973). Studies carried out by Wemmerlov and Hyer (1989) have shown that the main commercial advantages of adopting CM are reducing set-up times (by using part-family tooling and sequencing) and flow times (by reducing set-up and move times, wait times for moves, and using small transfer batches) to minimize inventory stocks and market response times. In conjunction with a number of cost-related benefits, these new team-based work arrangements are also seen to offer a 'key building block' towards more human-centred jobs. According to Badham and Couchman (1996), combining technical requirements with a social system of semi-autonomous work groups has become celebrated in Europe, and is viewed as a humane and positive manufacturing work trend of the future.

Group technology

Essentially, CM builds on the earlier principles of Group Technology (GT). In contrast to the traditional job shop layout, where machines are located together according to function, under GT machines with different functions are located adjacent to each other. (For a discussion of the history of cell-based manufacturing, see Benders and Badham, 2000.) Studies in the 1970s and 1980s demonstrated that significant improvements could be achieved by grouping technology (dissimilar tools and machining equipment) and labour (differing skills and trades) into work units or cells for the purpose of manufacturing related parts that are similar in their processing require-ments (Ham et al., 1985; Opitz and Wiendahl, 1971). These group-based approaches contrast sharply with the traditional job shop layout where machines are usually grouped by function. For example, all grinding machin-ery is located together and all drilling machinery is installed at a separate location within the same plant (Blackburn et al., 1985). The succession of operations necessary to manufacture the components would often require semi-finished parts to be moved to several locations throughout the entire plant, incurring considerable costs in the routing and storage of parts in various stages of completion. This functional layout of machinery also encourages the manufacture of parts beyond current requirements, in order to achieve an apparently high level of operating efficiency through maximiz-ing machine utilization (see also Venugopal et al., 2001). In short, through grouping different operations plants can operate more efficiently by being restructured around a component's processing requirement rather than a machine's functional purpose (see Biddle, 1993; Huq et al., 2001).

TEAMWORKING

The main human resource objective behind applying these principles (espe-cially in a number of European automotive plants, such as the twentieth-century Volkswagen programme in Germany) has been to improve levels of job satisfaction by breaking away from the individual-based assembly line-paced systems to more humane and group-based forms of work organization. In Sweden, for example, the success of the work redesign programme at their Kalmar automotive plant provided an early practical example of Social Technical Systems (STS) theory (Trist and Murray, 1993). This interest in cellular forms of work organization continues, and has been further strengthened by the growing interest in work arrangements that support teamwork (see Procter and Mueller, 2000; Sohal et al., 2001).

In the growing body of teamwork literature, there is a broad range of studies covering a wide range of social science disciplines (Benders and Van Hootegem, 1999; Buchanan, 1994; Dyerson and Mueller, 1999; Procter and Mueller, 2000). For some commentators, the growing emphasis on teamwork signifies the emergence of jobs that provide greater autonomy and promote the development of high trust relations (Wellins et al., 1991). For others, teamwork is simply a clandestine form of management control which attempts to manipulate the hearts and minds of workers through peer group surveillance (Sewell, 1998). The potential for increased surveillance and control over employee behaviour has been highlighted by Sewell and Wilkinson (1992). They describe how a Japanese-owned plant, manufacturing consumer electronics, used a combination of new management techniques to increase managerial control. Minimum performance targets were set and visual displays provided detailed information about the quality performance of the team and its individual members. The displays took the form of 'traffic light' cards suspended above the production line. Green cards signalled no incorrect insertions of components; amber – between one and four incorrect insertions; red – four or more incorrect insertions. This visible performance monitoring system enabled management to determine whether the production line was too fast or too slow, and whether particular individuals were having difficulties. Although there was some sharing of workplace responsibilities with operatives, controls over employee behaviour were significantly tightened through improved surveillance techniques (Sewell and Wilkinson, 1992).

In looking at the growing uptake of teamwork arrangements, an alternative perspective has centred on the move from the more Taylorist and mechanistic structures towards flexible specialization (Piore and Sabel, 1984) and more organic forms of organization (Burns and Stalker, 1961). These participative high trust cultures represent a shift from more direct forms of control to strategies of responsible autonomy (Friedman, 1977) and the emergence of 'postmodern' organizations (Clegg, 1990). Autonomy is a key concept. Teams of flexible multi-skilled workers are characterized as new model employees who work with others in taking responsibility for product output and quality in the organization and control of work. As Buchanan (2000: 34) describes, the concept of teamwork combines connotations of collaboration and comradeship with joint decision-making and shared skill in groups that range from three to over 30 members. The flexibility of this concept helps explain the history and rediscovery of teamworking and, as Buchanan (2000: 34) notes:

> Here is a management idea – the team – that is eminently plastic, which can mean whatever one wants it to mean in any given situation, but which at the same time appears to possess significant immunity from terminally damaging attack. One potential consequence of the plasticity of the concept is that teamwork is intrinsically indefinable, adopting different expressions over time and in different contexts.

The need to examine the context in which teamwork practices are adopted is supported by the work of Danford (1998) who advocates the importance of case studies in detailing the political process and outcomes of change initiatives. In some cases, teamworking may simply represent management rhetoric of empowerment and participation that masks the realities of shop floor operations; in others, greater forms of autonomy and worker control may be achieved. Similarly, Badham (1999: 5) argues that it is important to understand and take account of the role of organizational actors in shaping 'the teamwork agenda to create the forms of teamwork that they desire'. He maintains that the political process of organizational choice and the unfolding of workplace change cannot be fully explained from a single perspective that centres on issues of either control or autonomy. Increasingly it is argued that unlike the team-based initiatives of the 1970s, greater strategic importance is placed on the use of work teams in organizations and in particular on the use of team-based cellular manufacturing (TBCM) (Badham et al., 1997). Under these new work arrangements, greater responsibility for operational decisions is devolved to groups; supervision is redefined, with a greater reliance on peer group pressure and self-supervision; job tasks are allocated by members of a self-managing group; and these tasks are often rotated by agreement. However, as Baldry et al. (1998) have argued, employees may find team-based structures no less coercive than the individual-based work regimes that they replace. As McCabe (2000: 217–18) concludes in his study of teamworking at an automotive manufacturing company, employees may variously support, oppose or simply be indifferent to or nonplussed by change:

> 'Bewitched' employees were broadly supportive of teamworking, although the intensity of their support varied sharply. Although a number of employees noted that the 'normative' rhetoric of teamworking did not live up to the reality, this did not detract from their overall support. . . . Employees who were 'bothered' by teamworking were alarmed by the 'normative' bombardment that accompanied its introduction. It was this that they opposed rather than the 'technical' dimension of teamworking. . . . By contrast to those 'bewitched' or 'bothered' employees, those who were 'bewildered' by teamworking saw it as nothing new. They neither welcomed nor opposed it and indeed the normative dimension seemed to be background noise for them. These employees tended to be older individuals who lamented the past and regarded the present in strictly parochial terms.

Although there can be various responses to change, the findings reported in Chapter 6 indicate that it is a myth to assume that people of a certain age will respond to change in a certain way. In practice, these simple causal links do not exist: it is a combination of factors under emerging contextual conditions that shapes individual and group response to change. In the Washdale case reported in this chapter, local management support these myths in their portrayal and understanding of why people resist change. For these managers, it is obvious that older workers will resist change and yet, as we shall see, history and culture are central to understanding the nature of the conflict and the resistance. Finally, as mentioned in Chapter 1, Washdale Manufacturing is a pseudonym and is used because of the content of some of the case material (the company did not request anonymity).

CELLULAR WORK ARRANGEMENTS AT WASHDALE MANUFACTURING

Washdale Manufacturing is a washing machine factory divided into two sections. In one (the machine shop), the gearbox/transmission for the machines are made; in the other, the washing machines are assembled. The manufacturing cells in the machine shop are comparatively small, from two to six machines, and are run by two people. Cell operators are skilled in the use of a range of machinery in carrying out all operations. Once the components are finished they are transferred to one of a group of larger cells (six or seven employees) for assembly. Although the coordinator of cell operations is called a team leader, in practice there was little evidence of direct leadership tasks. In the small machine shop cells, employees tended to work closely with their colleagues in what was observed to be an open and equal partnership.

Since 1998, over a million dollars has been spent on technology (such as computer numerical control equipment), and this has reduced the labour requirement. Electronic gauging has also been installed so that the quality manager can maintain electronic surveillance of components and monitor whether any parts are outside of the prescribed quality parameters. Taken as a whole, changes at the plant have involved the uptake of cellular teamwork arrangements; heavy investment in new technology which has facilitated greater statistical process control of operations; an overall reduction in the number of employees; and a reduction in shifts from three to two. In the process of implementing these changes, management have developed and adapted strategies to accommodate potential problems and to overcome factional resistance to their longer-term restructuring objectives. The nature of some of these problems is outlined below and issues of resistance and control are discussed.

SLEEPERS WAKE: STAMPING DOWN ON THE CUSTOM AND PRACTICE OF NIGHT SHIFT OPERATIONS

Management at the plant were aware that there was something amiss with operating practices on the night shift (due to the high incidence of machine breakdowns), but they were uncertain about the cause. CM provided a useful opportunity to reassess night shift operations. At this stage, they did not realize that night shift operators had modified their work patterns to enable some 'sleep time' prior to the arrival of the morning shift. This behaviour became part of the custom and practice of night shift operations and there was considerable group pressure for new members to conform to this method of organizing work which, as one employee recounted, 'made life easier for all'. As a consequence of working the machines as hard as possible for the first part of the shift, there was a higher incidence of machine breakdown on the night shift than on the other two shifts. Aware that something was going on, management decided to install a system to monitor machine cycle times. As a manager recalled:

> When we looked at it there was a question of what the night shift were actually doing. They were making the numbers but things just didn't really gel. So we actually put read-outs on the main circuit board so that every time there's a machine cycle of course you get a little blip, so you can actually count the cycles, how many they do and all that sort of thing. They were actually manipulating the controller and speeding up the cycle – we were having a lot of maintenance on the machines and that was one of the reasons, they were running them too hard. We were having a lot of breakdowns on the circuit boards and things. They were actually speeding up the cycle that fast and then there were these long gaps from about two o'clock to about five o'clock. There was this long gap of nothing and yet the next day they had the numbers there. You know, how can they do that? So we checked it for a while and there was a definite pattern. The same time every night nothing was happening and the next day they had the product.

Although management remained in the dark for a number of years, other operators were well aware that their night shift colleagues were working machines beyond their limit in order to meet their targets as fast as possible so that they could create a 'sleep space' during the shift. By investigating the machine breakdown and productivity problems on the night shift, the local management team discovered the regular stops in production and decided to pursue the matter further. From their perspective, an absence of supervision and management control on the night shift was the probable cause and so they decided to find out for themselves what was going on:

> We came in one night about midnight, sat up in the office and did a few things. The machine shop was working and then about two o'clock there was no one. You know, we left it for a while, wandered down, no one around. We went into the lunchroom and we had to wake them up. So yeah, we don't have a night shift anymore. Their first response was 'Well we're just having a break'. They

didn't know that we'd been watching them for the whole shift. And this wasn't a one off, they'd been doing it for years. They had makeshift beds and little alarm clocks to make sure they'd wake up before the day shift people came in and all that sort of thing. The amazing thing about it was, because we were here, when people from day shift started rocking-in they think: 'Gee, what are they doing here at this hour?', you know. And when word spreads around what has happened, and these people are in the office and they're on the mat, staring down the barrel. The response from the people out there in the machine shop and that: 'You beauty, about time they did something about that. About time you fixed those guys doing that.' And you say, well, why didn't you tell me? Why didn't you say? 'Ah no, couldn't do that.' They wouldn't tell the boss and dob them in, but they were glad to see that someone had finally done something about these people bludging on night shift. . . . Yeah, they left the company. (Manager, Washdale Manufacturing)

This precursor to the introduction of CM was a clear signal to employees about the position of management and how they were not going to tolerate 'inappropriate' behaviour. Their strategic intention was to improve operational efficiency by the restructuring of workplace arrangements. For many on the night shift, peer group pressure and the local night shift culture did not allow them to do anything other than adopt standard practice. Work routines and expectations had become reinforced over time through the development of group values and beliefs that supported certain behaviours and prevented or discouraged others. These 'controls' emerge and are developed within groups. They are not simply a reflection of the systems developed and implemented in the design of work, but rather reflect the mutual shaping of structure and action within the context of a working environment. Given that night shift employees had little choice but to adopt common practices, it could be argued that many of these 'victims' of change were treated harshly in not being given a second chance under different contextual conditions.

Interestingly, day shift operators showed little concern over this outcome (viewing the night shift as an easy option that had been going on for too many years) and generally supported the hard-line stance taken by management. Local management also commented on the positive feedback they received from day shift employees. Paradoxically, by disciplining the night shift employees, management were able to raise morale among other members of the workforce. This not only highlights how different groups of employees may respond differently to management strategy, but also the importance of context in making sense of employee attitudes and behaviour. This hard-line approach was also used to overcome factions of resistance that emerged during the transition to CM. In this case, however, management combined their approach with the development of a programme for employee involvement which had the support and backing of the union. The events reported below illustrate how management were able to dislodge key individuals in militant shop floor areas and overcome employee resistance to change.

MANAGEMENT STRATEGY AND MACHINE SHOP RESISTANCE TO CHANGE

During the 1990s, senior management raised their concerns over the operational performance of the factory, and the factory manager set about the task of planning for change. There had been a barrage of programmes from many different consultants but there had been no lasting change in productivity. From the perspective of the factory manager, there was clearly a need to change methods of work in order to improve operational efficiency and remain competitive. One area in which production problems were most in evidence was in the transmission and gearbox section (the machine shop). About 90 per cent of the work in the machine shop was for gearbox components. As a long-standing and comparatively autonomous unit of operation, the machine shop had developed an independent culture based on the trade skills of employees. As an employee commented:

> I mean I have only been here five years and when I started here, it was like, you cross that line into that area and you could feel the change in atmosphere. You know, you could feel as if people were looking at you asking, you know, what's he doing in our area. So there's a real culture there and also there are little factions within the one area. Certain people hung around and stuck together, like the Italians would sort of stick together and other people would sort of stick together. When it came to the area and people and change, there was like one culture. When it came to other things, like who should be doing what jobs and that sort of thing, like things that happened inside the area there were like these other groups. But of course, I didn't know any of that when I started here. The day-to-day functions and everything, the duties were handled by a team leader in there. Basically, one team leader operated over three shifts. There were 34 people in there over three shifts working Saturdays, every weekend. The way it was set up is that, there was like a batch production set-up. There were individual machines and every machine had an operator. Now some of these people had been working there 15 years working the same machine, making fairly well the similar sort of part. They'd come in, they'd clock on, and they'd work there and keep pumping all these parts out whether we wanted them or not. Then they'd go home, come in the next day and do the same thing.

Under the batch production set-up, a lot of work-in-progress was generated and the operational efficiency of the shop was called into question. Plant management decided to have a look at going from a batch production set-up to a CM arrangement. With the appointment of a new graduate engineer, a computer-based package to simulate the effects of changing to teamwork arrangements was purchased.

> You could put all your variables in and that, and you could simulate the process. You could see how it runs, change a few things on the computer which is really easy and run it again, until you get the best result.

Using the software, they came up with the design for a cellular-based system that would reduce a lot of the non-value-added work and work-in-progress.

In pursuing a strategy of employee involvement, key stakeholders were invited to take part in the detailed design. A pilot was set up to prove that the change to CM was both possible and commercially viable. Volunteers were used in the pilot and they turned out to be not only willing participants in change but strong advocates of the benefits of this new form of work organization. As a local manager reflected:

> The fastest and most successful change comes from early involvement of employees and at the very least of all of the stakeholders; that is, consultation and involvement in the planning and development stages coupled with an open management style is a recipe for success . . . The plan doesn't matter. The planning does.

However, in the machine shop (located in the middle of the plant with 37 people), there was open hostility towards attempts to involve them in the process and it was here that considerable conflict and resistance occurred. As a local manager recalled:

> They had over 30 employees in the machine shop all traditionally operating one machine each. From a manufacturing engineering point of view the machine was dictating the rate. And in fact what was happening was that the cycle time for the machine might have been one minute and the people element of that would have been ten seconds or 15 seconds. You know, we had something like an 80 or 90 per cent waste cycle for labour. So you know, I actually put forward to them that we were going to change that to a different layout and the response initially was that 'Better people than you have tried it and haven't been successful'. It is highly unionised. In fact it was the hot spot for unions within the whole place. Because they are all trades people they see themselves as the workers elite. Untouchables almost, they wouldn't even let somebody come in and do a time study without walking off the job. Consequently, it took a bit longer and we involved them all the way. We used computer simulation to be able to show them graphically the changes which could take place. We used video, so that they could see for themselves their wasteful practices and we used machine labour cycle diagrams to show them how we could couple three or four or five machines together and do it comfortably. Consequently, about 18 months later they were down to about 24 people [from 37] in the same area with increased volume in the plant. We actually believe that the labour in washing machine manufacture was reduced by 5 per cent with that one change.

With the change to cellular design, personnel was reduced from 37 to 22 and there was an approximate increase in output of 30 per cent. Eventually, seven manufacturing cells were introduced and the time for the manufacture of new products (from customer order to the delivery of the product) was reduced from two years to five months. However, the change also necessitated the redeployment of staff, as one interviewee recounted:

> At the end it went from 34 people, three shifts, lots of overtime, every Saturday full crew and that sort of thing. Heaps of work-in-progress down to 22 people, two shifts, hardly any overtime, and hardly any work-in-progress. I think it was something like $400,000 to the bottom line of the business. That includes labour and work-in-progress.

Reflecting on the process, the factory manager claimed that the easy part was getting the software, simulating the change and planning what had to be done. The hard part was implementing the change and getting employees to accept the benefits of moving from the traditional machine shop set-up to a cellular-based system. Specifically, it was getting people to accept change and to get involved in the process. The factory manager suggested that it was perhaps the supervisor who acted as a major block to change. He was a gatekeeper between employees and local management. He was often relaying his own views and yet he would forward these as the views of the shop employees rather than his own. (See also Chapter 6 on the experience of supervisors and older workers.) As the manager reflected:

> He would say things to me like 'the people would not want to do that' you know. He was always the spokesman, no one else came and spoke to me. Even though you invited them to, he was always the one who would come and talk. But I think looking back now it was a case of he didn't want them to, you know what I mean. It was a case of he was controlling everything.

This resistance to change was highlighted in an early meeting which sought to involve employees in the process and communicate the intentions of management.

> We actually got everyone together and we had a brainstorming session and we said, look this is the way we believe people work well. And yes, there will be a reduction in labour but those people will not lose their jobs, we will give them a job somewhere else. That didn't go down well. That didn't go down well at all. And then, out of, I guess frustration, after trying to get them involved it was, well, you might as well get on the bus because this is going to happen anyway. And of course that just made them worse, because from then on when you asked for their involvement it was, 'Ah, well it doesn't matter because you're going to do it anyway aren't you?'. So it was very difficult to get them involved. We even tried with the layout, because we had to change the layout of the machine shop, we put up a layout which we could see had flaws in it purely for a starting point for them to say, no, that's no good, you should have it like this and you can do it like that. We didn't get any involvement. The only involvement or suggestions were from the supervisor.

In an attempt to overcome this problem, the local management team presented the layout and tried to make suggested improvements into a competition. They told employees that the group that came up with the best suggestion would be rewarded with something fairly significant. However, again the only suggestions came from the supervisor. Consequently, the cellular redesign of work arrangements within the machine shop was finalized without the involvement of employees. Once the design had been finalized the process of implementation began.

> When things started to change was when we got a reaction, when we actually started to move machines and put them into the cells. Then all of a sudden the people out there must have gone, 'Shit it is going to happen, they are really going to do this'. Even though we had been over this they actually had in their

mind that it was not going to happen – they've talked about it before and it's not going to happen. When they actually saw it start to happen we actually had a few people come up with ideas, you know, 'Why don't you put it there?'. You know, just a trickle at the start, but it was good.

In bringing about these changes, employee concerns were raised and the change strategies of management were questioned. However, management had already negotiated an enterprise agreement with the union stating that employees would be awarded pay increases on condition that they supported the introduction of new techniques (best practice management and lean manufacturing principles) that would raise productivity. Lean manufacturing is characterized as a system that lowers inventory through the use of just-in-time techniques to order stock when it is required, achieves continuous productivity improvements through employee involvement in group problem-solving and teamworking and reduces labour requirements by developing multi-skilled employees who are able to achieve higher rates of output through a more efficient and 'lean' use of resources. The agreement stipulated that management were required to involve employees in a consultation process prior to implementing change. In the pre-change meetings employees were not unduly concerned; it was only when the consequences of change became clear that workers started to object. Tensions between management and employees resulted in open conflict and the union was approached and asked to support the position of the employees. Unexpectedly (from an employee perspective), the union blamed the employees for not taking a more active part in the consultation process and suggested that they should put any personal antagonisms to one side and get involved in steering the change process. But, in practice, it was largely management who were politically active in leading the programme of change and overcoming factions of employee resistance. As the factory manager explained:

> Basically, the employees went to the union several times, but when the union responded we answered their questions. . . . You know, the enterprise agreement – which I was a negotiating member of – shows that you've agreed to a pay increase based on productivity improvements and the philosophies of lean manufacturing etc. And I deliberately used broad terms in our enterprise agreement – which is the legal replacement for the award in the area stated – so we used broad terms like world best practice and lean manufacturing principles and practices. All I had to do then was verify that they were best practice and part of lean manufacturing and they had to comply. The other thing which they came back with was that they were saying that they weren't consulted enough with some of the changes. . . . The union went back to them and said, 'Hey you guys you better be careful, part of the enterprise agreement is also to work together on the consultative process and it's not all one-sided, you guys have got to be part of that as well'. From that point on there was a hell of a lot more involvement from the employee side.

In the process of winning trade union support and developing a policy that encouraged employee involvement, local management attempted to steer the change process in a direction that circumvented or undermined barriers to their longer-term objectives. In this political process, the securing of support from other powerful groups in developing networks and setting up agreements were central. Moreover, due to the factional nature of resistance, there were always some groups who supported the decision by local management and so provided greater 'room to manoeuvre' in the political process of managing change. However, even after the changes had been implemented in the machine shop, the tension between local management and a small group of employees continued. As the factory manager explained, there were islands of resistance that were difficult to break down:

> There were factions. It is interesting actually, there were factions. We had a barbecue for the success of the changes and one faction warned the others that if they attended the barbecue that they would be black-balled and the faction were the outspoken guys. There was probably about four or five guys in the whole group that was forcing the others not to participate. What we did eventually – unfortunately for those people – is that we earmarked who they were and in the downsizing we redeployed them into quite low-skilled jobs like assembly. We left their salaries the same, we never changed them, but we put them into fairly demeaning-type jobs like putting screws in washing machines and then they were forever, after that, asking to come back into the machine shop. Yeah, so there is a way of handling this.

CONCLUSION

Washdale Manufacturing provides a good example of a politically hard-line and somewhat unscrupulous approach to change management. Drawing largely on the reflections of management, the data highlight how the local management team carefully modified and adjusted strategies to ensure they achieved the outcomes they desired. They were able to divide existing groups and by gaining the support of day shift employees and the union, they were not only able to achieve their objectives, but they were also praised by others for taking such a firm hand in bringing about change. Interestingly, while participation was taken to be central in planning for change, management viewed this planning as more important than the plan. Clearly this case raises questions concerning the degree to which employees and their union were manipulated through a series of clever political manoeuvres that serviced the aims of management and paid little real attention to the needs of Washdale employees. Participation was more about winning over employees to a management viewpoint than listening to and accommodating real shop floor concerns. This lip service participation took place within a context where management were making sure that they documented their attempts to involve employees so that there could be no recourse to union intervention later. As it turned out, when employees sought support from their union they were informed that they had been acting outside of a pre-negotiated agreement. Management had carefully planned their position and had successfully manipulated other significant parties to secure the objectives they sought. Although the company must remain anonymous, Washdale Manufacturing provides a clear illustration of some of the darker sides of change management strategies. The case demonstrates the importance of history and culture in shaping employee behaviour, and how the use of electronic surveillance techniques can identify 'inappropriate' employee operating practices that might otherwise remain hidden. Management's discovery of these operating practices provided them with a justification for closing down the night shift which simultaneously reduced the number of staff and enabled an overall increase in productivity. The extent to which this may have always been an intention of management remains open to speculation, but it certainly provided them with an opportunity to bring about a change which might have otherwise proved difficult.

On the question of teamworking, Richard Cooney (1999) draws attention to the considerable variation in the implementation and operation of cellular team-based work arrangements (see also Benders and Badham, 2000). He questions the degree to which there can ever be universal company adoption of these new concepts of group work, and spotlights the importance of contextual factors in shaping outcomes. Cooney (1999) also questions whether the new design criteria for empowered work groups represent any major advance from the autonomous (composite) work groups based on socio-technical work design theory. In this case study, the change did bring about the reorganization of work from individual-based jobs to teamwork arrangements in the new manufacturing cells. However, this did not signify a shift towards 'empowered' work groups that were of a different order to those associated with socio-technical work design. Moreover, this transition to team-based cellular manufacture was strongly supported by some employees and fiercely resisted by others, and the experience of the resisters has been the focus of this chapter.

In the machine shop, the distinct autonomous sub-culture that was rooted in custom and practice militated against employee involvement in the implementation of new teamwork arrangements. It was not the plan itself but the process of planning that enabled local management to identify barriers to employee involvement and to develop strategies for overcoming workplace resistance. As already noted, although a participative approach to change was formulated by local management (they achieved early involvement and support of the union), in the context of employee group resistance management became more forceful in their approach to change. This response went beyond actual restructuring and involved management in identifying individuals whom they purposefully removed from the machine shop to break up old established factions. Although management emphasized the importance of participation and employee involvement, pockets of employee resistance were quickly identified and strategies were revised to overcome them and bring about preferred outcomes. In this sense, change is a political process and, as Buchanan and Badham (1999) describe, often involves 'winning the turf'. However, not all parties start on an equal footing (it is not a level playing field) and, in this case, local management used their power in a way that serviced their own political ends. As players within the political process of change they were successful, and yet some shop floor employees suffered the consequence of that 'success'.

Upon reflection, if Machiavellian politics is associated with 'the use of devious political tactics . . . particularly in the context of organizational change' (Buchanan and Badham, 1999: 104), then the methods used by management in this case can be described as Machiavellian. Their shrewd and somewhat unscrupulous approach raises moral issues about how far change agents should be indiscriminate in their political manoeuvrings to achieve certain preferred objectives. From a Machiavellian position, moral scruples simply impede political success and individual achievement. In this example, the underhand, clever and manipulative behaviour of management suggest that their Machiavellian political tendencies enabled them to force through change in the face of considerable resistance from a longstanding and traditional power-block on the shop floor. But when does the balance shift from acceptable, if somewhat undesirable, behaviour to behaviour that is deemed unacceptable and amoral? A question worthy of further discussion and not one that can be resolved here.

8 Globalization and strategic change

> Almost every business today is under severe technological and competitive threat; in the USA the change in the rankings of the top 500 companies is twice that of a generation ago; look what happened to IBM. (Giddens and Hutton, 2001: 13)

Over the last decade, the speed of organizational restructuring has increased to accommodate the opening of trade across national borders and the development of the global market. For many companies, a focus on the traditional home market is no longer sustainable or commercially viable with the onset of competition from international players. As a result, an increasing number of companies have found themselves facing strong overseas competition and, for some, these changes have brought decline, takeover or even collapse; for others, the process of internationalization has brought with it a whole range of challenges, constraints, opportunities and threats. In this chapter, the views and experience of senior management are recounted in an examination of the emergence and growth of Faulding, a South Australian pharmaceutical company that has been transformed from a local company into an international player. The research was carried out over a number of years in collaboration with Margaret Patrickson of the University of South Australia. The main period of data collection was between July 1997 and December 1998. It involved document analysis, observation and a series of repeat interviews with the senior management group (see Chapter 1).

The development of erythromycin, known as Eryc (a delayed release antibiotic) and the acquisition of David Bull Laboratories (DBL) provide examples of Faulding's push towards developing a global technology forum from which it could compete on world markets. The distinct operating culture and 'family business' environment of DBL are also used to illustrate some of the social and organizational issues that companies face when trying to incorporate the 'culture' of other organizations. It is shown how there were both tensions and developments around strategies of centralization/decentralization and the process of merging new acquisitions. On the one hand, Faulding has needed a strong corporate identity in order to integrate newly acquired operations into the general company philosophy;

on the other hand, they have also recognized the importance of providing a certain degree of autonomy to acquisitions so that different operational arrangements and work cultures can coexist within a more broadly defined whole. But before presenting the senior management perspective on the critical events and change issues that arose during the pursuit of a strategy that sought global repositioning within a fiercely competitive industry, the next section provides an overview of some of the main debates around the controversial issue of 'globalization'.

GLOBALIZATION AND ORGANIZATIONAL CHANGE

According to Manuel Castells (2001), globalization is widely recognized as a fundamental feature of our time. He argues that while it has historical roots – with developments in information and communication technology and the deregulation of capital and securities markets – the 1980s and 1990s have witnessed the emergence of a 'new economy'. The infrastructure for this new economy has been 'the rise of the network society' based on software developments, microelectronics, computers and telecommunications (Castells, 1996, 2000). It is this technological infrastructure that differentiates the nature of change and competition today from early developments in international activities and trade. Castells argues that while the internationalization of economic activities has an extensive history, there has been a shift in both the character of competition and the nature of the companies developing within this new economy. Unlike corporations of the old industrial age, these new century companies often employ far fewer people while sustaining a far higher market value. As Castells (2001: 52) explains:

> Productivity and competitiveness are, by and large, a function of knowledge generation and information processing; firms and territories are organised in networks of production, management and distribution; the core economic activities are global – that is, they have the capacity to work as a unit in real time, or chosen time, on a planetary scale. Not everything is global. In fact, most employment is local or regional. Yet the strategically crucial activities and economic factors are networked around a globalised system of inputs and outputs, which conditions the fate of all economics and most jobs.

In other words, while there has been a significant change in the growth of the global economy, the experience of work remains grounded and contextually shaped within particular localities (see also Bradley et al., 2000 and Chapter 11).

In debating the concept of globalization, Giddens argues that this is not a single event; rather, it reflects four overlapping trends: developments in worldwide communications and the Internet; the 'instantaneous nature' and 'enormous turnover' of global financial markets; the collapse of communism and the emergence of capitalism as the dominant social and economic order;

and the growing equality between women and men (although Giddens recognizes that this development still has a long way to go in many parts of the world) (Giddens and Hutton, 2001). Giddens and Hutton both agree that while there are historical continuities there are also significant changes. In summarizing some of the controversy around the concept of globalization (see, for example, James, 2001; Shaw, 2000), Giddens states that:

> There is an enormous controversy going on at the moment about just what all these changes amount to and how far there are either continuities with the past or parallels to be found in previous eras. There are two quite opposing views. On the one hand, there are some who say there is nothing new under the sun. . . . They argue, for example, that a hundred years ago there was just as much globalisation as there is now. . . . At the other extreme are the 'Gee-whiz' types, who are so impressed with all the changes happening today, especially those to do with technology, that they see a world breaking quite radically with its past. As usual, the truth is probably somewhere in the middle. But on the whole I tend more to agree with the Gee-whizzers. (Giddens and Hutton, 2001: 3–4)

In the ongoing debates on globalization the immediacy of worldwide connections through the networked society, the increased interconnectedness on markets, and the growth of powerful global corporations (that may disinvest in certain countries or restructure and shift investment to low cost areas such as China) are variously identified as key elements of this process. At the same time, the local still remains important especially in studies that seek to understand how people experience workplace change (see Hirst and Thompson, 1999). For example, Collins (2000: 42) highlights how the 'forces of competition and change do not strike all with equal ferocity' and argues for a need to refocus attention away from the environment of competition to the context of business. He is concerned with the tendency to view globalization as an external force that is all-determining, leaving no space for individuals, groups or governments to actively shape their own futures. This concern, which is echoed by Hirst and Thompson (1999) and Bradley et al. (2000), reasserts the importance of human choice. As Collins (2000: 381) states, 'since our globalized futures are not yet written, and since viable choices remain within globalization, we should reject the simplistic, intellectually conservative, and imperative-driven ideas of the "gurus"'.

Since the late 1980s many major national organizations have restructured their operations to reposition themselves in a broader and more open market place (Ohmae, 1991, 1994). For some companies, narrow national markets became increasingly unsustainable as they found themselves facing fierce competition from overseas. Established international industries such as pharmaceuticals, where heavy costs are involved in developing new products to the level acceptable to stringent drug administrations in major user markets such as the United States and Europe, have been at the forefront of such movements (Hazelmere Group, 1978).

This process of internationalization has been facilitated by sophisticated technology and typically involves heavy investment in infrastructure to improve systems of communication across geographically dispersed operating units. For many industries, new product development outlays are extensive and can only be recouped by those companies who can earn worldwide revenue through the delivery of their product on the international market. Hodgetts and Luthans (1997), for example, cite earlier work by Main (1989) who reported how the time and cost of developing a new pharmaceutical product had risen from four to five years and US$16 million in the 1970s, to eight to ten years and US$250 million by the late 1980s. Since only huge conglomerates can underwrite such costs, smaller organizations may need to combine their resources into a consortium with global connections so that costs can be recouped quickly. For example, establishing joint partnerships may provide the capital, the technological knowledge and the understanding of varied marketing and distribution systems necessary for more global activities. This form of partnership arrangement may also contribute to the defrayment of high-level fixed costs, although, as Woodside and Pitts (1996) stress, particular care should be given to the choice of partnership arrangements.

On the question of managing across borders, Bartlett and Ghoshal (1991) have argued that organizations can no longer afford to base their strategy on a single focus. Rather, it must be complex and multi-faceted, reflecting the complexity they now face. Every part of the structure needs to collaborate in solving problems collectively. They offer a 'transnational solution', suggesting that companies have tended to adopt a strategy based on either an international, multinational or global approach (Bartlett and Ghoshal, 1991; Ghoshal and Bartlett, 1998). Under an international model, the home-based company sets up operations overseas in order to exploit the technology and products of the parent organization. Strategic decision-making, research and development and innovation remain at the home base with the gradual worldwide rollout of products and services. The multi-national approach centres on setting up a number of different nationally-based operations that can service the needs of a particular national market (allowing for product differentiation and quick response to national environments). The global approach rests on the standardization of goods and services to meet the demands of world markets (Ghoshal and Bartlett, 1998).

However, all of these approaches are untenable in the long run and reflect the outmoded mindset of managers and old strategic fit contingency models (that is, that there is an appropriate structure for organizations given prevailing environmental circumstances). Thus, Ghoshal and Bartlett (1998) advocate the adoption of a multi-dimensional strategic capability that emphasizes efficiency and responsiveness while recognizing the need to draw on company knowledge in the development of new competencies and innovations. These new forms of transnational organization require a new type of manager who is not constrained by company customs and traditions, but actively questions convention in developing new visions and innovations. However, as Collins (2000: 366) indicates, we are never given any descriptive analysis or insight into how these elements may operate in any particular context:

> It is difficult to avoid the conclusion, therefore, that the transnational solution promoted by Ghoshal and Bartlett works to disembed action from context, and so fails to investigate how people, real, living breathing people conduct their lives and live out their ambitions within organizations.

It is with an examination of a particular case, and the way senior management set about shaping the future direction of their company, that the remainder of this chapter is concerned. The analysis that follows presents a narrative account of how one small pharmaceutical company in Australia, which developed a new technique for modified drug release, was able to capitalize on its innovation and become an international player in the health care industry.

THE COMPANY: F.H. FAULDING & CO. LTD

Faulding was founded over 150 years ago as a small retail pharmacy located in Rundle Street, South Australia. Since those early days the company has grown substantially, investing in manufacturing and research facilities, and negotiating licensing agreements for the international marketing of its popular products. As well as the development and manufacture of pharmaceutical and household products, the company has also been heavily involved in wholesale and distribution operations. It is a worldwide health and personal care company encompassing generic oral and injectable pharmaceuticals, consumer health products, the provision of distribution and retail management services to pharmacies, and logistics management services to hospitals. The company is represented in over 70 countries and has over 4300 employees. In the 1999/2000 financial year Faulding delivered annual revenues of AUS$2.33 billion. The company continued an upward trajectory in the year ended 30 June 2001 with a 17.5 per cent increase in sales revenue to AUS$2.734 billion, a 35.4 per cent increase in net profits.

During their early years in Adelaide, Faulding manufactured a number of natural products, such as Solyptol (derived from eucalyptus oil). Following the formation of a partnership with Luther Scammell in 1861, the company grew and by the late 1890s had expanded to Perth in Western Australia. In the 1940s, a plant was built to produce penicillin and shortly afterwards Faulding became a public company (although all but one of the directors were family members). Throughout the twentieth century the company continued to expand their Australian operations and by the mid-1970s, with the development of Eryc (a delayed-release form of erythromycin), the international push into the development and production of innovative drug delivery systems had begun.

In 1977, Eryc was introduced on the Australian market and was soon a commercial success worldwide. These achievements on the world market were followed by the development, production and marketing of other products, such as the antibiotic Doryx, which by mid-1987 had captured 12 per cent of the US market (Donovan and Tweddell, 1995). In 1988, another sustained release drug was marketed, but the theophylline drug for asthma (Austyn) proved to be a technical rather than commercial success. During the 1980s Faulding also acquired the Melbourne-based David Bull Laboratories (DBL) which produced generic injectable anti-cancer drugs. In September 1985, an office and distribution centre for DBL was opened in the UK.

By the early 1990s, all of the Faulding manufacturing facilities were concentrated in new premises at Salisbury in South Australia and in January 1993, Faulding Pharmaceuticals and DBL merged to become the Faulding Pharma International Division. One of their most successful products of the 1990s was Kapanol, a controlled release morphine product first manufactured on the Salisbury site in 1994. In an attempt to expand the company, a strategy for more Australian acquisitions was embarked upon. However, senior management were blocked by the Trades Practices Commission who were concerned about the consequence of further growth for restrictive competition within Australia. This judgement sent a strong signal to Faulding that alternative strategies would be required to increase market share in the future. In response, they turned their attention overseas and acquired an operation in New Jersey (Kalipharma) which traded under the name of Purepac Pharmaceutical. During this period, they also acquired a 90 per cent interest in Fosham Horizon, located in Guandong province, China. The facility manufactures western pharmaceuticals and is also involved in the production of traditional Chinese medicines.

In managing growth and change, Faulding has continued to focus on the provision of innovative health care delivery systems which serve the changing needs of the health industry. Within this focus, they built up considerable knowledge and expertise on product and process development, manufacture and distribution. There is ongoing investment in new technology for plant and equipment. The main outlets for their products are retail pharmacies (chemists), hospitals (including nursing homes), general practitioners and the supermarket/grocery store. In developing their strategy for the future, the senior management team have concentrated their attention on what they term 'continuous innovative thrust' rather than investing large sums of money in long-term projects which may (or may not) provide the 'strategic leap' of a new product.

With the growth of the company and an increase in the number of employees, questions of how best to organize the human resource management function came into sharp focus. For example, during the 1980s there were only three people the human resource (HR) team. It was located at corporate head office and provided operational support through regular visits to various sites. Since the early 1990s, a far more decentralized HR support team evolved through the placement of HR staff within the divisions. This shift away from a centralized system was driven by a number of factors, not least of which was a response to the growth and expansion of the company. As Faulding continued to expand and to take on more staff, it became increasingly difficult (from a corporate standpoint) to keep abreast of what the real issues were at the operational level. It was decided that the divisional HR function needed to align itself far more closely with what was actually happening on the ground. Placing HR management within the divisions enabled the HR function to become a part of the divisional planning process and also brought HR personnel closer to the 'voice' of the employees they were serving.

Monthly meetings are held for corporate HR staff and all the divisional HR managers in Australia. During these sessions, various site issues are discussed as well as those of a more global nature, and the implications of change for the various divisions are examined. If there is something that is going to be developed on a group-wide basis, such as competency framework strategies or motor vehicle policy, they will be discussed at these meetings. Once an agreement has been reached, local implementation strategies are often adjusted to accommodate contextual site conditions. Interestingly, one of the most sensitive issues for change was parking, as this was something that nearly everybody had a vested interest in.

At the corporate level, there is also regular liaison between the various group leaders. For example, the group HR manager maintains an ongoing dialogue with the vice president of development and operations. As the latter indicated:

> Ultimately I am the person responsible for the outcomes of the endeavours of 800 people and I have to have a reasonable degree of freedom to get that working in an optimum way. Just as long as it doesn't violate fundamental corporate values and does not compromise what is going on in other divisions. There is that general sort of balance which you have to take into account. You certainly couldn't go into a free car policy, if another division which is actually a part of the group had a policy which goes in a completely different direction. That is where it is very, very important to have this liaison and balance.

With growth, Faulding adjusted their management of HR by maintaining open communication across decentralized HR functions. In the view of senior management, they needed staff who could not only recognize the importance of the local, but could also see Faulding as a small but growing global player in the health care industry. HR managers needed to liaise with their opposite numbers at different geographical locations and be aware of the need to accommodate local cultures and operating conditions.

GOING GLOBAL: BEYOND THE LOCAL PERSPECTIVE

In moving from a local mind frame to a more global view of the place of the company and its operation, the senior executive recognized that they were going to need a different type of manager, not just in HR but throughout their organization. As one senior staff member commented:

> The one trait I look for is definitely inter-cultural skills. You know people that can relate to different cultures. Now whether it is the culture of manufacturing versus accountants, whether it's the culture of feeling reasonably comfortable with the Japanese person, German or Serb, it doesn't matter. It's just feeling that sort of comfort. You know people who don't see boundaries around themselves. People who can get into the health culture and see that overview. That's what attracts me and those are the people that we want along.

In reflecting on his 11 years with Faulding Pharma International, the innovation director recounted some of the difficulties associated with moving from being a family business to a global organization. He noted that there was security in being part of a large company based in Adelaide and that this inhibited the drive for change, especially among some employees. Those who were part of and sustained the local culture were cautious about breaking away from a familiar world to a more uncertain and competitive future. For some managers, the risk of letting go of the concept of a 'family business' in embarking on growth and a push for global recognition held them in check. During this period, there were a number of managers who were unable to fully embrace change that would steer the organization into the global market place. As the innovation director explained:

> I guess when I came the perception of Faulding which was given to me by very many people – and I think was very true – was that it was an organization which couldn't decide whether it was still a family company or whether it was really serious about being a late twentieth-century publicly listed company.

During the 1980s, when Bill Scammell was Chairman of the Board and Chief Executive Officer (CEO), the company sought to expand while at the same time maintaining its historical roots in Adelaide. At this time, most of the board members were South Australian businessmen and Bill Scammell acted as a strong paternal figure in setting the strategic direction of the company. The CEO was viewed as an 'entrepreneur' with an 'ability to identify worthwhile projects'. For example, one of the big contributions that Bill Scammell made (in collaboration with Bill Davies) was recounted as follows:

They realised that if you were going to spend the money and devote the resources to develop a prescription drug product you had to look at the world as the market, not whether we would make a profit in Australia. They did that with Eryc. For many years with that product, every time they sold a bottle of it in Australia the company lost money. But they recognised that you had to be selling it in your own country before you could convince other people to do it. (Senior Management Interview)

This was also a period of uncertainty in the company as it was unclear whether they were developing drugs for Faulding to sell or whether the company should be developing them for overseas pharmaceutical companies to sell. These fundamental questions have remained with Faulding for a long time. For example, it has only been since the turn of the century that the company has crystallized the position it should take within the world market place. By examining the existing organization, Faulding's research capacity and the cost of developing future 'potential' drugs, the emphasis is now on the commercialization and distribution of products and on 'delivering innovative and valued solutions in healthcare'.

In its ongoing drive towards becoming a player in the global market place, Faulding continued to expand its operations worldwide while remaining an Adelaide-based company. This international model of a home-based company was combined with the setting up of nationally-based operations in China and a more global approach to product development and manufacture. Their strategy never fitted into one of the simple categories of international, multinational or global; it has always been more complex and multi-faceted (Ghoshal and Bartlett, 1998).

By the late 1990s, Faulding had become a global organization and yet it sought to sustain its historical links with Adelaide. The culture of Faulding during the Scammell years was still an integral part of the way senior management viewed the company, while also recognizing that great change had occurred. For example, a number of senior managers voiced the need for Faulding to be closer to global markets while also outlining the benefits of being more distant from their major competitors. As a result, head office remained in Adelaide at a time when business growth in America drew attention to the need for a head office overseas. When asked to explain this decision, senior management generally agreed that, while there were some drawbacks with South Australia, there were also a number of distinct advantages. The three main benefits mentioned during the interviews were:

1 *Staff turnover*: there is a low turnover of staff and once people settle in Adelaide they tend to stay.
2 *Test marketing*: you can do a lot more test marketing in Australia without it getting into the mainstream track.
3 *Security*: the isolation and distance from the main markets mean that it is less susceptible to industrial intelligence and espionage.

However, the decision to remain in South Australia created a recruitment problem. There was growing pressure to recruit staff with global experience and yet it was difficult to attract these people to a largely unknown city in Australia. For many people who have been active in Europe or America, Adelaide can appear rather small and isolated from the large pharmaceutical markets. In an attempt to counter-balance this location issue, senior management have invested heavily in technology to sustain and further develop their global communications network. Nevertheless, as one senior manager reflected:

> If you started from scratch nobody in their right mind would place a global pharmaceutical company in Adelaide. It's as simple as that. If you put yourself in the global perspective of the market place that we're competing in you would base us in New Jersey, California, London or Osaka.

The history and culture of Faulding had a powerful influence on corporate decision-making about the location of head office. Their South Australian base provided a strong historical identity, and promoted a sense of stability and continuity within a context of strategic change and innovation. This sense of the past and its place in helping to shape the future direction of the company are captured in the following quotation:

> One of the key things in all of this is not to lose contact with the past. The last thing a new generation of managers should do is to come in and say that the past is rubbish. Which is a huge tendency for new managers. You need absolute respect for the achievements, for what people have done and built up.

A GLOBAL TECHNOLOGY FORUM: THE DBL ACQUISITION

> The commercialisation of Eryc gave Faulding a unique global technology platform. Because technology by itself doesn't get you anywhere. (Senior Management Interview)

The modified release drug Eryc highlighted the need for a global technology platform if Faulding was to compete successfully on the international market. Although successful in Australia, Eryc had remained a doubtful commercial proposition until it gained access to the larger pharmaceutical markets overseas. After satisfying the demands of the US Food and Drug Administration, a ten-year licensing agreement was negotiated with Parke-Davis. Under this agreement, Parke-Davis were given access to Faulding technology and were able to sell Eryc in America. The success of the product drew attention to the need to commercialize, which included a marketing and distribution organization. At the time of Eryc and later Doryx (an antibiotic that Parke-Davis also acquired the American licence for and that captured 12 per cent of the market) Faulding did not have this capacity. To resolve this block, a strategy for the acquisition of DBL was put into place. This new acquisition – which was a fully vertically integrated injectibles business that was just beginning to grow in sales in the UK and Europe – made the first step towards the globalization of the Faulding business possible. In other words, by expanding into a niche market (injectibles), Faulding was able to break into, and become a significant player in, the international arena. At the time, however, DBL was an expensive purchase and there were problems assimilating the DBL culture with that of Faulding. As one senior manager explained:

> It has really only been in the last three or four years that the people who have been involved in that business have started to appreciate that there is the global company Faulding which they are a part of. . . . I think a key factor was a couple of years back when we started to change the name. So at the moment we still have DBL as a brand name because it was such a well known brand name it didn't make sense to change that. But in terms of the business name, it is out of the business name altogether now. The other thing was when we had some changes at the senior management level, and we actually had people who were managing this site also managing the Mulgrave site. Some of that was good, some of that was bad, but I think that started the integration.

It is perhaps ironic that, at the very time that Faulding was moving away from its historical legacy of a family business, it purchased a family company. The management of DBL sought to maintain 'business as usual' and resisted attempts to change the culture of the company. The paternalistic attitudes of management prevented either a quick or smooth integration, and for these reasons it took a long time to change the culture of the DBL operation at Mulgrave. At the time, a consequence of this change was the unanticipated tendency for Mulgrave personnel to view Faulding as the main customer rather than as a global pharmaceutical industry. Working within this framework, a lot of time and attention were diverted into projects which, while proving to be technically successful, did little to improve the position of Faulding internationally. Under these circumstances, employee morale suffered. One of the main reasons was that although staff were achieving excellent technical results, they were not producing commercially viable products that would generate a profit. As stressed by one interviewee, this remains one of the major challenges facing Faulding:

> I think that the real challenges are trying to get people to understand the demands of the customer. And that begs the question who is the customer and that is not always easy is it? But understanding the demands of the customer and the environment in which the customer has to work. And that is the toughest one I think. To a large extent, for most of our workforce here, it's theoretical and abstract; they haven't experienced it emotionally yet.

Shifting employee attitudes towards a more global mindset is a difficult task and not one that can be achieved overnight. One way in which Faulding is tackling this issue is through the recruitment of senior managers who have had considerable experience working in other international pharmaceutical companies. This developing group of senior managers are formulating strategies and implementing change initiatives to further the cultural shift from being a 'national company' to being a 'global player' in the health care business. But as one manager noted, 'It is actually quite hard to get that global mentality'.

This process of 'globalization' is ongoing in Faulding and represents an essential element of their strategic change initiative to create a more responsive and adaptive operational system. Being aware of both the internal and external contexts, and being able to take a more holistic and multi-disciplinary view are part of the transition, or cultural shift, towards a less parochial and more global mindset. In treating context seriously, management recognize that there cannot be a single solution, plan or operational strategy that will service the different operating conditions in the various sites and divisions. In managing these changes, there is also recognition that there will inevitably be some resistance to policies that redefine traditional ways of working and thinking. As one senior manager explained:

> Initially there was a scepticism or resistance because people have a belief that what works in one place will automatically translate into another. I don't think you can be further from the truth. Each situation has a unique set of circumstances that have to be addressed.

In moving away from a focus on discrete achievements within manufacturing or research and development (R&D), the links between business development, project development and manufacturing have been made explicit. The emphasis is not simply on manufacturing, or product development, or the launch of a new product, but rather on the links between these areas and the benefits to the company as a whole.

STRATEGIC OBJECTIVES: TOWARDS THE SEAMLESS ORGANIZATION

In developing a strategy that emphasizes the links between all stages in the commercialization process from R&D, to product manufacturing, to marketing and distribution, to selling the product in the global market place, Faulding is attempting to move towards its objective of a 'seamless global organization'. As one interviewee noted:

> We are aiming to have just a seamless, fluid organization. Where you have product development based on management risk and matching it to customer needs with seamless transfers into manufacturing. . . . Traditionally what has happened was as soon as an idea came up it was bolted down. The project was formally started; the specifications were set, just instantly galloped down at the bench. And what you do of course is that you carry that risk and you haven't reconfirmed with the customer if this is actually what they want. Oh and by the way, nobody has checked to see if it is manufacturable. Pretty simple things when you look back, but that is actually the history of most product development in the company.

Under the old way of working, the risks for new product developments were carried a lot longer than they are now, and failure rates were consequently a lot higher. Some of the older products that have been 'saved' have nevertheless presented manufacturing difficulties. In the case of their operations in South Australia, Faulding have implemented an approach where the focus is placed on commercial viability and potential customer demand for new products. The main concern is with getting the prototype right, working out whether it can be manufactured, estimating costs and evaluating potential sales and profits. In this way risks are reduced and unfeasible projects are identified far earlier than previously. As one senior manager explained:

> The other inherent problem which this organization has was that it could never stop projects. You always had what I called a cockroach syndrome. Someone would say look this is not going to fly. You would stomp on it then someone else would say that's my project. You throw another million dollars at it. The years go by, tick tick tick tick.

In assessing the future direction of Faulding, all senior managers stressed the need to expand and develop as a niche player in the global market place. With regard to Australian-based health care, Faulding has just over a 40 per cent market share of the distribution business and it does not envisage any growth in this area. In fact, holding on to this level of market share in Australia is viewed as a hard enough task. For the senior management group, the main issue is how to engage in a successful strategy of lateral diversification, and how to identify and develop products to meet the changing health care needs of the twenty-first century:

> One scenario is the growth of a health care business stepping into wellness, self-medication and retail. Further down the track you can say, well, stepping out to getting some of our brands globalised in the retail side. It's a tough slog but it is doable. Then if you were to look back onto the Pharma side of it . . . the issue is how can a very small player like Faulding – and we are small – carve out a niche and be recognised in that. I think there are two ways. One is we've got to be ruthless in our focus on what we are good at. What we are good at is injectibles. That's the only business in pharmaceuticals where we are vertically integrated. We develop, manufacture, distribute and access end-user, and that end-user is the hospital. . . . But the future for injectibles is a lot of geographic expansion. To move into Latin America, selectively into European countries, and obviously selectively in Asia. You've seen this with the roll out strategies that we've got at the moment and our subsidiary base, but it's cautious expansion and constantly building up the product portfolio. (Senior Management Interview)

Since the turn of the century, the company has come under increasing pressure to establish a firmer footing in the large markets of Europe and America. On 1 July 2000, Faulding's worldwide oral and injectible pharmaceutical businesses commenced operation as a single division, Faulding Pharmaceuticals, and relocated their head office to New Jersey. In moving out of their Australian base, the Faulding group CEO Ed Tweddell noted that:

> Faulding is now ready to take the next step of integrating and streamlining its pharmaceutical businesses under more concentrated leadership, based in the

northern hemisphere where the majority of our major customers and business partners are located. This move will enable us to be more responsive to key market needs and opportunities. It will also upgrade our capabilities through the increased allocation of management and technical resources to the United States and Europe, and through the recruitment of senior personnel with local market knowledge and experience.

From its manufacturing facility in Elizabeth, New Jersey, Faulding Pharmaceuticals manufactures approximately two billion tablets and capsules each year under the Purepac™ brand. The company has also purchased an additional facility at Piscataway, New Jersey. Taken as a whole, the division experienced a strong growth in sales revenue during 2001 that amounted to a 29.8 per cent increase in earnings before interest and tax (an increase from AUS\$91.3 million in 2000 to AUS\$118.5 million in 2001). At the same time, the Australian-based health care operation, comprising consumer health care products, logistics and retail services, became the other main division, Faulding Healthcare. This division also experienced growth (although at a lower rate) with an 11.6 per cent increase in earnings (AUS\$77.7 million), and remains an Australian-based operation.

CONCLUSION

In the words of one of Faulding's senior managers, 'there is only so much we can do in Australia, we have to grow globally'. In charting this transition, the initial push for the more global commercialization of a product occurred with Eryc in the 1980s. However, in seeking a quick passage to becoming a global company, the importance of gaining the appropriate mix between various elements of marketing and technology was overlooked. This may have been due in part to enthusiastic ambition linked to limited experience. Since the 1990s, a new and expanding set of strategic alliances has been formed and during this period Faulding emerged as a small global player with a range of licensing agreements for the overseas marketing of its Australian-developed products. Faulding entered into a technology licensing agreement with Dainippon Pharmaceutical to manufacture Kapanol for the Japanese market; the company acquired an injectibles manufacturing facility in Aquadilla, Puerto Rico; and in the UK, the marketing of Faulding's morphine product (under the trademark Morcap) was carried out by Sanofi Winthrop. These and other alliances have been used in the worldwide commercialization of Faulding products and have been an integral part of strategic developments in managing the process of 'globalization'.

One of the key elements in this transition from being a local Adelaide-based company to becoming a global player in the pharmaceutical industry has been Faulding's ability to adapt and change to shifting contexts and its capacity to identify new strategic opportunities. A spirit of entrepreneurship, a commitment to innovation, and a recognition of the importance of HR management to the successful implementation of corporate policy, have all been identified by senior management as central factors in the development and growth of F.H. Faulding & Co. Ltd. As one Australian senior manager said:

> I think you have got to come to the insight that all organizations pulse like amoeba. There is no single model of a whole. If anybody believes that they are nuts, absolutely nuts. The way of working and organizing yourself and the structure will vary according to external and internal forces. And that's exactly what is happening now. We've reached, I think, many of us that insight, that in a particular point of time we decentralise and another point of time you may need to centralise something. You may need to get that change going, to get that orientation effective and then you let go. It's no different to deep-sea fishing, in a sense.

The importance of breaking down barriers between individuals from different disciplines, operating environments and functional areas was also identified as a key factor in the successful transition from a small local company to a global business. The notion of the fluid, seamless organization that could respond to the needs of customers in the global market place by identifying, developing and producing commercially viable products was used to highlight the centrality of contextual adaptability and the value of developing employees with a broader global outlook. This strategic shift has been promoted by a new breed of senior managers who bring with them a global perspective in the search for and identification of new strategic opportunities. From the perspective of senior management, the future is about managing diversity by developing contextually sensitive policies and not seeking to transplant successful innovations at one site to all operations worldwide. Their 'transnational solution' centred on the careful choice of partnership arrangements; investment in technology and advanced communication systems; a focus on the development of new competencies and innovations; the recruitment of senior managers with a broader and more global outlook; and the discarding of simple policies and strategies. But this largely 'successful' strategy of growth and change also moved the company into the global arena of the pharmaceutical market place, and as a player they have once again become noticed by larger pharmaceutical companies. As it turned out, on 6 August 2001, in a letter to the shareholders, the chairman, Alan McGregor, stated that the directors were recommending that they accept the revised takeover bid for Faulding made by Mayne Nickless Limited. Mayne employs approximately 38,000 people worldwide and through the acquisition of Faulding in 2001, the pharmaceutical division is represented in over 50 countries worldwide. The main focus remains on the development, manufacture and marketing of injectable and oral pharmaceuticals. By August 2002, Faulding had achieved their strategic objective of being a global player, but in so doing they can no longer be regarded as an Adelaide-based pharmaceutical player operating in a niche market.

Trade unions and a shifting industrial landscape

Trade unions at the moment are in a very difficult situation because of membership and apathy from the general workforce. All it needs I guess is something like a metaphorical bomb underneath a group of workers to make everyone else feel threatened and that might shake them up a bit. But there's a lot of resignation to it, you know: 'What can you do? You can't do anything can you?' And also because we do have high unemployment and everybody knows somebody who's been looking for a job. 'I don't want to be out there looking for a job, so I'll accept the shit that they give me because I don't want to lose this job because I don't want to look for another one.' (Shop Steward)

This chapter examines change and trade unions. Unlike some of the previous chapters, the focus on trade unions is not linked to change processes within a particular workplace, but on trade unions as organizations operating in an industrial relations landscape which has itself undergone fundamental change. For some commentators, the purpose and place of trade unions have been called into question as their influence in representing the collective needs of organized labour has declined (see Belanger et al., 1994; Crouch, 1994; Hyman and Ferner, 1994; Niland et al., 1994). Clark (1995b: 593–4) suggests that this shift from a union-based system of collective bargaining to a more individual contract-based system of employee relations has (in parallel with the rise of HR management) undermined the position of trade unions and redefined the future of industrial relations. Although in the Australian context the institutions of compulsory conciliation and arbitration have historically marked out a rather unique industrial landscape (Baird and Lansbury, 2001; Howard, 1987), there has nevertheless been a decline in union membership as in many other industrialized countries. As Cooper et al. (undated: 2) note:

> It is clear that the historical protections offered trade unions by the state in Australia have not blunted the impact of structural changes in the labour market and growing employer militancy. In fact some commentators argue that the historical 'dependency' of unions on the state has made them less able to adjust to the conditions they currently face.

Since the late 1990s, the relationship of the Australian trade union movement to the state has been redefined with a movement away from centralized policies and the grass roots development of autonomous unions. Legislative reforms by federal and state governments have weakened the legal position of trade unions, for example the Workplace Relations Act 1996 allows for non-union individual and collective bargaining, and limits the access of union officials only to sites where the union already has members (Cooper et al., undated: 8). In the UK and Australia, an examination of these changing contextual conditions centres on two key areas: the response and strategies of trade unions to the changing business environment and work-place change initiatives; and the extent to which trade unions are themselves changing in order to renew their relevance to the contemporary world of work. Linked to these broader areas are others such as membership decline (Machin, 2000), deunionization (Korczynski and Ritson, 2000), changing legislation (Gall and McKay, 1999, undated), technology and shifts in the nature of employment (Marginson and Wood, 2000), union organization (Baird and Lansbury, 2001; Carter, 2000), and the barrier of male unionism to union renewal (Healy and Kirton, 2000; Wajcman, 2000). The case of the South Australian and Northern Territory Branch (SANTB) of the Australian Services Union (ASU) is used to highlight some of these elements by drawing on the experience and reflections of a number of union members and officials. This trade union provides a pertinent example. It is having to deal with the 'crisis' of declining union membership; to debate 'renewal' issues in attempting to redress the tradition of male unionism by promoting the place of women; and to tackle the 'ideological' and political issues associated with union amalgamation and change. As Kelly (1998: 54) points out in his iconoclastic book *Rethinking Industrial Relations*, although the intense political struggles by activist groups within trade unions are acknowledged, there is surprisingly little research in this area. The contemporary issues facing trade unions are both problematic and central to the development of union strategies and alternative approaches to meet the challenge of trade unionism in the twenty-first century.

THE CHANGING INDUSTRIAL LANDSCAPE AND THE DECLINE IN UNION MEMBERSHIP

Over the last 20 years there has been a fall in union density in the UK, the US and Australia. An increasing number of trade unions have witnessed a shift away from traditional forms of work and employment arrangements to new types of jobs, linked to a growth in part-time and casual employment. Complex patterns of sociopolitical events and business developments have contributed to a change in the industrial landscape including deregulation, global competition, shifting employment patterns, the use of new technology to create new types of jobs (for example, teleworking), and new forms of work organization (for example, call centres). In addition, various changes in government legislation have resulted in a general movement away from centralized systems of collective bargaining to more localized bargaining arrangements (see Marginson and Wood, 2000). A general decline in union membership – which in the UK fell by over 20 per cent between 1989 and 1997 to around 7 million - has been paralleled by legislative change and a barrage of new workplace change initiatives (Bradley et al., 2000). In Australia there has been a decline in union membership throughout the 1990s from over 2.6 million in 1990 to fewer than 2 million in 2000, with the first growth in union membership numbers for over a decade occurring in March 2001 (Cooper et al., undated: 27). This overall decline in union membership has occurred in a context of company change programmes that have tended to promote a traditional (unitary) perspective (Fox, 1974) on HR management. This view assumes that a common culture exists and that organizations are harmonious, conflict-free, cooperative structures. The rhetoric of 'togetherness', where new empowered employees work collaboratively in the pursuit of common goals, echoes through many of these new management techniques (Collins, 2000). In restructuring work and bringing employees 'on board', the employment relationship is viewed as something to be managed in a non-adversarial way without union interference. An anti-union management ideology has developed in some areas and a number of companies have attempted to derecognize the place of unions in their drive for deunionization (Bacon, 1999; Peetz, 1997). The importance of management ideology in steering this change has been documented by Kochan et al. (1986), who note that in the US, management anti-union stance has been a critical factor in the growth of the non-unionized firm. Kelly (1996) argues that many employers object to the very existence of trade unions and would actively support any programme that de-established unions. This trend toward strategies of union derecognition has also been identified in the UK in the work of Claydon (1989, 1996) and Millward (1994). However, Korczynski and Ritson (2000) argue that it is the pragmatism of UK employers rather than any growth in anti-union management ideology that has led companies away from centralized bargaining arrangements. They use the example of the oil and chemical industries to illustrate a type of dualism whereby a centralized bargaining framework operates for contractors involved in repair, maintenance and construction, and yet the same employers have successfully embarked on strategies of union derecognition for their internal staff. They note that there is

> little evidence to support arguments that a strong anti-union culture in the industries underlay employers' actions. Rather the evidence suggests that management have acted pragmatically in response to pressing short-term economic pressures. The different approaches to unions for the two sets of workers have been guided by the different economic objectives facing employers and by the different historical position of unions in helping or hindering to secure those objectives. (Korczynski and Ritson, 2000: 419)

In this case, the historical demarcations of internal craftwork were viewed by management as a barrier to workplace reform whereas collective bargaining for external workers was perceived as efficient. In other words, management viewed the collective representation of external workers by unions as aiding their economic objectives with contract firms while impeding their requirements internally. From these findings, Korczynski and Ritson conclude that unlike the anti-union ideological drive for deunionization in the US, the British experience is somewhat different – it is a pragmatic response to securing objectives rather than a value-driven strategy. They also note that following the 1999 Employment Relations Act, it is no longer an option for management to derecognize unions in cases where over 50 per cent of workers are union members. As a consequence of this change in legislation, some of the plants in their study may seek to regain collective bargaining rights (Korczynski and Ritson, 2000: 435). Since this period, a number of unions have seen their membership stabilize and there have been some cases of growth through the development of alternative recruitment practices. For example, Carter (2000) has identified a more widespread recognition within the union movement of the need to manage change and describes the movement from a more conservative 'servicing model' to an 'organizing model' where members are far more active. However, he notes that there can be different cultural traditions within unions and across different sites which, unless tackled, may limit change. As Marginson and Wood (2000: 494–5) point out: 'The decline in trade unionism in Britain appears to be more a matter of the failure of trade unions to organize new workplaces than of young workers having an inherent antipathy to trade unionism or there being a new individualistic or apolitical generation of employees'. Furthermore, Gall and McKay (1999) illustrate how the level of union derecognition has fallen significantly between 1994 and 1998, and that the number of new recognition agreements exceeds cases of derecognition. In a more recent study they highlight how this trend has continued and conclude that:

> the role of the trade unions may need to be given greater prominence, not just in lobbying for the creation of statutory mechanisms and a change in public opinion, but also in organizing campaigns to increase density levels whereby gaining union recognition in line with the thresholds becomes a more realistic prospect. (undated: 18)

In Australia, Peetz (1997) claims that the Australian union movement is facing a crisis following a sharp decline in union density (from 1982 to 1996 the proportion of employees belonging to a union dropped by over one-third). He argues that some HR management strategies that promote notions of 'trust' seek to remove unions from the workplace and yet there has been little discussion of the effects of workplace change on unionization. He provides evidence to show that over a four-year period in the early 1990s one in 20 unionized workplaces employing 20 or more people became union-free (Peetz, 1997: 27). Although there is little consensus within the literature about the effects of workplace change on unions (Kelly, 1990), deskilling (Crompton, 1976), increased job insecurity (Lumley, 1973) and work simplification (Hundley, 1989) have all been identified as factors that generally encourage unionization. In contrast, the more recent change initiatives which promote participation and seek to increase the commitment of employees to the organization have been associated by some with deunionization (Quinlan, 1996; Taplin, 1990).

Although deunionization may more often be a 'by-product' rather than an 'explicit objective', in 1995, Comalco (part of the large mining company CRA Ltd) implemented an explicit deunionization strategy at their Wiepa operation in Australia (Dawson, 1996: 19–20). The aim of CRA was to create a workplace without unions (a change they had successfully achieved in their New Zealand operations) where all employees would be offered substantial pay rises to move to an individual-based system of staff employment. Masked in the rhetoric of greater employee commitment for competitive advantage, CRA argued that such a change would encourage 'staff' to be actively involved in the search for and implementation of improvements to both strengthen the competitive position of the company and enable the company to sustain competitive remuneration packages (Dawson, 1996: 19). As it turned out, the Industrial Relations Commission instructed CRA to bargain collectively with unions (although in practice this did not rule out systems based on individual contracts).

In examining proactive union strategies, Cooper et al. (undated) draw attention to a number of active campaigns by unions to address the issues of falling membership and the growth of the non-unionized workplace. For example, they describe a campaign to unionize the Australian call centre industry and organize its predominantly unorganized labour into unions. All the unions with coverage rights in the industry (including the ASU) joined together in the *callcentral* campaign. Instead of following the traditional methods of drawing attention to poor employment conditions, the campaign set up a website to provide advice on employment rights of call centre workers. They also highlighted how the Community and Public Sector Union (CPSU) had attempted to reinvigorate itself through a collective decision in 1997 to move to 'organizing unionism'. As they explain:

> 'Recruitment', the traditional means by which Australian unions have brought in new members, involved a union official convincing an individual non-member of the merits of union membership, in a sales-like manner. The union chose to adopt the less passive 'organizing' approach instead. This has involved members, rather than officials, recruiting non-members, active campaigning around collective workplace issues and the nurturing of workplace union organization. This shift included the adoption of new tactics in organizing including organizing outside of the workplace, one-to-one organizing and activist development. (Cooper et al., undated: 18)

This shift towards more 'self-reliant unionism' spotlights the importance of change in developing new and more inclusive strategies for involving employees in unions. On this issue of strategy and trade union effectiveness, Boxall and Haynes (1997) critically evaluate the 'organizing' versus 'servicing' model in their study of trade unionism in New Zealand (see also Hyman, 1994). They question the simple dichotomy between official-led unionism which services members (consumers) and the organizing model where members are empowered to be a union in what Hyman (1989: 179) describes as a 'living collectivity'. In advocating the view that unions face choices for organizing that complement their servicing activities – for example, in developing cells of workers that may constitute 'pockets of effectiveness' (Boxall and Haynes, 1997: 573) – they argue that at critical junctures there is a range of choices that can be made, from strategies that promote selective activism to those that seek mass mobilization. Similarly, in the employer relations dimension, they reject the simple juxtaposition between 'adversarial' and 'cooperative' relations, arguing that any sustained form of relationship with an employer involves some form of cooperation. They argue that between the dimensions of union–worker relations and union–employer relations, there are four broad patterns of union strategic choice:

- classic unionism with adversarial employer relations and member servicing plus solid organizing;
- partnership unionism where credible adversarial relations include extensive cooperative practices;
- paper tiger unionism comprising a servicing model with formalistic adversarialism; and
- consultancy unionism characterized by servicing with limited organizing and some cooperative practices within routine adversarialism (see Boxall and Haynes, 1997: 576).

They illustrate how large unions may exhibit more than one pattern of unionism and conclude that, while servicing models are strategically vulnerable, the organizing model of classic unionism is proving effective in public sector services (although the astute political management required of partnership unionism is often difficult to sustain). In short, while presenting a more differentiated framework for making sense of union strategy, the question of how to revitalize and renew trade unionism within the shifting industrial landscape remains open and in need of more detailed contextual analysis. But before embarking on our case analysis of the ASU, it is important to draw attention to the influence of gender and changing patterns of work on unionization.

GENDER, CHANGING PATTERNS OF WORK AND TRADE UNIONS

An international trend that is evident in the UK, the US and Australia and that has important implications for trade unions centres on the changing patterns of work and the growth in part-time and casual employment. Many of these jobs are being created in the service economy and are outside the conventional work sites where unions are present. Consequently, many of the traditional industries in which unionism flourished, such as coal, steel and shipbuilding (whole communities of working-class male workers), have declined and are no longer central pillars of the trade union movement. Stubbornly, many of the values and traditions associated with this industrial past persist to the detriment of the renewal of the modern union movement. In particular, the gendering of unionism which has sustained unions as symbols of working-class men has prevented women from taking a leading role in the future development of trade unions (Healy and Kirton, 2000). Interestingly, even in the academic field of industrial relations there has been a tendency to sidestep or downplay women and gender issues (Wajcman, 2000). Although recognition has been given to equal pay and to areas where women predominate in the labour market (for example, call centres), gender still remains largely absent (or simply equated with women) in the study and theory of industrial relations. This absence is especially critical at a time when unions need to radically reappraise their future strategic direction and relevance. As Healy and Kirton (2000) argue, although there have been 20 years of positive action strategies to improve women's involvement in trade unions, there remains a significant discrepancy between the proportion of female union members and their representation at senior union levels (a factor raised and discussed in the case study that follows). They suggest that women's under-representation highlights power relations and gendering in organizations in which cultural images of gender are reproduced and main-tained. Similarly, Wajcman (2000: 195) draws attention to the need to address the gendered character of employment and trade unions, and not simply to conflate 'studies of women with gender analysis'. For Wajcman (2000: 196), this tendency downplays the 'role played by unions in institu-tionalizing women's subordinate position in the workforce'. Although the existence and maintenance of patriarchal relations in unions shape policy, institutional structures and the election of union officials, there remains an odd silence on the issue of gender and trade unions. Writing on Australian unions, Pocock (1997: 10) decries this absence:

> A failure to understand unions as masculinized organizations which reflect the habits and dominance of men has led to an assimilationist approach to women. Concepts of women's deficiencies and disadvantage have generally underpinned union analysis and action in relation to the 'problem of women' in Australian unions. Union action in relation to women's under-representation has been constructed around assumptions about women's anti-unionism, their low levels of knowledge, skills, confidence and their lack of interest in unionism. As a consequence, little attention has been paid to the structural and cultural machinery of unions themselves.

Pocock argues that assumptions about women's attitudes to unions and interest in activism are generally wrong and not supported by the evidence, and yet these false assumptions have served to advance men in their domination of unions. There has been a tendency to see the lack of achievement of women in gaining leadership positions as a reflection on women ('deficits in women') and not patriarchy ('deficits in masculinised unions') (Pocock, 1997: 11). Within the field of industrial relations, there is surprisingly little on the experience of women as trade unionists. It has largely been defined as 'male territory' (Forrest, 1993; Wajcman, 2000). In taking gender seriously it is important to examine not only the way patri-archal power relations shape unionism, but also differences within the broad categories of 'men' and 'women'. It is also important to understand the relationship of actors outside the workplace to issues such as union activism. As Pocock (1997) and Wajcman (2000) argue, factors such as domestic duties, child care and partner opposition can be critical in explaining differences between men and women in union activism. This again highlights the importance of contextual analysis which does not isolate work or union involvement outwith the domestic sphere of life. These and other issues are now addressed in a case study analysis of the ASU.

CHANGE AND TRADE UNIONS: THE CASE OF THE AUSTRALIAN SERVICES UNION

The Australian Services Union (ASU) is an amalgamated union which operates through a series of semi-autonomous branches with the main national office located in Melbourne and a smaller national office in Sydney. In November 2000 the union had approximately 130,000 members Australia-wide spread over 14 branches (some of the states had more than one branch), with 9000 members in the South Australian and Northern Territory Branch (SANTB). Although the ASU is an amalgamated union, some branches had not fully amalgamated (the SANTB amalgamated in 1995). Over 60 per cent of ASU members are women. They work in both large companies and small businesses and are in full-time, part-time, casual or temporary employment. It is the only organization in Australia that represents the special interests of clerical and administrative employees in both the public and private sector. The public sector includes energy and social and community services as well as local government. Clerical and administrative members in the private sector work in industries such as road transport, the retail sector, credit unions, small business, airlines and pro-fessional offices. Because it covers a broad range of industries, the union has had to deal with a host of change issues both in terms of company change and the broader politico-economic context. In addition, shifts within the union and the different approaches of the union branches have highlighted the political process of change and the need for a more strategic approach to member retention and recruitment.

As an organization, the ASU centres around the branch (which is far more in touch with ASU members), with national-level activities being more involved with research tasks that can service the union as a whole. There is an assistant national secretary (ANS) whose chief role is to act as resident expert on privatization and contracting out (this person works closely with British unions, especially their sister union UNISON). The National Executive of the ASU meets three times a year, bringing together all branch secretaries and various other union officers to discuss policy and union strategy. However, as the union remains a loose federation of branches and is still striving for full amalgamation (a theme of their annual convention held in December 2000), these arrangements can act as a barrier to the development and implementation of national policy.

> The nature of our union and the way the rules are is that nobody can impose anything on anybody. It's got to be a co-operative sort of effort. So what we do is we talk about it, you know, like this conference this week we'll try and talk about it. With 14 branches you might get, say, nine who'll say, 'Yep we'll be in that and we'll contribute money for it'. The others will say, 'No, we don't think it's of any interest to us'. There's not much we can do about it, except over time get more of them thinking nationally about the ASU.

The national office provides coordination and specific services to the branches, but its role is not directive; rather, it tries to ensure that the various branches work collectively for the common good of the ASU. As the National Secretary and CEO explained:

> We provide a service from the National Office to the Branches to help them do their job and it's sort of a complementary sort of arrangement I suppose. We have certain tasks that we do in relation to the kind of industrial relations system that we've got here. We have a number of industrial officers that work for us to look after National Awards, run national campaigns. That's complemented by the Branch doing their own local stuff with their union organisers and looking after their own State Awards. And what we're sort of moving to is more of a campaigning sort of role. Recognizing that many of our industries are downsizing and contracting out. We get involved in those sort of campaigns to either stop it happening, or if it does happen follow the members into the contract companies, you know, and still provide a service to them and still keep them in the union.

The SANTB amalgamated in 1995 in contrast to some of the other states where amalgamation has proven far more difficult and contentious. The main barriers to change seem to centre on political affiliation, gender (patriarchal power relationships, masculine leadership and shortage of female union officials) and ideological conflicts. Interestingly, the ASU is a union that not only covers a wide range of employee groups but also a broad political spectrum. As a consequence, there is the potential for conflict in bringing together diverse groups of employees into a larger amalgamated union (see also Kelly, 1998):

> We had a lot of tension, when you put council labourers together with white-collar workers, together with almost managerial types, across a whole range of sections which are not used to working together. It causes a lot of tension. But a lot of the tensions are personality, who's going to be the National Secretary, who's going to be this, who's going to be that. And my view is that amalgamations are terrific and the benefits will come in the next generation. When the

legacy is gone and the next generation comes in, they won't care whether they came from the clerks' union or the municipal workers' union, or the social and community services workers' union, they'll just say, well I come from the ASU. There will be a whole new culture.

As some branches are left wing while others follow the political right, there can also be considerable tension between various branches of the ASU federation and this has important implications for the formulation of national policy. The national senior leadership group (referred to by some at the annual convention as 'fence-sitters') tries to steer a middle course and spends considerable time and political energy ameliorating conflicts between the factions. This national group of leaders comprises a national secretary and CEO (the most senior position in the union), a national executive president and three ANS (within this top layer only one was a women in 2000, holding one of the ANS positions). However, the national office has no members as such, but exists to formulate policy and overview the running of the union as a whole. As one union official explained in discussing this structure:

> So the National Office hasn't got any members, however, it's got the same building, 28 staff, cars, all that sort of stuff, so it costs a fair bit to keep running. So all the branches pay. In 99 we paid $28 per member per year, so what's 9000 times $28? Say about $270,000 or $250,000 we give them to maintain the ASU name. Essentially it's like a big franchise. So, like, we're a separate branch but to use the ASU name we give them 250,000 grand, one of the bigger NSW branches gives over 400,000. So all the branches are always saying: 'Why in the hell should we give 250,000 or whatever it is, when that would employ three more people back home?' So it's always that sort of thing and we've never come to terms about being either a national union and operate nationally where all the branches are in tune with the national office, or a loose federation and that's what we are at the moment. Others would argue with that, trying to get something done, you know: 'Ah, my hands are tied because the men are playing dead.' And in some of the votes nationally it's not a clear left/right split, sometimes it'll be a man/woman split but then you'll bring in the left/right as well. So it is a brave delegate that comes in with an unprepared motion at National Conference because you just don't know which way it is going to go.

If you are not part of the national leadership group, then the only way to get a motion at the national convention is to go through one of the branches. In contrast, the National Secretary, National Executive President and ANS can develop their own motions and put them through the National Executive. This group consists of the national office members plus the branch secretaries and executive presidents (around 40 in all). However, voting rights on the National Executive are weighted by the number of members in the branch. The SANTB has nine votes out of approximately 128. Consequently, branches have to work behind the scenes to gather votes in support of particular motions or to resist policies they deem inappropriate. As the SANTB Branch Secretary explained, you have to lobby and make deals with other branch secretaries:

Sixty-two is the magic figure, so once we've got 63 votes, you can formulate or influence policy. We start from a base of 30 votes approximately as we enjoy good relations with Victoria and Queensland-based Branches. We then have to cobble together another 30 plus votes from the other branches which will involve trading support in other policy areas or supporting an individual for elected office within the union.

The SANTB views itself as a far more cohesive political branch than branches in some of the other states where 'branches are captives of both left and right committees' which can seriously impede change. At the national level, however, the SANTB can often be frustrated in its broader objectives since voting rights are based on membership numbers. A lot of political effort goes into trying to ensure that the National Executive is composed of members who can lead the union forward in a proactive rather than reactive way. This need for strategic trade unionism is deemed doubly important given the shifting nature of work and the major changes that are occurring to jobs and employment. However, once again, the importance of history and context is highlighted both in maintaining continuity (past traditions, values and beliefs) and in spotlighting the need for change in employment, government legislation and gender composition. The ASU case provides useful insights into the process of organizational change.

GENDER AND TRADE UNIONS: FROM MALE BASTION TO FEMALE FRIENDLY?

If you go through the entire union movement, right, just any union meeting you have, the men are out there running the show. Well, it's the same thing isn't it? I'm just talking about the full picture all over in Australia. If you hold a union meeting and you have ten delegate positions, nine out of ten will be men, and you might just get one female. That's just how it works. Just at the moment you're not going to change that.

With the growth in part-time work, casualization and the decline in employment in energy, transport and local government, the future recruitment opportunities for the union are shifting towards women. Typically, it is the more male-dominated areas of employment that are in sharpest decline and although there has been a significant increase in part-time male employment, the ratio of female to male ASU members is, under current trends, likely to increase. However, this broader labour market change also has implications for change within the union. For example, the New South Wales Branch has been a traditional male bastion. It is more right wing than the other branches, and has strongly resisted any attempts to re-invent the ASU as a 'women's union'. In contrast, the SANTB is seeking to address gender issues both in terms of senior union appointments and in its strategies for recruitment. As one union official explained:

In some of the branches it's worked and in other branches it's failed. If you were to take one of the New South Wales Branches, you know, it's run for blokes, by blokes. But that will change, that'll change. In our Branch, I mean, one of the things we consciously do is get the organisers to go out and recruit women shop stewards or workplace representatives as we call them because it's the shop steward that recruits most members and organises the workplace – sort of takes the bulk of that workload – so whenever we go into a workplace we encourage women to put their hand up to be the union delegate in that workplace. Then the other women in that area can see that it's not a bloke's union.

Strategically, the ASU is making a conscious decision to go after women and is currently repositioning itself as a women-oriented union. This reinvention is viewed by some union officials as being critical to the survival of the union; however, the history and tradition of Australian unionism do not lend themselves to easy transformation. These changes need to be seen not only in outward policy formulation and revised recruitment strategies, but also in terms of women holding senior positions in the ASU. Although real changes are occurring in some branches, in others, where the context supports traditional trade union values, these transitions are less likely. Also the more formalized committee structures were not seen as being female friendly, as a discussion with the Branch Secretary and Branch Executive Secretary of the SANTB highlighted:

> *Interviewee 1*: We've found that a lot of people, either through fear or whatever, say I don't want to stand for an elected position. However, I'm quite happy to hand out your stuff, phone up people and things like that. So don't call me a committee member of the local government and industry division, but I'm quite happy to be a workplace rep. or a contact where you can drop stuff off. So people either get scared over titles, you know, setting themselves up as a target. Or indeed what we are finding with the large women membership, you know, women traditionally have got their job at the workplace and then their job at home. And trying to get them to formal meetings and things like that, they just go, 'We ain't got the time'.

> *Interviewee 2*: They haven't got the time and often they're intimidated by those sort of structures. They don't want to sign up for something where they feel they might have to contribute. Or often they say, 'I wouldn't be able to say anything and I'd feel silly, and I don't know how meetings work, or meeting procedures'. But they would quite happily come along to a quasi-social event.

Many of the formalized structures were viewed as historical legacies from the smaller unions that existed pre-amalgamation and may have factional representations that are not conducive to improving the participation rates of women. They reflect traditional union structures and the relevance of many of these old methods is being called into question. In practice, the SANTB has not acted on too many of the resolutions from these more formal committees. Attention is being placed on networking and encouraging participation among members locally, and on trying to steer national policy in recognizing how traditional gender arrangements are detrimental to the future of the union. Major issues facing the ASU centre on rule changes and the campaign to see more women elected to union positions. The push to ensure affirmative action – in the election of women representatives to all the national structures – has been ongoing for a number of years. However, attempts to introduce rule changes that require the proportional representation of women have been resisted by the more traditional trade union factions. As a branch executive president described:

> Immediately you try and do something like that the old guard comes out of the woodwork to try and stop it, basically because they're threatened. They're threatened. There's old men that have held these positions of power for a long time and a) they don't want to lose their job and b) a number of our national members really don't think that women should be in the workplace let alone running the union.

This view was supported by the Branch Secretary who recalled how at the Canberra National Conference there was a major outcry by many traditionalists at a motion to ensure that same-sex couples got the same paternity/maternity leave. As he went on to recount:

> Yeah, '97. We still had the Western Australians getting up and saying that homosexuality was ungodly. Unhealthy, ungodly and you know if you come to the national conference at the right time, you know, that'll come up again and again. . . . They believe we should be going down a tax reform path to ensure that women are encouraged to stay home to look after the family, you know, they believe that's why membership has been declining, it's because we've let more women come back into the workforce when they should be home looking after the kids.

A policy has been drafted and endorsed that seeks to secure a higher representation of women in the senior ranks of the ASU. However, the more right wing factions of the union drafted this policy and although it addresses the issue at the branch and shop steward level (the policy is that the 2003 elections should have at least 30 per cent women candidates), it does not cover national officials. The SANTB is pushing for at least 50 per cent and has managed to get this position endorsed by the National Executive. As the Branch Secretary explained:

> We've just got our rules through, it just got confirmed on Friday that we're trying to push the envelope at least 50 per cent, in those areas where we've got at least 50 per cent, so it's a true proportional representation. . . . You see our rules have to be endorsed by the National Executive. So again, we had to wait for 62 votes. So if there were enough Branches obviously who thought well: 'What are they doing?' You know, 'They've gone crazy . . . they're just supporting the women a bit too much'. It could have gone down, but it's like a benchmark for the Branches. . . . We're fully amalgamated, we'll push the envelope on all progressive issues, and the real things that do actually mean something to our membership. The other Branches are seen to be, you know, sort of lagging behind. That's fine, that's their problem and they can explain that to their members – but they never do.

Essentially, the union has to take a more strategic approach and yet these changes involve an internal political process as the positions of the branches do not align. With a wide range of membership (with branches being on the left and right of the political spectrum), the traditions and culture of male-dominated unionism compete with the push by some branches for a more radical shift in the union agenda. In this sense, breaking the inertia and moving towards more agile unionism is not simply an awareness issue, but a socio-political process which ironically mirrors many of the workplace change issues faced by the union in representing the needs of their members. But are the internal political processes able to accommodate such a radical change? In the next section, new empirical data are presented to provide some insight into these issues through a brief analysis of the politics of union organization.

THE POLITICS OF UNION ORGANIZATION: VESTED INTEREST, GENDER AND TRADE UNION DEMOCRACY

Many union positions all around Australia were up for election in May 1999 (apart from honorary positions, there is a four-year term for all positions). Strategies were devised to ensure preferred outcomes, although it was recognized that unanticipated consequences could result from too heavy a push in particular areas. This was discussed as a complex political process where it was all too easy to 'knock off the wrong bloke'. The system of election is not preferential but first-past-the-post. Nominations opened on the first Wednesday in March 1999 for a period of 21 days, after which there was a week to withdraw nominations. A few weeks later ballot papers were sent out and members had three weeks to lodge their ballot. (As it turned out, both the Branch Secretary and the Executive President of the SANTB were re-elected unopposed.) As would be expected, these periods are highly political and there is a lot of manoeuvring and positioning of candidates. However, the outcomes of these political processes are also critical to aspects such as the continuation or decline of traditional forms of male unionism, determining the left/right political composition of the union, and in selecting the groupings within which future policies will be developed and discussed. As one interviewee recalled at the annual convention when reflecting on the 1995 elections:

> Leading up to the '95 election there was the Wollongong conference and negotiations got downright dirty and ugly. 'I'll ruin you, you ruin me' all that sort of stuff. And it didn't get resolved at national conference, you know, everyone came along, you know, did their bit, said, 'We'll see you at the ballot box'. Then in December almost everyone got nervous and we got summoned to Melbourne. I was the only one from our group so what came out of that meeting was an agreement to support X, Y and Z for all these positions. . . . It was not a formal meeting of the union, it was a meeting of the factions of the union. But what happened was that a deal was worked that people would nominate for the various positions but no more nominees would be in those

positions, so it didn't have to go to a ballot. . . . Unions hate having elections of the members because you can't control it, so if you can control it by controlling the nominations for the ticket, then that's usually how things are sorted.

These deals are common practice in unions and serve to maintain some form of stability in the branch leadership. They can also serve to maintain certain political configurations and sustain patriarchal relations, thereby limiting women's access to key union positions. Although anyone can be nominated (provided that they have two other paid up members to nominate them, they have been a fully paid up member for 12 months and they accept the nomination), agreements are often made across branches. For example, a New South Wales Branch might make a deal with a Queensland Branch for mutual support in the case of a leadership challenge. These deals can become even more complex if it is necessary to encourage left wing members to vote for a right wing candidate in another state:

> It's like the Federal election really because it's sort of like the ALP [Australian Labour Party], you know, the factional heavies hate each other, but come an election they all sign up to the ALP. And so, you know, you'll get right wingers campaigning in left wingers' seats, and vice versa, and helping as much as possible just to get the party over the line. This is a bit different, because we're not being threatened by an outside organization you know. Like you said, any of the 130,000 members could drop a nomination in and when that happens obviously we have to look at the nominators and check that the person's financial [paid up].

During the interviews prior to the election, the question of the ballot was high on the list of a number of group agendas. Typically, people wanted to hold on to their positions and under the ballot system there would be a high degree of uncertainty over outcomes. Nevertheless, for some, maintaining a position that actively sought to prevent members casting a vote for those they wished to lead the union was at odds with trade union democracy. Moreover, it was suggested that such a position might be a contributing factor to the decline in union membership. As one elected official reflected:

> One of the reasons people are leaving unions in Australia is because they see them as undemocratic and blokey. Bastions of blokes hanging on to their extremely well paid jobs and extremely beneficial superannuation benefits. So, you know, it's my opinion that at some stage or other there should be ballots so that the members feel that they actually do participate in deciding who runs their union, and while it's safer for me to stitch it all up beforehand it's also not necessarily a good thing because the members will see us as also part of the machine. We'll be seen as looking after our own interests.

It was pointed out that while an election is a 'scary thing', the demands of meeting short-term objectives in order to influence long-term goals can 'take you down a track which may not be in keeping with your overall beliefs'. There can be conflicting responsibilities and the water is rarely clear in the murky process of trying to influence and steer trade union strategy in keeping with a wider political cause.

ECONOMIC RATIONALISM AND THE CONTEXT OF CHANGE

In the case of the SANTB, there have also been a number of contextual changes that have shaped union strategy and change. Many of these socio-economic changes have been brought about in the name of economic rationalism and the so-called pursuit of competitive advantage. For example, the outsourcing or privatization of public utilities and the amalgamation of local councils resulted in a decline in union members at a rate of about 120 a month. A number of voluntary separation packages changed the union membership landscape of South Australia, but as with union membership worldwide, there has been a range of legislative and labour market shifts which ASU recruitment strategies have had to accommodate. For example, there has been a big increase in part-time work and, in particular, casual work. Although the gender distribution has not changed overall (around 60 per cent women and 40 per cent men), there are noticeable differences across the old traditional areas of work, such as railways, buses and energy (still around 80 per cent men and 20 per cent women), local government (with a more even distribution) and the growing financial services area where there is a higher ratio of women (around 70 per cent women and 30 per cent men). As the SANTB Branch Secretary and Branch Executive President pointed out, job security is a major issue facing their members:

> Trying to develop some form of job security for the members. That's what they want. Everybody has been downsized, restructured, turned around, turned upside down. The members have just had enough, you know, 'We actually want some permanency and some type of security, we used to have it, now we haven't got it'. So that's going to be part of it, as well as trying to make a viable financial base out of the membership that you've got. In the last couple of months, the membership decline has gone back to a more manageable level. Earlier this year it was about 200 in a month, now it's back down to 100 to 120. Well if we can maintain that and get back to our recruiting – we used to recruit 120 a month – so as long as you can break even on that you're pretty much okay.

In the case of the downsizing of public sector employment and the shift towards the smaller private sub-contracting business, the ASU has been strategically well placed to accommodate a movement of its members from the public to the private sector by covering both sectors. However, in some states such as Victoria, where the right wing government of Kennett introduced compulsory competitive tendering in local government, the ASU branch lost approximately 54 per cent of its membership. In contrast, the SANTB has remained relatively stable, although again members were lost through the amalgamation of local councils and the consequent rationalization of operations (with an overall reduction in staffing numbers). Furthermore, with the election of a Liberal state government in the 1990s, compulsory unionism for local government ceased. As one ASU official recounted:

So now people do not have to join the union, so you actually go out and organise and recruit them individually. In South Australia, in local government in 1995, the state government determined that the number of councils, which was about 118 at that stage, should be reduced. So now we have 67 councils and that's where the redundancies have come, because it's a much bigger operation so of course they had duplication of services so they got rid of the staff that they didn't need anymore. But as those employees move out of public sector employment into private sector employment we can follow them because our rules allow us to cover people in the private sector. So as a union, strategically, we're placed extremely well to continue to represent employees.

In tackling some of these changes, ASU workplace representatives have regular programmes of visitations in areas where they have members and they continually seek to arrange access to companies where they think there is potential to recruit new members. Once they have gained entry to a new workplace and signed up a few members, organizers will generally target an activist to become the union delegate. This employee is then given the responsibility of recruiting new members, sorting out issues on the job (as far as they can), implementing union policies, and so forth. In discussing some of the problems of recruiting, the growing number of people who are taking part-time employment, pay and contactability are highlighted as major barriers. As one union official explained, 'If they're working part-time they're often working shift work. So to actually get an organiser to find them when they're at work is difficult.'

TRADE UNIONS, TECHNOLOGY AND THE GEOGRAPHICAL DISPERSAL OF WORK

Along with the economic rationalist strategies of government, gender, and the barriers to change of traditional male unionism, developments in technology are another factor that has serious implications for trade unions. Unlike the 1980s and early 1990s, where developments in information and communication technologies were largely used to transform work functions such as drafting, accounting or word processing – in what Zuboff optimistically labelled 'informatize' or 'automize' (Zuboff, 1988) – the late 1990s and early 2000s have witnessed a much more ambitious change programme integrating across functions, obliterating processes that do not create customer value, enhancing the control potential of employers, and enabling new forms of telework. As one union official reflected on the problems of recruitment with computer-mediated work:

It's very hard. You know, the concept of people working from their own homes at the end of a computer and all that. I suppose there are still big groups of members working in big establishments and they're the areas you tend to concentrate on. They're the easy ones to go for. We've thought about how do you sign up people who have no concept of solidarity, of being in the union and working in a big office or a big depot or factory. How do you sign up people who are working from home, you know, it's bloody hard. . . . The old traditional way is still the way it is mostly done.

With advances in communication and information technologies, it is possible to carry out procedures and routines across time and space, making what Castells (1996) labels 'working together apart'. The growth in this type of work, which can be spread across regions, countries and continents, is a potential threat for organized labour (Leisink et al., 1996). Although institutionalized units of unions have historically had trouble handling workplace change that cuts across the turfs of different union groups, these issues are now at the forefront of union change strategies:

There is an increasing number of those types of workers [virtual workers] and we are slowly addressing them. It is one of the things we would hope our National Office would be a bit more proactive about. These are national concerns and already many of our Enterprise Agreements have clauses dealing with the issue of people who are in employment but choose to work at home. And that works okay, as long as they're attached to a local government authority or something where you can cover them. But the real problem is when those people are contracted in their own home or have no contact at all with the workplace.

The problem of how the union makes initial contact with this growing number of workers is one that the union is attempting to address, but it is not any easy issue or one that they feel they have adequately tackled. As the SANTB Secretary commented:

The problem is it's highly mobile, you know, set up anywhere in the world, anywhere there's going to be a telephone. They're quite clever this one mob in Melbourne, they're near the university and one floor is like a café and lounge, while employees are killing time between lectures they will be invited to wait in the lounge with a coffee and then be called in for a couple of hours' work. It's incredible what they do. On Friday nights instead of the happy hour they close the café down, turn it into a bar and have bands playing there. So people are in there listening to bands and stuff like that and the supervisor will say: 'Ah look Patrick, you know, can you just duck up and cover the phones for a couple of hours?' It's like a little city and they provide all these benefits and pay them shit. Then you go and try and organise those workers and say, you know: 'You're getting paid ten bucks an hour, people who are doing this work get $18 an hour.' But the answer comes back: 'I'm a student. This is not my career. I'm only hanging around because I'm waiting for a lecture. And I'll pick up a couple of hours' work, 20 bucks in the pocket and I might come back a bit after the lecture and see if anything's happening.' So it's a big social thing as well. So while they're having a coffee there's the potential to earn 20 bucks for two hours' work.

The growth in this area of non-unionized casual labour is not dissimilar to grape-picking jobs and other forms of work in the black economy. But in this case, modern technology and new methods of recruitment are used to engage people in a new type of casual low-paid labour. In Australia, as in other parts of the industrial world, the ability of companies to shift elements of their operation to lower-paid economies can threaten national employment opportunities. As one union member commented:

> Yellow Pages have set up their call centre in Vietnam and this Australian was over there with the manager setting it up. Consequently, Yellow Pages – 'of course we're committed to Australia' – but underneath there is this implied threat that if you push too hard they'd just unplug the phone here and plug it in Vietnam. And 'the only thing we have to manage is the time zone'. But, you know, 'We can get a 24-hour shift going up there'. You know, 'for one-tenth of the cost that it's costing us here in Australia'.

This international dimension of shifting patterns of employment and the growth in contract work are major issues facing the union and were the main themes for the ASU national convention in Adelaide, as the National Secretary and CEO commented:

> The main issues cover the whole breadth of our membership really. Downsizing, contracting out, privatisation, decline of unionism and just trying to get people back into the party. So that's what this conference is about. The theme of the conference is 'Organizing for Your Security'. Because what's happened in this country like most of the other Western countries is that jobs are no longer guaranteed. You know, the concept that in the old days you'd start work as a kid with not too many skills for the local council, and you could work there for the next 40 years, and make sure that your kids got a job on the local council. Or you'd get a job with Qantas and you'd be there for the next 40 years, you know, all that sort of security has gone. It is very precarious these days. There's a huge growth of casualisation and part-time work in this country.

In this shifting industrial landscape, the union not only has to address strategies for dealing with change in the form of technology and new forms of work, but also internal issues such as union organization and gender. But as already noted, power relations and political process still remain deeply rooted in 'masculine priorities and privileges' (Wajcman, 2000), although some attempts to redress this imbalance are being undertaken by the SANTB.

CONCLUSION

This chapter has set out to identify and discuss some of the main change issues facing trade unions today. The place of the traditional trade union institution has been called into question and yet there clearly remains a need for the collective representation of employees. As one trade union activist stated:

> You can see it now in the workplaces. People are fed up with the job insecurity, being put on by rapacious management. With organizations who are only in it

for the dollar and don't care about people. You can see the tide starting to turn where the workers are starting to say enough is enough.

With the pace and range of workplace change initiatives, many employees are showing signs of fatigue and dissatisfaction with management, and the consequence of change for their work. The rhetoric may speak of 'empowerment' and 'working smarter rather than harder' but, in practice, it is often fewer employees producing more by working longer hours. This tendency towards work intensification is likely to further disillusion employees and may provide a fertile ground for the recruitment of members and the development of a more strategic form of trade unionism, one better able to service the needs of the employees it represents. As Giddens and Hutton (2001: 22) note:

> It's clear that unions are weaker than they were, but I would not write their obituary just yet. Workers feel very exposed to the harder, shareholder-value-driven capitalism with its demands for intensifying work effort, making jobs more insecure and laying people off. There are signs that workers are becoming readier to join unions; membership in Britain is stabilizing for the first time in twenty years. They are still a constraint on capitalism, and may re-emerge.

Unions need to take responsibility for a critical appraisal of their position in redefining their future development. If unions are inactive or simply respond to management change strategies, then the influence of unions in shaping change will be largely ineffectual. In Australia – with the demise of compulsory unionism – such inactivity may lead to deunionization and the political peripheralization of the union movement. Many unions in the UK, the US and Australia are now finding themselves on the edge following the decline in union density and the shift away from trade unions and collective forms of representation towards part-time, casual and non-unionized labour which may be geographically dispersed. As Cooper and colleagues (undated: 24) conclude in their study of union revitalization in Australia:

> It is yet to be seen whether the trade union will embrace the changes necessary to organize an increasingly dispersed and casualized labour force. Some unions have shown that they can move beyond traditional means of organization to attract the type of workers who have historically not joined a trade union. However, this approach needs to be more broadly adopted in order for the revitalization of the Australian union movement.

As well as responding to the external changes and shifts in the social, political and economic conditions of work and employment, unions also need to examine their own internal arrangements and policies. One significant area highlighted by this chapter is the need to incorporate more women into senior union positions. As has been shown, gender is a major issue facing trade unions and one which requires continual political pressure for change. Male-dominated trade unionism is not gender blind but, rather, actively seeks to sustain traditional male-based assumptions about the position of women in work, employment and society (see also Bradley,

1999). As the ASU case illustrates, attempts to suppress the strategic significance of reinventing the union as a more women-oriented union are prevalent among some of the old surviving male bastions. Resistance to attempts to push gender as an important political and strategic issue is evident in the reactive gender defensiveness of certain individuals and groups. Gender blindness can no longer be blamed on ignorance, nor does it stand as a viable position for trade unionists. Rather, the gender lines have been drawn in political processes involving those who seek a proper interrogation of gender issues in policy formation and those who continually drive for gender suppression in their attempts to maintain the male-dominated trade unionism of the past (see also Linstead, 2000; Wilson, 1996). In these debates and in the political manoeuvring within and between factions, it is not a question of gender outwith political affiliation (whether politically more left or right wing) but, rather, there is a more complex contextual and political struggle in which support is gathered on packages of positions. Again, this can create the anomalous situation where, in order to strengthen long-term support for an issue, there may be the political necessity to support an individual who is diametrically opposed to the strategic objectives of the group. This complexity needs to be understood by key stakeholders who seek to influence the strategic path of unions in the real-world political process of steering change in certain preferred directions.

It appears that the trade union movement has reached a critical juncture where, although collective forms of representation may be needed by a growing group of dissatisfied employees, the conditions under which this change is likely to flourish are not so clearly understood in the new landscape of employment relations and socio-economic change. What is clear is that unionists need to curb the marginalization of trade union influence on workplace change initiatives. Although this may be a by-product, a deliberate anti-union strategy, or the consequence of pragmatic management, unions should not ignore marginalization. In taking strategic action, trade unions need to align internal change perspectives and issues to offset the inertia regarding traditional union customs and practices, and adopt more flexible and agile perspectives. With the overall decline in union membership and the emergence of a new industrial relations landscape, there is increasingly a need to recruit members from the non-traditional workplaces. Unions also need to develop policies that members can identify with; to educate the younger workforce about the history and value of collective representation; and to renew unionism by setting aside the culture and traditions of a masculinized industrial past.

In short, there is an urgent need for greater union agility both in leading with strategic purpose rather than remaining marginalized in the *post hoc* responses to company change, and in discarding outmoded practices in the development of more inclusive strategies in an ongoing process of union renewal.

10

The quality management experience

In this chapter our attention turns to an area that has been at the forefront of change initiatives in industrial economies over the last 20 years – quality management. Quality initiatives have been developed and implemented in all areas of business, and debates on the appropriateness and need for quality systems capture public headlines, are raised by governments and are often an integral element in change programmes. There is now a considerable body of work on quality management in academic journals (see, for example, Dawson, 2002; Dawson and Palmer, 1995; Dawson, 2002; Wilkinson and Willmott, 1995; Wilkinson et al., 1998), as well as an array of publications by consultants and quality management gurus (see, for example, Crosby, 1980; Deming, 1981; Feigenbaum, 1961; Juran, 1988). Although the popularity of quality management as a discrete change initiative reached its peak in the late 1980s and early 1990s, the market-driven and government-backed push for accreditation and quality assurance systems continues to force many organizations down the quality path. Furthermore, quality management has been absorbed into many other management initiatives, such as best practice management, lean production, business process re-engineering (BPR), and employee improvement/empowerment programmes (Hackman and Wageman, 1995; Tuckman, 1994; Valentine and Knights, 1998). But this brave new world of quality has also been linked with strategies for downsizing, outsourcing and delayering where resultant tongue-in-cheek commitment may become a mask for individual survival. Company collapse, plant rationalization and relocation, and more wide-scale industrial and commercial restructuring signal an uncertain world where quality becomes yet one more task to accomplish with ever decreasing resources. While the 'enlightened' and 'accountable' organization may espouse the value of a committed workforce, they may offer little to ease the growing pressure of work intensification that follows the growth in quality management demands. The pressure to deliver more with declining resources and increasing demands is an ongoing concern for many manufacturing and service industries in both the private and public sectors. For example, the demand for teaching quality assessment in higher education has sparked an ongoing debate over the future of university education (Baty, 2001). Higher education quality management programmes have been developed and introduced in Australia, New Zealand, England and Scotland. For some, the standardization of course proposals and the bureaucratic difficulties of introducing change simply stifle teaching innovation and creativity. The Russell group of universities in the UK have been openly critical of the Quality Assurance Agency (QAA) and, as a result, less intense and more hands-off methods of assessment have been advocated for England. As noted in the *Times Higher Education Supplement* (2001):

> The QAA stressed that it was . . . 'a possible operational model' for the new quality system, planned for September next year, which will slash the amount of subject-level inspection in favour of an institution-wide audit approach. Audits could take just four days . . . thus reducing the number of 'reviewer days' spent on each university by almost 90 per cent.

In Scotland, the Scottish Higher Education Funding Council (SHEFC) has decided to abandon this traditional approach to quality assurance. As Wojtas (2002: 4) reports, 'academics would be "jumping for joy" as the bureaucratic burden was lifted'. In conjunction with QAA, a Research Assessment Exercise (RAE) has also been put in place to audit research excellence to make 'transparent' a 'league table of excellence' (Goddard, 2001). In practice, the RAE has diverted attention from teaching, stimulated political game-playing, and distorted the broader and more balanced academic endeavour. For example, there has been a tendency to downplay dissemination of research in favour of publication in typically less widely read but reputable academic refereed journals. It is perhaps ironic that the quality systems imposed may militate against achieving the 'excellence' they purport to enable through a supposedly more accountable and transparent system. As I have noted, 'it is the rhetoric and bureaucracy of quality management which requires scrutiny and criticism, if companies and their employees are not to fall foul of a totally questionable method' (Dawson, 1998: 18).

Over the last 20 years, the shine on the golden face of quality has dimmed and the place of pedantic paper-pushing consultants is no longer readily accepted by organizations struggling to survive. In this chapter, an analysis of the findings of a longitudinal study (funded by the Australian Research Council) on the introduction and effects of Total Quality Management (TQM) on a number of Australian and New Zealand organizations is presented (see also Dawson and Palmer, 1995). The project was undertaken by two research teams, one located at the Key Centre in Strategic Management at Queensland University of Technology under the direction of Gill Palmer with research support from Cameron Allan, the second at the University of Adelaide under the direction of myself with research support from Verna Blewett. Additional case studies were commissioned in Western Australia and New Zealand. In all, eight organizations were studied: Pirelli Cables Australia Ltd, State Bank of South Australia, Vicbank, Accom Industries, Laubman and Pank, Alcoa, Tecpak Industries and Hendersons Automotive Ltd.

This chapter draws on material from the eight longitudinal case studies to clarify the nature of quality initiatives through a contextual analysis of the change process. The findings from the research question many of the assumptions that lie behind prescriptive conceptions of quality. The data are also used to draw out some practical lessons on change management both for those involved and for those at the receiving end of change. Any attempt to distil practical lessons draws attention to the link between theory and practice in analysing the assumptions that lie behind different levels of understanding. The next section provides a brief introduction to quality management.

QUALITY MANAGEMENT: THE NEW COMPETITIVE ADVANTAGE?

> Customers – both industrial and consumer – have been increasing their quality requirements very sharply in recent years. This tendency is likely to be greatly amplified by the intense competition that seems inevitable in the near future. (Feigenbaum, 1956: 93)

There is nothing new about notions of quality. Craftsmanship and the development of expertise in the creation of items of value can be traced back to early empires in China, Babylonia and Egypt. It was around 3000 to 2500 BC that the first manufacture of iron objects is believed to have occurred. In the sixteenth century the superiority of Japanese craft products was discovered by Dutch and Portuguese explorers (Grun, 1991). However, it was not until after industrialization, with the growth of the factory system and the expansion of commodity markets, that attention gradually shifted from low cost competitive advantage to methods for achieving the large-scale manufacture of quality products. Apart from an early concern for the quality of mass produced military products, western manufacturing industries have been comparatively slow in the uptake of new quality management techniques. Although Armand Feigenbaum (1956) emphasized the competitive importance of quality in the 1950s, it was the Japanese who were the first to embrace many of the quality ideas promoted by Juran (1988) and Deming (1981). In part, the readiness of Japanese companies to embrace new methods of organization reflected their weak post-war position and their need to improve the quality of their products to compete on growing world markets. In the 1950s, Japanese goods were often viewed as cheap, poor quality imitations of western products and yet by the 1980s they had become a dominant force threatening the competitive position of many western companies. Over the last two decades, the views of Deming and Juran have been widely sought by western management; for example, Deming ran a four-day seminar in America during 1987 that attracted some thousands of executives (Allan, 1991: 30). In Australia, several visits by Juran and Deming stimulated the uptake of quality management initiatives that culminated in the Australian Prime Minister Bob Hawke launching an 'Australia for Quality Campaign' on 2 April 1984.

Since the 1980s, there has been a broadening of quality management in the development of initiatives that attempt to engage all employees in the systematic effort for quality. No longer is quality promoted as a simple operational manufacturing technique, but rather it is seen as a potential strategic weapon for bringing about large-scale cultural change in the quest for competitive advantage. The definitional confusion and ambiguity of quality management (and its various forms, such as service excellence and TQM) have allowed it to accommodate new and emerging concepts, such as benchmarking, and to incorporate non-manufacturing companies and areas of operation. On this issue, Chiles and Choi (2000: 186) claim that while as a body of practical knowledge TQM has had an 'unparalleled impact on modern business history', it has largely remained atheoretical, amorphous and conceptually hazy. The fluidity and ambiguity of terms also reflect the influence of different stakeholders who have a vested interest in differentiating their 'products' and 'services'. For example, competing consultant groups continue to advocate the benefits of their own 'unique' methodology for the successful implementation of quality schemes; quality organizations broaden and redefine their objectives to justify their continued existence and to secure future funding (see Navaratnam, 1993); and popular quality exponents argue for the adoption of their own 'distinct' set of principles (see, for example, Albrecht, 1992; Crosby, 1980; Imai, 1986; Ishikawa, 1985). In short, the substance of quality management is composed of a number of elements which can be combined, redefined and implemented in a number of ways. Part of the popularity of these programmes stems from their meaning different things to different people (Tuckman, 1994). For our purposes however, there are a number of common characteristics that can be distilled from the work of some of the main exponents of the quality management movement (see also Clark, 1995a: 189; Hill, 1995: 36–40; Tuckman, 1995: 65–6).

There are several common elements in company quality initiatives:

- the notion of a comprehensive approach where quality is an integral part of all operations and involves every employee of the company, as well as external operating practices and customer–supplier relations;
- the use of a range of statistical methods and group problem-solving techniques in applying a systematic approach to quality problems;
- strong senior management commitment to, and responsibility and support for, the achievement and maintenance of a quality system;
- the importance of getting it right first time and developing a system based on prevention and not inspection;
- the institutionalization of a system of continuous process improvement that ensures the steady commitment and ongoing involvement of all employees; and

- the development of small group activities (through quality circles and TQM teams) where employees with different skills meet together to solve common quality problems.

In practice, different combinations of these elements characterize typical company quality initiatives. However, in the popular and prescriptive literature there remains a view that such initiatives will not only improve company performance but also the quality of working life for employees. As Wilkinson (1998: 45) points out in his discussion of empowerment, a common assumption is that:

> workers are an untapped resource with knowledge and experience and an interest in becoming involved which can be released by employers providing opportunities and structures for their involvement. It is also assumed that participative decision-making is likely to lead to job satisfaction and better quality decisions, and that gains are available both to employers (increased efficiency) and workers (job satisfaction), in short an everyone wins scenario.

Since the middle of the 1990s, greater attention has been given to some of the failures of quality management projects and a growing body of critical material has emerged in the US (Hackman and Wageman, 1995), Australia (Dawson and Palmer, 1995) and the UK (Wilkinson and Willmott, 1995). In their analysis of TQM, Hackman and Wageman argue that one of the main problems with quality management initiatives is that once new improved work practices are identified and documented they may be implemented throughout the organization, leaving a vast number of employees with no say over the new work arrangements. In their view, this is simply a new form of 'old-time scientific management', only in this case the new designs for work originate from peers working on cross-functional quality teams (Hackman and Wageman, 1995: 327). In Australia, workplace studies have shown how the solutions identified by a small group of employees may be imposed on others who may be unable to participate in group problem-solving because their first language is not English (Dawson and Palmer, 1995). Moreover, through assuming the benefits of and need for a common unitary culture, many of these quality initiatives are unable to accommodate or even account for the possibility of cultural heterogeneity – a common characteristic of many multicultural workplaces in Australia. The unthinking endorsements of these programmes may exacerbate workplace conflict in spotlighting the tensions and divisions between groups (Dawson, 1995). In the UK, Valentine and Knights (1998: 84), in their comparison of TQM and BPR, conclude that 'there is too much prescription in the management and organizational literature and insufficient critical reflection'. As Darren McCabe (1996: 30) notes, 'TQM may prove to be far more problematic and uncertain than is often assumed to be the case'. In short, all these studies draw attention to the practical consequences of TQM principles and the way in which company outcomes can be reconfigured during the political process of change. They also highlight the importance of studying processes of change 'as-they-happen' in the organizational introduction and development of TQM initiatives.

COMPLEX OUTCOMES: A PROCESSUAL ANALYSIS OF
CASE STUDY DATA

The data reported in this section are drawn from a programme of research funded by the Australian Research Council and conducted by a research team co-directed by Gill Palmer and myself (see the Appendix). From a processual analysis of the eight empirical case studies the importance of contextual factors in colouring the nature of the TQM experience emerged as central (Dawson and Palmer, 1995). Although there was general support for an ideology of participation and collaboration by involving employees in managerial decision-making, the level of senior management commitment varied across the case organizations. For example, Accom Industries is a small company which had only just begun to start thinking about the benefits of adopting a TQM programme. Accom is part of the anti-corrosion engineering industry and has three main areas of business: selling its technology and engineering expertise in anti-corrosion; providing a specialized blasting and coating service; and custom building fibre-reinforced plastic (FRP) items, principally for industrial use. It has both service and manufacturing sides to its operation, and work is carried out both at Accom and on site at its customers' premises (see Blewett, 1995a). Although they were committed to quality assurance and accreditation, the conflicting views of the managing director and the general manager on the benefits and problems of employee involvement programmes put into question the level of management commitment behind the 'possible journey towards TQM'. In other words, while they can be identified as an organization committed to quality management, Accom management were not united in their commitment to employee involvement. In practice, the absence of strong, active support among the senior executive severely limited the potential for TQM to become a mainstream management philosophy of change. In this example, TQM was treated in a similar vein to other piecemeal initiatives such as quality circles, and suffered the same types of setbacks and problems.

On the question of continuous improvement, findings from the research programme illustrate how TQM group-based activity is by its very nature temporary. The notion of continual TQM improvement is a misnomer since the activities are typically project-based and oriented to solving discrete problems in a predetermined timeframe. This was highlighted in the formation of Process Improvement Teams (PITs) at Alcoa's Kwinana plant where teams were formed to solve discrete problems. The Alcoa alumina refinery at Kwinana was originally established in 1962 and is located on the heavy industry coastal strip just south of the Perth metropolitan area in Western Australia. It has an annual capacity of 1.7 million tonnes of alumina. The Australian operation of Alcoa employs some 6500 people in total; the Kwinana refinery has a workforce of approximately 1100 employees with some 850 involved in direct operations and maintenance activities (see

Brown, 1995b). In this case, two initial PITs (PIT) were formed to act as test cases for TQM and process improvement. The Kwinana example is interesting because the company introduced what they termed 'natural teams' comprising employees with common concerns who worked together to improve productivity and levels of workplace efficiency. Although the cases illustrate a general trend towards teamwork on the shop floor, TQM teams were typically cross-functional teams set up to tackle particular problem(s) over an explicit timeframe. In many cases, the initial TQM teams were established to tackle company problems that had already been identified by management. Consequently, while initial projects may solve problems and save the company money, in the longer term, the benefits of TQM may become less evident as achievements are restricted to minor system changes.

In evaluating the application and use of appropriate quality control techniques the emphasis has to be on the word 'appropriate'. What was deemed important at the outset changed considerably during the process of introducing TQM. While all the companies identified some benefits by establishing benchmarks from which improvements could be gauged, these were often far simpler measures than those promoted during the initial periods of change. For example, on the question of the shop floor use of statistical techniques, the empirical evidence suggests that these methods tended to be over-emphasized in the training programmes provided by consultant groups. In the case of Pirelli Cables Australia Ltd (PCAL), the statistical quality tools formed a central part of the Blakemore Consulting training programme and were seen as a critical factor by senior management during their initial search and evaluation of a range of TQM change consultants. Initially, this 'hard' approach to change was positively appraised by senior Pirelli management, who argued that the successful introduction of TQM should result in a disciplined approach to shop floor activity, combined with a shift in culture towards greater employee involvement and participation. Prior to TQM, problem-solving was haphazard and largely ignored shop floor employees as a key resource for identifying, measuring and solving production problems. The TQM approach was seen to offer a programme of culture change directed at increasing employee involvement and worker harmony through the formation of TQM groups versed in the use of statistics. The approach also supported the managing director's view that changes initiated from the shop floor were more likely to be accepted by employees than those imposed by management. However, in studying this change in three different Pirelli sites over a period of 18 months, the emphasis placed on statistical quality techniques in the training period did not translate into a change in workplace practice. Observations and interviews revealed that employees did not always understand or use the range of statistical techniques available; rather, they relied on one or two individuals to provide visual graphs to monitor the group's achievements. In the case of Tecpak – a small New Zealand plastic container manufacturer in Dunedin – training in statistical process control was identified as a need later in the change process and was provided by an external quality manager. This external consultant spent a weekend training five key staff members in the use of simple statistical techniques, such as Pareto charts, fishbone diagrams and machine process control charts (see Batley and Andrews, 1995). Like Pirelli, a small number of staff (the 'experts') became responsible for the visual presentation of shop floor data. In short, the statistical side of TQM tends to be emphasized in prescriptive material, consultant packages and training programmes, and yet the vast majority of employees made little use of these methods in practice.

With regard to the group problem-solving of process operations, the techniques that tended to dominate were simple numeric measures and the more group-oriented approaches (for example, brainstorming techniques were often used in initial TQM meetings). In Pirelli, measuring the scrap rate of a particular machine, brainstorming the problem, implementing one or more possible solutions, then measuring any changes in the scrap rate, was a simple, classic example of how fairly basic measures were used as indicators of the success or failure of TQM team solutions. In such cases, the key activity was group problem-solving. In these groups easy communication, good internal relations, an open-minded approach, a willingness to listen to different views, and a good facilitator or group coordinator were all identified as important ingredients. This highlights how many of these quality training programmes could be redesigned to reduce the emphasis on statistics and increase the focus on interpersonal skills, group dynamics and communication. In the case of Tecpak, an early emphasis was placed on 'talk skills'. A communications consultant was hired who provided staff training in interpersonal communication. However, in organizations such as Pirelli, whose employees comprise a multicultural workforce, employee participation was found to be limited to those fluent in English. In this sense, TQM was not well suited to building employee commitment in a workforce that was culturally diverse. It demonstrates how TQM has been influenced by the managerial practices associated with the extraordinarily homogeneous society of Japan.

TQM has been heavily influenced by the managerial practices of Japan, and by Western management's desire to emulate the culture of employee commitment to organizational goals, seen to result from Japanese management. However the context in which Japanese organizational cultures have developed is very different from those in the West. Japanese management arose in the context of an extraordinarily homogeneous society. Japan was deliberately protected from external influences for the centuries before the Meiji restoration in 1868. Cultural norms support homogeneity, not cultural pluralism. After the Meiji restoration, the political economy of Japan was built to create a hierarchy of economic organizations; it was not based on notions of individual rights, entrepreneurial and economic freedom or the value of competition between competing interests. The social controls that developed in this context assume the need to administer group activities towards common goals; they emphasize structures of co-ordination and hierarchical control. In contrast, the managerial controls of Western cultures have developed more techniques to build alliances between stakeholders who have different allegiances. Western employment relationships tend to be based on an open market for labour, and on individualistic rewards and sanctions. (Dawson and Palmer, 1995: 169)

The focus on internal and external customer–supplier relations was another common feature of many of the quality initiatives studied. Many companies wanted to improve external relations and to break down some of the internal barriers between departments and units. For example, Hendersons Automotive (SA) developed a new company strategy based on the need to be 'customer-driven'. At the South Australian manufacturing division of Hendersons Industries Pty Ltd, a fully owned subsidiary company of National Consolidated Ltd (NCL), Hendersons Automotive consolidated operations in the niche market of automotive seating. This was a deliberate strategic move into a market not easily entered by overseas competitors because of the shipping costs associated with the cubic size of the product. This market is also unattractive to potential importers because its small absolute size, fragmentation and distance exacerbate communication problems and lead times. In the Australian market, Hendersons have also managed to build a well-established position with the adoption of supplier preselection by most of the Australian automotive manufacturers. There are also technical barriers to entry for competitors because Hendersons hold certain key licences and technical agreements with global automotive seating manufacturers. At the time of the study, Hendersons was the major manufacturer of seating components in Australia outside of the major automotive manufacturers (see Blewett, 1995b).

In the uptake of their quality management initiative, Hendersons' initial focus was on improving internal customer–supplier relations and facilitating more open communication within the company. On this count, the programme was positively appraised by shop floor personnel and following an improvement in internal relations, management set about developing a programme to improve their external customer–supplier relations. For example, over a 12-month period 40 suppliers attended a seminar conducted by Hendersons to communicate their requirements for quality and to inform suppliers about recommended systems for quality assurance. On the customer side, regular weekly visits were made by a small group of shop floor employees plus a quality inspector to their major customers in South Australia (interstate customers, such as Ford and Nissan, were visited fortnightly). In this way, their quality programme was seen not only as a new management approach to improving external relations, but also as a vehicle for achieving greater communication and establishing new networks in existing structural arrangements. In some companies, however, the principle of internal customers and suppliers has only been partially accomplished. One of the major practical issues that the TQM literature does not adequately address is how to accommodate multiple intra-organizational relationships. For example, in cases where an individual or group may have to service multiple customers (such as next stage in the process as well as opposite numbers on alternate shifts), a conflict of interest may result and offset the benefits associated with a system based on a simple linear customer–supplier progression. In practice, therefore, the assumption that by operating a system of internal customer-supplier relations more cooperative work environments will be created and sustained is but one of a number of quality management myths.

The commitment to employee involvement varied across the companies studied. For example, the Accom study demonstrated how conflicting managerial views about employee involvement influenced a company's commitment to such schemes. In the case of Laubman and Pank, confusion over the direction of their Service Excellence Programme (SEP) and different cultural groupings all served to shape employee experience of change. Essentially, Laubman and Pank is an optometry company involved with eye examinations and prescriptions for individual customers, and the dispensing of glasses and contact lenses. Trained optometrists are employed to examine the eyes and visual functions of clients and to prescribe visionary aids. In addition, an optometric assistant or 'dispenser' will assist the optometrist in dispensing spectacle prescriptions. Dispensers may also deal with prescriptions. The Laubman and Pank Group are also involved in the manufacture and supply of lenses, spectacle frames and contact lenses through their laboratories set up under the organization Tescol Pty Ltd (see Dawson, 1996: 112–28).

In the Laubman and Pank case, although senior management recognized the potential for TQM to develop high-trust relationships and encourage employee involvement, there was a tendency to focus on TQM (particularly within the laboratory setting) as a scientific method for identifying and establishing documented procedures and quantifiable indicators. Moreover, while there was a certain public agreement about the need for a shift in the culture of the organization and a movement towards greater employee involvement, there was also a general belief that conservatism still dominated senior management decision-making and that there would be some resistance to embracing programmes of change that sought to radically transform existing cultures and operating philosophies. Hence, while it was not uncommon for management to verbalize a commitment to employee involvement, in practice it was often restricted.

The final common feature of TQM programmes centres on developing a climate of trust and cooperation, and a non-adversarial system of industrial relations. Findings from the case studies illustrated how there were not only considerable differences between companies but also between plants of a single company located on the same site. Contextual dimensions and the politics of change were important determinants shaping the outcomes of change on employee relationships and the system of industrial relations. This was illustrated in a case study of change in the banking industry in Victoria. Originally, Vicbank was a building society established in 1959 and at this stage it offered only a narrow range of financial products, such as home loans and small personal loans. Through the 1960s and early 1970s the organization grew slowly, having just 200 staff in 1974. But in the late 1970s and early 1980s it actively sought to expand its market share through media advertising and the expansion of its branch network. Within a decade, the organization had assets of $1 billion and had developed into a successful bank. However, given the highly competitive nature of the financial services market, the company was aware of the need to further improve its effectiveness and competitiveness. Quality management was seen as a potential vehicle for achieving such a change (see Allan, 1995).

The Vicbank attempt to introduce quality management was far from straightforward and provides a good illustration of the political and non-linear process of change. In the first period, Vicbank selected TQM as an ongoing method of process improvement and brought in outside consultants to set them on the path to organizational change. But the implementation of TQM was never clear-cut. Although adopted successfully in some areas of the organization, the TQM programme had minimal impact in others. The central difficulty stemmed from the character and politics of middle management resistance. In the second period, senior managers revised their implementation strategy and developed their own novel solutions to gain management commitment through cultural change. These experiments also failed to secure total management commitment. In the third period, Vicbank brought in outside expertise to help them develop a clear sense of direction and provide them with a step-by-step improvement methodology. During all three periods, developing a climate of trust, cooperation and a non-adversarial system of industrial relations was never fully achieved. An interesting dimension to this case was the persistence and determination of Vicbank managers to continue in the face of opposition and to continually adapt their implementation strategies in the light of unforeseen events (a practical lesson on change management taken up in the next section).

In the case of Pirelli, although the same implementation strategy and change consultants were used for the uptake of TQM at all their Australian sites, two very different experiences emerged from the shop floor observation and interview data drawn from studies of two adjacent plants operating on the same manufacturing site. The Pirelli example also demonstrates how companies that are downsizing may find it particularly difficult (if not impossible) to build trust in a context where job security is threatened. While TQM offers the potential to develop network relations and better communication channels within an organization, it will not by itself solve the problem of poor employee relations. On the contrary, the introduction of change initiatives that talk of a brave new culture of trust and cooperation may simply exacerbate intra-organizational conflict. Once again, it is important to stress that organizations comprise a range of different sub-cultures and that while TQM may represent espoused values and change the surface levels of culture, deeper levels are far less open to change. In short, quality initiatives provide no panacea for management–union conflict or for poor relations with staff, even if they can be used as a means of improving communication and employee relations.

From this necessarily brief overview of some of the main findings of the research programme, it is possible to distil a number of practical guidelines for understanding and managing change. Several of these are developed and explained in the following section.

USING CASE STUDY DATA TO IDENTIFY PRACTICAL GUIDELINES FOR CHANGE

One of the main lessons that can be drawn from a processual analysis of these eight longitudinal studies is that there is no single best way to manage change. Any fixed approach will not be able to accommodate the unexpected, the unforeseeable twists and turns of events which have not yet occurred. Although there is great value in planning for change, any benefits are lost if the proposed schedule becomes cast-in-stone and not open to renegotiation and adaptation. Change management strategies must be sensitive to the character of the change, the context in which change is taking place, and the views and reactions of employee groups and key political players. Change strategies that prove successful in one company may be entirely inappropriate in another comparable company, or even in a different plant in the same company. If we look across the case organizations we can see both comparisons and contrasts in the type of change strategies adopted. For example, the State Bank of South Australia formed a cross-functional implementation team and adopted a top to bottom approach whereby employees at lower levels in the bank's organizational structure were progressively introduced to the philosophy and practice of service delivery. This cascade method centred on progressively training and educating each level of staff about the values, the mission, the strategy and the management principles of the new service quality philosophy. Four levels were included in the cascade training process:

- level one: the top 20 members of the executive team;
- level two: 200 members of the senior management group;
- level three: 700 managers and supervisors; and
- level four: the remaining 2500 staff members.

The final level was preceded by a large-scale staff function known as the 'One Day Event'.

This change strategy proved very successful and is comparable to the Vicbank approach. As part of Vicbank's implementation strategy, a consultant group was contracted to train and acquaint all levels of management with the tools and philosophy of TQM. The consultants ran a series of small workshops for managers, beginning with the most senior team and progressively moving through to the lower levels of management. These sessions normally took half a day and provided managers with an overview of the origins of TQM concepts, the major TQM tools and how they might be applied. A full-time person, the Organizational Development Manager, was appointed to be responsible for overseeing and supporting TQM imple-mentation. However, in contrast to the State Bank's initiative there was no high profile 'One Day Event', nor was there a general acceptance of the commercial benefits of TQM. Some employees viewed it as simply unneces-sary while others criticized the TQM training sessions and formed the view that TQM was superficial and of no relevance to their own functional areas. They were particularly scathing about the consultant's method of presenta-tion. It was seen to be too blunt and forthright, and based on extensive manufacturing rather than service-oriented examples. Unlike the State Bank, Vicbank had not fully taken on the responsibility for implementing TQM; it had largely left the programme of change in the control of outside con-sultants. In contrast, the State Bank spent considerable time and effort planning and preparing a comprehensive training programme which was tailored to the needs of a financial services organization. Thus, while there are some general lessons about making the change programme relevant and clearly communicating intentions to all employees (bearing in mind that these outcomes also reflect political processes), how this is to be achieved cannot be generally prescribed. As the Vicbank case illustrates, organizations are themselves changing and what may be an appropriate implementation strategy in the 1990s may not prove effective in the 2000s.

A second and related lesson is that change is a non-linear dynamic process, whose outcomes cannot be assured even with the best made plans of experienced, professional change agents. Large-scale operational change generally unfolds over time and consists of management omissions and revisions as well as unforeseen employee responses, technical problems and contingencies. Once again, Vicbank provides a good illustration of this point, where the initial introduction of TQM was met with significant middle management resistance. Consequently, senior managers had to revise their implementation strategy and develop their own novel solutions to gain management commitment through cultural change. Similarly, in the case of Tecpak, initial attempts to implement TQM proved unsuccessful and senior management set about revising their strategies and using an external consult-ant to communicate the philosophy of TQM to their staff. In short, major organizational change is a task that will take a number of years, require considerable planning, involve numerous revisions and modifications, and is unlikely to be marked by a line of continual improvement.

This last point leads on to outcomes common to organizations under-going large-scale change and is one that relates to the unevenness of the change experience. Individuals and groups will experience change in a range of ways, and their expectations and views of change are likely to be further modified as the change unfolds. For example, at the outset of a major change initiative there may be a certain degree of excitement and anxiety. The excitement may be hard to sustain even among enthusiasts as the realities of managing large-scale change hit home: enthusiasm wanes, the high profile of change agents is replaced by the pressures of meeting output targets and deadlines, and with the possibility that only a few may actually meet or exceed their objectives, staff commitment to change may waver. Those already anxious and concerned about change may view these 'failings' as an indication of the need to reject change. For example, in both Pirelli and the Alcoa refinery, there were some downsides and failures associated with the adoption of TQM. One of the most common frustrations stemmed from the failure of TQM teams. In the case of Pirelli, the acceptance of TQM in the cable processing plant can be partly explained by the success of the original TQM team, in contrast to the experience of the cable manufacturing plant. Similarly at Alcoa, one of the initial teams failed while the other reported significant improvements. The successful team proved instrumental in shifting the view of one supervisor from being highly sceptical to being a strong supporter. Conversely, failure brought with it employee disillusionment and disgruntlement with the change initiative. The findings from these case studies indicate not only the importance of recognizing the diversity of employee experience, but also the need to recognize so-called 'failure'. In other words, organizations should learn from all experiences of change and not just concentrate on 'successful' change stories. For example, in the case of Alcoa, the team from Building 46 failed for several reasons including the lack of clearly defined goals, unrealistic team expectations, inadequate management support, absence of an implementation strategy and limited training. To blame the team, rather than focus on how to learn from the experience, perpetuates the myth that lessons for change are embedded in 'success' (an issue taken up and discussed in Chapter 11). In many instances, organizations may learn more from their failures than from successful implementation strategies (which are generally praised rather than critically evaluated). In the studies briefly discussed in this chapter, it was only those organizations that could manage the downside of change that were able to successfully develop and refine their change programmes over time – another important lesson on managing large-scale and radical change.

The substance of change

In examining the substance of change, there was considerable variation in the characteristics of TQM programmes across companies. The main features of these programmes tended to reflect the assumptions and views of the major change agents. For example, in cases where consultants were used the packages were generally predefined and laid out in a very structured series of steps. The content of the programmes was generally adaptations of material derived from popular exponents of quality management, such as Deming, Juran and Crosby (see Dawson, 1996: 55–77). There was also a tendency to overplay the importance of statistics, perhaps because this is an area in which expertise can be easily justified and one in which the relevance of training programmes can be supported. The statistical focus of many of the consultant packages also added 'scientific' credibility to their proposed schemes. Nevertheless, measurement mania was a problem encountered by some companies during the early experience with TQM. For example, Hendersons

Automotive recognized some of the benefits of measurement at an early phase. Statistical Process Control (SPC) was seen to provide 'as-it-happens' information that would allow process problems to be detected and adjustments made. However, in their enthusiasm for measurement there was also a tendency to measure first and then question the reasons for the measurement later. On this point, Verna Blewett (1995b) notes that an instance was observed where the workers regarded a particular type of SPC charting to be worthless, as it did not add to their knowledge of the quality of the component. After discussions with the quality inspectors, the engineering department and the materials manager, it was agreed that the workers were right and a more meaningful measure was introduced. In short, it was often common for organizations to try and measure too much too soon without regard to the practical value of such measurements. This is, of course, a lesson particular to the introduction of quality management systems, although attempts to evaluate the 'success' of change by simple financial parameters often fail to account for the broader effects of change.

A related problem identified by many of the companies was the tendency to try to do everything at once. For example, too many teams were created without due care and attention being given to what those teams would be able to do. It was assumed that the more TQM teams you had, the closer you were to becoming a total quality organization. Companies just beginning to implement TQM also had a tendency to over-emphasize the importance of gaining some immediate returns that could be balanced against the cost of quality. This was particularly noticeable at the outset of change, when there was a tendency for companies to underestimate timescales and to focus on achieving immediate quantifiable results as indicators of 'success'. It was only in retrospect that senior management tended to reflect on the longer-term nature of trying to establish and sustain a major change programme. In reflecting on these timescales, senior management emphasized the importance of communication both prior to implementation and throughout the change process. In the cases of Tecpak and the State Bank, communication was identified early on as a central element to change management. For example, Tecpak introduced 'Roadshow Meetings' where staff were encouraged to discuss company operations, make observations and express concerns, while the State Bank organized their 'One Day Event' which aimed to communicate senior management's intentions in an atmosphere of 'gaiety and entertainment'. For some organizations, such as Vicbank, it was often only after problems of implementation had arisen that senior management became aware of the importance of communication. A general lesson that emerges from these studies is that with large-scale operational change it is important not to try to do everything at once and to regularly communicate intentions to employees.

Training was another issue raised by the substance of TQM programmes. Two main weaknesses were identified. First, there was a tendency to train as many people as possible regardless of whether they were going to be involved in change. In some cases, training and the formation of teams were misaligned. Thus, one lesson is that training should be aligned with the uptake and operational use of new techniques and it should be organized on a needs basis. A second problem arose when training programmes focused on statistical elements and ignored the human skills requirements for group work. For example, the senior management of Laubman and Pank identified training as a key ingredient in the successful introduction of a service excellence programme. They stressed the importance of customized training packages that would fulfil the needs of different groups. In contrast, the experience of Vicbank illustrates the problems caused through the use of inappropriate training materials, which in this case emphasized statistical measurement for manufacturing industries. In Tecpak, training was an ongoing issue with the problems of poor communication and interpersonal skills identified as major barriers to the adoption of TQM. In all the organizations studied, training was an essential element to change. Training was important both in the 'softer' (interpersonal skills and group dynamics) and in the 'harder' (statistical methods) elements of TQM.

During the process of implementation both the internal change agents and the employees who formed the initial problem-solving teams often modified the substance of the change programmes. It was not uncommon for an organization to modify their TQM scheme (to enhance some elements, revise others, and downplay or reject others) and develop their own custom-ized version. In fact, a common characteristic of 'successful' companies was that they had substantially modified TQM to fit their own organizational requirements. On this count, the State Bank (although no longer a financially successful company) did develop a particularly effective change programme which was modified to meet their own organizational needs. Similarly, Hendersons Automotive adapted a whole range of quality techniques to fit their requirements, and continue to revise and modify existing policies to meet the managerial objective of developing a highly specialized and flexible workforce that can adjust rapidly to new production arrangements to meet changing market conditions.

The context of change

The context of change raises a number of important considerations. The external context has been influential in promoting the uptake of TQM. For example, a number of government-supported agencies have publicized TQM and offered incentives for companies to take on accredited consultants to help them introduce quality management programmes. Internally, a central contextual dimension that was often ignored during programmes of change centred on the history and culture of local operations. In Pirelli Cables, for example, the contextual differences between two adjacent plants operating on the same site resulted in very different employee experience of change. In this case, factors such as gender, ethnicity, professional identity and language were all important elements that were not adequately taken into account in consultant packages and descriptive guidelines. In the context of Australia and the UK, notions of a unitary organizational culture are misplaced as they fail to account for the cultural pluralism of many Australian and UK workplaces.

Political process is central to change and a simple lesson arising from this research is that the greater the support for change by all employees, the higher the probability that change will occur and progress. However, the likelihood and intensity of political contestation are more marked under radical change programmes which fundamentally shift resources and turf domains. In the context of a serious threat to company/plant survival, there are often greater opportunities to steer the political process and orchestrate vested interests in shaping the process of organizational change. Senior management commitment and support are central to radical change initiatives. Without them, change can only ever be partial and is unlikely to form an integral part of management strategy. In terms of barriers to change, the absence of supervisory involvement was one of the most commonly mentioned factors. For example, in both Laubman and Pank, and Vicbank, middle management resisted attempts to 'empower' employees by instigating a change that placed greater emphasis on the knowledge of operative staff in correcting and adapting day-to-day operations. In the middle management view, such a change would simply undermine the traditional authority base of the supervisor. Both cases highlight the need to involve supervisors at an early stage in the change process and to clarify the ways in which their position may or may not change. In redefining supervision it is important to make the expectations of the new position clear, not only to incumbent supervisors, but also to operative staff and the senior management group. Along with this redefinition, appropriate TQM training must be provided at the supervisory level. It is perhaps ironic that supervisors are key players in programmes of change and yet they often remain forgotten. Interestingly, gaining trade union support was not an issue faced by the companies we studied. Unlike the UK, in Australia TQM was not a major trade union concern. At the time of the research many of the Australian unions were actively and deeply involved in award restructuring and elements of enterprise bargaining. In the case of Tecpak, unionization has been actively discouraged and since 1984 there has been only one trade union member on staff. In this largely non-union firm, there have been few problems and staff have not looked to outside representation for support. Although unions were informed of TQM programmes there were no major industrial relations disputes in any of the companies studied.

These, then, are the major lessons on change that can be drawn from these case studies on TQM. As has been shown, there are no simple recipes for 'successful' change and yet there are practical lessons to be learnt from company experience. Lessons such as the need to align training programmes, to communicate widely, to muster support, and to maintain flexibility in order to accommodate the unexpected can ultimately only provide general guidance rather than a clear set of detailed prescriptions. The lessons draw attention to some of the critical elements that need to be considered in steering change. They also spotlight problem areas that should be avoided, but they do not provide universal solutions to the complex task of managing large-scale change. However, such a framework and guide can help and educate those involved in managing change to make sense of their own change experiences and to extend their knowledge of the change process.

CONCLUSION

The introduction of quality management initiatives occurs within the context of other ongoing changes. Although the case studies reported in this chapter demonstrate the diversity of approaches towards establishing a quality management programme, it is also possible to identify a number of common organizational trends. For example, there was a general movement away from individual-based work towards teamwork and an increase in employee involvement through the formation of group problem-solving teams. In some case organizations, new collaborative networks have emerged and developed which support more open communication and the comparatively free provision of information. Among external customers and suppliers, increased value is now being placed on the quality of goods and services provided, and there has been a general movement towards longer-term relationships with fewer suppliers. In terms of the more common features of TQM programmes and the principles espoused by quality exponents, the case studies highlight the degree of variation in the scale and nature of the changes being introduced. There has been a tendency to overstate the statistical side of quality management and to underplay the cultural dimensions. The bureaucracy of some quality management programmes that emphasize standardization and global procedural requirements may not achieve the transparent quality systems they aspire to and can often hinder innovation and change. Programmes are needed that do not follow rigid guidelines, but can be adapted not only to the needs of different companies and groups, but also to the changing requirements of an organization undergoing change. While the simple scientific approach to quality management is likely to remain an attractive and saleable package to companies seeking quick-fix solutions, these empirical findings show this to be a quality management myth which should be discarded and replaced with longer-term and more culturally sensitive strategies of change. In short, quality management neither is nor should be a rigid set of principles, nor can it provide a panacea for all organizational ills. These and the other lessons outlined in this chapter underline the weakness of importing overseas change programmes and the importance of being critical of consultants who propose simple solutions to complex problems. Finally, as stated at the outset, if the rhetoric of change does not align with the substance of change, then employees who find themselves having to do more with less resources are likely to become cynical about management change initiatives and to view TQM as a totally questionable method.

Living with change in the twenty-first century

The main intention of this book has been to broaden our understanding of organizational change by drawing on processual case study data collected over two decades of research. Interviews with individuals and groups have been analysed in the presentation of accounts which have sought to illustrate the different perspectives and views of those who experience change. Simple linear models of change and the neat prescriptive accounts of the popular management literature have been criticized. There are no golden rules or universal lessons to be derived from approaches that make simple distinctions between the 'rights' and 'wrongs' of managing change. On the contrary, a driving concern of this book has been to bring out the contradictions, ambiguities and untidiness of change. From the perspective of the senior executive team through to the views of older workers, union activists, local management and branch employees, there has been divergence and disagreement as well as common purpose and concerns. It is argued that attentiveness to processes of change is central to the development of a critical reflective awareness that can provide both greater understanding of change and insights on how to actively shape change processes. As illustrated in the case study chapters, it is necessary to move beyond simple cookbook approaches in developing new processual skills for making sense of change.

BEYOND THE COOKBOOK APPROACH: THE NEED FOR CRITICAL REFLECTION

Many of the cookbook approaches use company 'success' as their starting point for identifying a list of ingredients for the successful management of change. The development of consensual relations is viewed as a central tenet in developing cultures of participation and involvement which then foster autonomy, entrepreneurship and innovation. Anecdotal evidence (often involving unsystematic and questionable data collection techniques) has been used in the formulation of stage models on how best to manage change.

These 'recipes for success' generally ignore the contradictions and ambiguities of change, and tend to view conflict and resistance as obstacles. This contrasts sharply with the findings presented in this book which draw attention to the importance of political processes and context in making sense of the diversity of employee experiences of change. It has been shown how this divergence of experience combines with the existence of multiple change stories which are open to continual revision and redefinition. Individual accounts can remain silent or untold within broader group accounts which are negotiated and refined over time. These manifold voices and competing histories of change highlight the murky and complex nature of change processes and the existence of 'silent' individual and group stories spotlights the significance of power and politics. Far from being neat and tidy – as many of the popular recipe approaches would have us believe – change has complex boundaries that continuously shift and re-form. A major argument of this book has been that there are no simple solutions to the complex problem of managing strategic or large-scale operational change. To put it another way, there is a need for more critically reflective processual accounts that go beyond the cookbook approach.

A second and related warning arising from our research is that companies that place too high a reliance on past stories of success may unknowingly promote programmes that paradoxically undermine company survival through stifling other perspectives and voices on change and innovation. In other words, retrospective evaluations of change strategies that simply elaborate 'success' factors ultimately constrain and limit our understanding of the change process. This may also explain why so many change initiatives – often based on past experience – fail in practice.

A third caveat that we can draw from our research is that, although companies need to have a view of their future and be aware of the need to change, inappropriate change strategies – whether too rapid expansion, a poorly planned change initiative, or heavy investment in new technology – can hasten company demise. Companies need to consider and critically reflect on change, and not simply adopt the latest fashion or fad. Critical reflection ensures that companies do not simply focus on the need for change but are also able to make decisions about when not to change. Consideration should be given to the voices of resistance that may shed light on change options and strategies, and draw attention to alternatives otherwise ignored in the pursuit of fashionable change initiatives.

Another common misconception promoted by a number of guru consultants is the need for and possibility of bringing about 'revolutionary' change. Simply the plethora of supposedly earth shattering change initiatives cast doubt on this notion and in the current climate – where change fatigue is often more of a problem than change management – the concept of continual revolution is highly questionable. For many, change at work is familiar territory and is more likely to promote cynicism and frustration than anticipation and euphoria. In analysing employee experience of change, there has been little to suggest that these experiences have been 'revolutionary' or that they have captured the hearts and minds of employees. Conversely, the case studies provide insights into the nature of change in their accounts of the anticipated and unexpected, and in the relaying of employee experiences that spotlight the variety of emotions and the diversity of outcomes that are part of living with change.

In drawing on the daily stories of those who experience change from low-paid, temporary, part-time employees to highly-paid senior executives, the process of change has been studied 'as-it-happens' and within context. The intention has been to convey the complexity of change in a readable and accessible way that will stimulate further debate and reflection. In many areas the doorway to the debates on change has been opened and it has been argued that any search for the definitive answer is misplaced. In this concluding chapter it is worth spending some time drawing out some of the theoretical implications of our research for addressing some of the ongoing debates over the future of work, and some of the more practical implications of the data. Since commencing this book in 2001, there have been some dramatic changes in the world, such as the attack on the World Trade Center, the Enron debacle and the decline of high profile telecoms companies such as Marconi and QWEST Communications. In the section that follows, some of these more recent events and general trends are discussed in the light of our broader understanding of change. This is followed by a discussion of the practical implications of our research. Although, as argued above, there are no universal panaceas for change, it is appropriate to draw together some of the more general findings on the contemporary experience of change for people in work and employment.

ELEPHANT, FLEA, SEAL OR GAZELLE? CHANGE AND THE FUTURE OF WORK

It is common for books on innovation and change to look towards the future, to the creation of a world that contrasts sharply with our current way of doing things. Our place in the world requires reconsideration, with the inevitable need to shed old assumptions and traditional ways of doing things. Each new bundle of innovations brings in its wake the seeds of a genuine revolution which calls forth doom and gloom from pessimists and enthusiastic endorsement by optimists. In either event, we are typically presented with a new landscape, whether it is postmodern, post-industrial or a new dot.com society, where past rules are viewed as inoperable and outmoded. And yet our own experience informs us that, in this world of radical change and innovation, continuity remains and old ways of doing things re-emerge. For many, changes at work have not resulted in greater feelings of empowerment and a sense of belonging; rather, they have created ever greater demands on already busy work regimes. In examining the contemporary experience of change, it is argued that although real innovations are occurring in work and employment, the degree of change should not be overstated. Change is part of our society and there are many examples of radical innovations: the developments in transportation with steam power and the building of railway networks, the use of electricity at work and in the home, the microelectronics revolution of the 1980s, and the digitalization of global communication systems. Just as our parents and grandparents lived through great change, so we now consider ourselves to be in the midst of enormous change, no doubt heightened by the symbolism of a new century and the concept of globalization. As Hutton and Giddens (2001: vii) note:

> What gives contemporary change its power and momentum is in the economic, political and cultural change summed up by the term 'globalisation'. It is the interaction of extraordinary technological innovation combined with worldwide reach driven by a global capitalism that gives today's change its particular complexion. It has now a speed, inevitability and force that it has not had before.

This backdrop of globalization can be used to further our understanding of the experience of change for people at work. Although there is nothing new about international trade, the growth in multinational corporations has resulted in decisions being made in one locality having major implications for work and employment elsewhere. These major corporations (what Handy terms 'elephants') are in many ways a new power elite, able to influence government legislation in formulating their decisions on where to invest and where to develop their global operations. However, as Bradley and colleagues (2000) also usefully demonstrate, the effects of these changes on work and employment are not mirrored in any global sense, but are played out and contextually shaped in particular localities. They use the example of the northeast of England to show how global initiatives are mediated by government intervention strategies and the 'region's social, cultural and political heritage' (Bradley et al., 2000: 30). This highlights the need for caution in our interpretation and understanding of concepts such as globalization, and the need to be wary of the emotive, turbulent imagery that is commonly used to spotlight the need for rapid innovation and change at work. But this leaves open the polemical question of whether we are experiencing a genuine revolution, or is it just more of the same packaged and delivered in different ways?

The polarization of views in debates on the future of work is not peculiar to this century but reflects a tendency to emphasize either the positive (optimists) or negative (pessimists) possibilities for change. Although for some the context of established practice and conventional thought can be a major obstacle to new ways of thinking – in steering attention to past successes rather than future opportunities – a number of popular commentators advocate that people now have far more possibilities than in the past to be activists in shaping their own futures (Handy, 2001). On this count, Handy (1999) argues that we are entering a new world where the new entrepreneurs create something out of nothing; they are what he terms the 'new alchemists'. He relates his own experiences with work and how he has moved from working with large stable organizations ('elephants') to working in a more insecure yet independent freelance world ('fleas'). As he states:

> What is the world of work going to look like in the e-age, with its new mixture of fleas and elephants, with many more fleas, I believe, and fewer but even grander elephants? What is the future of capitalism and how will it change given that value is now vested in knowledge and know-how rather than land and things that you can see and count? How will we manage the new, ever-expanding corporations, and to whom will they be accountable, given that many of them generate more revenue than most countries? How will society adapt to a more virtual world where territorial boundaries are eroded by the Internet? (Handy, 2001: 11)

For Hamel (2000), there is a new agenda that builds on and goes beyond our previous concerns with product and process innovations to a concern with non-linear innovations and what he terms 'business concept innovation'. Hamel (2000: 26–9) charts three major historical innovation regimes. The first centres on securing new wealth through the application of science and technology during the innovation regime of the industrial age. The second focuses on the development of marketing strategies in the post-war consumer society where the mass production of similar products was differentiated through marketing innovations and advertising. The third and most recent innovation regime is that of the imagination, where inventiveness and creativity are used in the development of new business concepts which compete for attention and support in a more open and democratic market. Hamel (2000: 28) suggests that the old barriers of class, qualification, experience and age no longer determine who the new innovators are:

> Big science is an elephant dragging a hardwood log up the steep incline of scientific enquiry. Consumer marketing is a trained seal – a consumer who has been taught to respond to the inducements and blandishments of clever marketers. The new innovation regime is a gazelle leaping again and again above the tall grass of precedent. Cisco, Yahoo!, Amazon.com, Sycamore Networks, Red Hat, CMGI – these and a thousand other industry revolutionaries are the children of this new regime. But if they are to succeed more than once, they must become its students as well. Gray-haired incumbents and acne-faced newcomers alike must embrace a new innovation agenda, one that builds on the two that have come before – and then goes, far, far beyond them.

Hamel (2000: 314) views this new age as the 'age of revolution' in which dreams are possibilities and where 'for the first time in history our heritage is no longer our destiny'. He concludes by calling us all to be activists in leading the way forward. However, Hamel's optimistic view of the future presents a world that stands in stark contrast to the world of those who have been made unemployed by the shifting fortunes and geographical repositioning of large business corporations, and of those who struggle to make ends meet on part-time and non-standard forms of employment. To these and many others, Hamel's brave new world of the imagination offers nothing new. This rather limited view of the contemporary experience of people at work simply paints honeymoon scenarios and provides little insight into the world of change that most of us would recognize. Furthermore, as with all books that draw on exemplars of this new regime, it makes some rather grand claims that have not stood the test of time. For example, it is perhaps ironic that Enron is used to illustrate how to unleash the spirit of innovation and harness highly motivated entrepreneurs in an analysis where Hamel (2000: 218) states that: 'at Enron, failure – even of the type that ends up on the front page of the *Wall Street Journal* – doesn't necessarily sink a career'. However, by August 2001, the CEO of Enron, Jeff Skilling, resigns for 'personal reasons', the company files for bankruptcy in December 2001, and by summer 2002, the enormity of the collapse and the consequences of creative accounting practices become evident: 'the company had in fact made millions of dollars of losses, which were being hidden by financial chicanery' (*Sunday Times*, 2002: 4) – an example that on reflection testifies to the need to develop and sustain a level of business ethics and moral behaviour that questions such practices which, while imaginative, may break moral and ethical limits in their 'creativity'. Clearly, change strategies driven by vested interests with little concern for other employee interests, or broader social and community responsibilities, is not a future most people would support.

This decline in fortune is not peculiar to Enron. The early 2000s have witnessed some significant shifts in profitability among a number of large multinational corporations. In the automotive industry – a driving force for economic prosperity in the twentieth century – company decline, downsizing and operational restructuring have been ongoing. Ford, for example, announced in 2002 their decision to axe their American flagship car the Lincoln Continental and their intention to cut 35,000 jobs worldwide. As Cowing (2002: 22) described:

> Car manufacturer Ford last night stunned workers as its chief executive slashed 35,000 jobs, axed his own pay for the next year and ended one of the company's best-known names. The company, which made a £4.6 billion profit last year, is expected to report its third consecutive quarter of losses later this month and yesterday announced a £2.8 billion restructuring plan.

The terrorist attacks of September 11 acted as a trigger for change in the airline industry (which had already been operating on small profit margins), exposing its weak financial position and threatening its commercial viability (Ashworth, 2002). During 2002 the New Zealand government provided Air New Zealand with a NZ$1 billion rescue package, and British Airways experienced a serious decline in premium air traffic, as Mortished (2002: 42) comments:

> BA is not alone . . . Sabena of Belgium and Swissair, carriers with histories that stretch back to the start of commercial aviation, have been dragged through the bankruptcy courts. Aer Lingus is teetering on the brink . . . BA, Air France and Lufthansa will probably survive but KLM has thrown in the towel, predicting its own assimilation by one of the leaders.

Other long-established companies, ranging from well-known high street retailers such as Marks & Spencer, Woolworths and BHS, to large corporations such as Motorola and Marconi, to smaller less well-known companies such as the 154-year-old bookseller James Thin (one of Scotland's oldest family-owned firms), have seen a turn in fortune with declining turnover and a fall in profits. Although Marks & Spencer have initiated a change strategy to renew and revitalize their company, the future of the James Thin stores (with a debt of £5 million) is doubtful (O'Donnell, 2002: 5), and Marconi's British workforce declined from 15,000 to 7000 people over an eighteen-month period to August 2002 (*Times Business*, 2002: 25).

PRACTICAL LESSONS ON CHANGE: BEYOND STORIES OF SUCCESS

The whole tenet of this book centres on the diversity of the change experience and the complex nature of change which make the distillation of simple recipes impossible. It would be inappropriate to simply list a series of 'must do' prescriptions that decontextualize the findings. It is also recognized that any attempt to draw out broader organizational lessons on change can be criticized for over-simplifying what is a complex process. As Collins (1998: 75) indicated in an earlier piece of work published in 1994: 'Dawson's willingness to translate and to codify these notions for practitioners does little to communicate the complexity inherent in these matters.' And yet, there is value in trying to draw out practical lessons from detailed case studies on change. In Chapter 10, some of these lessons were described in the context of the introduction and uptake of quality management programmes in seven Australian and one New Zealand organization. In addition, the opening section of this chapter outlined a number of change caveats that can be drawn from a processual analysis of the data presented in this book. These and some of the other main organizational lessons that can be drawn from a more critically reflective processual approach are summarized below. It should be noted that the main aim is to be of practical value while broadening our awareness of critical change issues, rather than to present a set of prescriptions in a 'how to change' recipe approach.

The first lesson is that there are no universal prescriptions on how best to manage change, nor are there simple recipes for competitive success. However, this will not prevent continuing company demand for such solutions. Consequently, it is important to be aware of the limitations of these step guides for change and to challenge – where possible and practicable – the assumptions behind linear packages for 'successful' change. This is perhaps why, notwithstanding our current knowledge and experience of organizational change, 'the brutal fact is that about 70 per cent of all change initiatives fail' (Beer and Nohria, 2000).

Second, change strategies should be sensitive and adapt to the shifting character of change, the context in which change takes place, and the views and reactions of employee groups and key political players. Political sensitivity and astuteness (the ability to manoeuvre through shifting terrain) are often well-honed skills in those individuals and groups (change agents, trade unionists and the like) who are able to shape change.

A third and frequently stated lesson is that major change takes time. Radical large-scale strategic and/or operational change requires extensive planning – including numerous revisions and modifications to planned changes – and is unlikely to be marked by a line of continual improvement.

Fourth, the experiences of change recounted in this book testify to the fact that not only will individuals and groups experience change in a variety of ways, their expectations and views are likely to change over time. For example, if the individuals or groups that question change are viewed as obstacles, then they are unlikely to respond to or experience change in a positive way. Similarly, casting a jaundiced eye on 'failed' projects may result in negative employee experience and thereby inadvertently support the assumption that the problem rests with employees and not with other elements of the change programme. Such a view can create a self-fulfilling prophecy which can be hard to overcome especially where this position appeals to commonsense assumptions about why individuals and groups resist change. This clearly highlights the importance of and need for continuous critical reflection in order to question taken-for-granted assumptions.

Fifth and as already discussed, it is important to learn from all experiences of change and not to focus solely on 'successful' change stories or the views of those in dominant positions. Such stories are often *post hoc* rationalized accounts constructed to convey a preferred message to an intended audience. The experiences and views of different groups and individuals at various levels within an organization are all potential sources of knowledge for understanding and shaping change processes.

A sixth fairly general lesson (noted elsewhere) is that employees should be trained in new techniques and procedures when needed and as required. The misalignment of training programmes with change initiatives is not uncommon in large, complex change programmes and can be a major influence on employee experience of change.

Communication is the seventh area in which practical lessons can be discerned. Many writers would agree that communication is central to change, but it also needs to be understood in context. As supported by much of the literature, communication with employees should be ongoing and consistent. However, change often involves competing narratives, which draw attention back to the political process of change. The choice of what, when and how to communicate as well as the release of disconfirming information are often political issues. Communication is an important vehicle both for those seeking to steer change in certain directions and for those wishing to resist the preferred change outcomes of others.

The eighth lesson centres on the importance of context and substance. The external context can be influential in promoting certain change initiatives or packages over others, and the internal context helps to explain variation in employee experiences of change. Similarly, the substance of change is generally modified, reconfigured and redefined throughout change processes. It is not a static element. A simple lesson is that recipe approaches to change that promote well-defined programmes that support notions of unitary culture and context are ultimately misplaced. There is nothing so impracticable as a packaged, prescriptive, linear change initiative.

The ninth practical demonstration arising from the case studies is that change is a political process. Or to put it another way, political processes are central in shaping the speed, direction and outcomes of change. The greater the support for change, the higher the likelihood that change will take place and move in expected directions across unknown terrain. Although the results of change may be presented in the form of some objective demonstrable outcome, the route and progression of change (as well as evaluations of 'success' and 'failure') will be shaped by political processes.

The tenth and final lesson is perhaps the most straightforward of all, and that is that change is a complex of interweaving and sometimes contradictory processes. These processes have an ongoing history that is never static but open to change as the past is rewritten in the context of the present and in the light of future expectations. The substance, context and politics of change interlock and overlap over time. Once again, this draws attention to the value of a processual approach in understanding the theory and practice of change.

These, then, are ten general lessons on change emerging from the studies on the contemporary experience of change for people at work. However, the case studies also highlight coping strategies employed by individuals and groups trying to make sense of their change experience, and the ways others actively seek to shape change outcomes. For example, the Australian Services Union case study illustrates the influence of tradition and established patriarchal relations on attempts to reinvent the ASU and to tackle long-standing gender issues; the cellular manufacturing case spotlights the Machiavellian practices of local management in forcefully seeking 'revenge' on those who resist change; the Dalebake case draws attention to the importance of customer–supplier power relationships in making sense of the pace and pattern of change and innovation at work. This new empirical data is presented in a way that encourages the reader to address a number of critical change issues – such as age, gender, technology, globalization and the growth in non-standard work – within the context of a particular case or set of employee experiences. The interviews with shop floor employees, senior executives, trade unionists, local management and others pose issues and raise questions for further investigation in the context of the data presented and in the light of readers' own experiences. My hope is that these unresolved and yet coherent and accessible 'stories' will enable readers to draw out their own insights and to reflect critically on their own assumptions. By design, the chapters do not present a neat set of solutions or conclusions; rather, they leave room to manoeuvre in the further development of interpretations that will stimulate debate on the theoretical and practical dimensions of change.

The need for greater critical reflection on change and a broader understanding of the political processes behind the scripting of change stories are also demonstrated by the collapse of the giant energy trader Enron. This is a good illustration of how the commercial pressure to maintain a public 'success' story even when major problems are occurring can mislead and disguise processes of change. This form of company spin can be used to masquerade the realities of change, presenting sanitized and rational accounts which often elevate the individual manager to the role of charismatic leader, or executive teams into innovative visionary managers. However, such an emphasis on spin may result in creative accounting techniques that purposefully hide problems of profitability and poor, uncontrolled decision-making. Caught in a culture where performance is critical to any chance of competitive success, individuals and groups may find themselves under pressure to present a positive spin even under conditions where the very survival of the company is threatened. Contrary to the claims of the popular management literature (for example, Peters and Waterman, 1982) and tales of how to lead the revolution (Hamel, 2000), practical lessons on change cannot simply be distilled from spin doctor accounts and anecdotal executive stories which revel in their own self-mastery and innovative skill. These are simply social constructions and *post hoc* rationalizations that tell more about the storytellers than about the successful management of change. In practice, the politics of performance and accountability encourage senior management to engage in power-assisted steering (Buchanan and Badham, 1999) to ensure that their version of reality is the 'story' that is believed.

However counterintuitive, one should not be misled into assuming that stories of successful change provide a fertile ground for identifying lessons on how to 'successfully' manage change. 'Success' is itself bound up in the political process of change. It is argued here that such an imbalance can promote a blame culture in which individuals and groups that are identified (often wrongly) as the cause of company problems can have very negative experiences of change. Rather than cast groups who are unable to secure their objectives as 'failures', attention should be paid to a critical appraisal of the entire process of change. There is often a lot to learn from, for example, why a change initiative runs into difficulties in one section of an organization and yet appears to offer benefits in other areas. That is, different aspects of large-scale change may be labelled as being either a 'success' or a 'failure', while other elements may simply be ignored or remain hidden. And yet all these dimensions not only contribute to our understanding of the change process, they also provide useful material from which we can glean practical lessons on change. But alas, in studying these processes, companies usually prefer to talk about positive change experiences in highlighting their 'success' rather than allow researcher access for a critical examination of problem areas. Equally, employees who experience difficulties are generally not expected to analyse the nature of their problems in order to propose alternative solutions or to draw attention to how the company might learn from their experience. More often, the tendency is to downplay and turn away from these groups while celebrating the short-term wins of others (see, for example, Kotter, 1996).

In contrast to this emphasis on company success, it is argued here that all facets of the change process require examination and analysis. Practical lessons and insights can be gained not simply from evaluating projects that 'fail' or 'succeed', but also by examining the political processes by which stories are created, sustained and rewritten over time. As the experience of change will vary across individuals and groups in an organization, it is important not to prejudge the standing, value and contribution of these views and experiences. For example, the case studies and analyses presented in this book challenge some of these commonly held assumptions, such as the view that change is generally a positive development done for the 'right' reasons and that resistance to change is a negative response that requires action. The reasons why individuals and groups support or resist change cannot be assumed. For example, people are increasingly aware that resistance to change, however appropriate, may send a negative signal that ultimately questions their company 'loyalty' and professional 'capability'. In such circumstances, a willingness to embrace change may be uncritically assumed to mean endorsement and acceptance, rather than a true reflection of employee views and beliefs. This misreading of the situation limits opportunities for discussion, constrains knowledge and leaves no room for critical reflection. And yet simple recipe approaches that ignore these important issues continue to guide practitioners on the 'successful' management of change. What is required is a fuller understanding of the complex process of change, so that different experiences and viewpoints can be critically examined to further our knowledge and insights. I hope that this book has gone some way to redressing this imbalance in the literature, but there remains much more work to do in promoting the theoretical and practical value of more critical perspectives on change management.

CONCLUSION

There is no nook or cranny of the economy where change or the potential for change is not happening, driven by technology, markets and powerful corporations, with all the knock-on consequences for patterns of working which in turn refract into our personal lives and relationships. (Giddens and Hutton, 2001: 3)

This book opened with the view that change is an integral part of all our lives. We live in a world full of change. Some changes we seek to shape, and in harnessing these processes we attempt to steer change towards some preferred outcome. At other times, change may simply pick us up and sweep us forward on an uncertain journey. Whether we feel in control of change processes or not, we are all riders of change. For the most part, the experiences of change related in this book centre on the meaning of organizational change for people in work and employment. However, these experiences do not occur in a vacuum; they are part of a broader social context. Changes in the family and home, and in society at large, influence the way we experience change at work. The separation of our working experience from other aspects of our lives is false. Increasingly, we are coming to realize the importance of this interweaving of contexts as part of a greater tapestry that is our experience of change. For example, Richard Sennett (2001) illustrates how people tell different types of stories depending on what they want to explain. Their life narrative not only has to be continually recast to accommodate socio-economic change, context and experience, but also the story they construct for others has to be continually refined to take account of their audience and the aspects of their identity that they wish to hide or highlight. In this world of change, people seek to make sense of their experience and to have others confirm and engage with their narrative of change. Consequently, although we may not all be leading major company change programmes, we all encounter and have to make sense of the consequences of change in our experience of work. What some of these changes are and what they mean for people in work and employment are a central foci of this book.

Sadly, the main concern in the change management literature remains rooted in a search for key ingredients of 'success' in order to sustain competitive advantage. This has resulted in the production of managerial prescriptions for change which are generally presented in the form of a rational, historical development with each new development representing an improvement on previous ideas. In this way, new recipes for change are often presented as combining the best of earlier movements. For example, quality management can be shown to combine social and cultural ideas from earlier human relations and socio-technical systems theories with technical and administrative prescriptions from scientific management and bureaucratic theories. However, academics who have sought to explain organizational change have been quick to show that there can be significant variations in the adoption of managerial ideas; that any fundamental change is likely to engender at least some employee distrust and resistance; and that different strategies and structures may be appropriate under different circumstances. These and other competing views have resulted in a large body of empirical research and the development of a number of competing perspectives on change (see Aldrich, 1999; Carnall, 1999; Hayes, 2002; Henry and Mayle, 2002; Jaffee, 2001; Paton and McCalman, 2000; Senior, 1997).

The processual approach advocated in this book views change as a process that takes time and is shaped by context, substance and politics. I argue that simple recipe approaches to change are not practicable, as change strategies need to be able to adapt to the unforeseen and the unexpected. It has also been shown how the experience of change will vary over time and across individuals and groups. The data illustrate how there can never be a single authentic story of change as there will always be multiple narratives and competing histories of change. Although many of the views and experiences of employees may be ignored, quashed, invalidated or remain unspoken in the power plays and political struggles associated with radical organizational change, they nevertheless provide useful insights into processes of change. Absences of the less powerful (the unheard voices) in the presentation of the story of change are a major flaw and common weakness in much of the change management literature. Moreover, many of the changes occurring in the workplace are not isolated, context-independent events but form part of a myriad of overlapping, interlocking and at times conflicting change initiatives instigated by others for a series of competing reasons. To those wishing to steer, resist or promote change, the political process of information management is critical both in the timing and release of information and in the creation of change stories that may influence decision-making. Essentially, it is substance, context and political process that shape our various contemporary experiences of organizational change. I hope that the material presented in this book has gone some way to providing further insight into this complex and murky phenomenon. With these insights we may be better equipped to accommodate and steer change processes, but we can never be fully prepared for all eventualities. This is perhaps what ultimately makes change such an interesting subject to study and debate – the essential unforeseeable character of change means that the process cannot be predicted and that outcomes are often only understood in retrospect. We can learn from our experiences and the experience of others, but we cannot foretell how the process of change will unfold before the event. Change is by its very nature a complex dynamic process.

APPENDIX

THE TQM RESEARCH PROGRAMME AND GUIDE FOR INTERVIEWERS

Total Quality Management Case Study Programme

Australian Centre in Strategic Management at Queensland University of Technology

Objectives

The Total Quality Management (TQM) case study programme is funded by the Australian Research Council (ARC) and is designed to ascertain the ways in which TQM techniques have been introduced into a number of Australian firms and a New Zealand organization. The main objective of the programme is to assess the introduction, the implementation and the effects of TQM in Australia and New Zealand. In order to study the change process over time, a longitudinal element has been built into the research design with case study data being collected over a period of 18 months to 3 years. In the collection of new empirical data, an emphasis has been placed on the way TQM affects management, workers and their organizations, suppliers and customers and the organization of work.

TQM is difficult to define and is understood to mean different things to different groups. This programme will employ case studies to explore the substance of TQM in a range of firms and TQM will be taken to be those practices that the firms themselves regard as TQM. The study will not assume characteristics of change on the basis of the label attributed to the change.

The Project will be undertaken by an Australian Centre in Strategic Management research team, headed by Gill Palmer of the University of Wollongong with Research Assistant Cameron Allan, and by a University of Adelaide research team headed by Patrick Dawson with Research Associate Verna Blewett. Other case study workers in Sydney, Perth, Queensland and Otago are being organized and will come under the direction of either Gill Palmer or Patrick Dawson.

Outcomes from the project will be a series of journal articles and a book based on the research findings.

Research Themes
This research aims to determine if, in multi-plant firms, TQM is being implemented in different ways in different plants. Further, it is hoped to determine to what extent the practice matches the rhetoric. The following themes are to be examined:

A. **The Spread of TQM – The mobilization of a movement and the influence of change agents**
   1. The role of consultants in the transmission of quality management practices.
   2. The role of government (e.g. NIES programme) in the transmission of quality management practices.
   3. Ideologies/fashions of managerial reform movements.

B. **Customer/Supplier Relations**
   This research will study the effect of TQM on the networks of customers and suppliers around the firm and with the firm.
   1. Changes in perceptions and processes for external and internal customers.

C. **TQM and HRM – The nature of the changes generated and their impact on the flexible use of labour**
   1. The use of labour, changes in the structure of training, skill formation, recruitment, promotion and reward systems.
   2. Changing communication and influence systems. Changes in the nature of the psychological contract between employer and employee. The creation of a new culture. Contrasts between administered and market relations.

D. **TQM and IR**
   1. Quality initiatives and structural efficiency/award restructuring.

E. **Process of Change**
   1. Continuous improvements vs freezing/unfreezing: Organizational Behaviour and Organization Theory literature.
   2. Competing histories of the change process from different perspectives.
   3. Key symbolic events.

Methodology
Interviews will be conducted with the following personnel.

Key Player Interviews
- Senior level management and TU officials
- management, especially those instrumental to the introduction of TQM
- consultants

Employee Interviews
- a subset in a part of the company where TQM was implemented: managers, supervisors, shop delegates and workers.

Questions/Areas to Be Covered

1. Background Information about the Firm
- company size
- number of employees
- industry sector/s
- recent history re: grown/decline in market share/profits/workforce/ competition for last 5–10 years
- perception of change – the competing histories
- patterns of HRM/IR (look for changes due to TQM)
  - adverbial vs co-operation IRs?
  - relations with unions?
  - what type of appraisal/evaluation/reward systems?
  - any career routes?
  - what kind of security, recruitment, dismissal, grievance procedures?
  - what use of subcontractors, casual labour?
- any other attempts to reorganize work or change management labour relations in the recent past?
  - collective employee representation, traditional role of union delegates, previous experience of joint involvement in managerial issues.

2. The Decision to Change
- what were the circumstances in which the decision to try TQM was made?
- why was it thought necessary to introduce TQM: was it a statutory requirement, was it a directive from head office, was it related to company performance, product or labour market conditions, etc.?
- who made the decision?
- what were the justifications?
- what were the expectations?
- why use a TQM approach over others?
- to what extent did union representatives feel involved in the decision to change?

- were there other mechanisms for involving employees in the early decision-making process?

3. Planning the Change

- was there any planning?
- was there any type of consultative committee setup to discuss the issues or objectives of introducing a TQM package?
- who was involved: management, trade unions, employees, consultants?
- what were the objectives, e.g. to reduce stock, to increase worker involvement, etc.?
- timeframe
- costing justification
- expectations

Package

- what package/s were introduced?
- what techniques were they comprised of: statistical techniques?
- what did it cost?

Consultants

- who and why were these particular consultants chosen?
- what was their brief?
- what processes did they use and how influential were they in the implementation?
- was NIES support an important factor; were they subsidies?
- was there any worker involvement in the decision to *introduce* a package?
- what role for the unions?

4. Implementation of Change (TQM)

- what were key stages in the process?
- timeframe
- what problems encountered?
- what levels of management were involved in the implementation of TQM and what was their role?
- in what ways have workers been involved in the introduction of the TQM?
- were the unions involved?
- what involvement did the consultants have in the introduction and implementation of the TQM package/s?

5. Effects of Change (TQM) – evaluated by the participants

Union perspective and views

- any change in union's attitude?
- views of shop delegates?

Management perspectives
- any changes to the role and responsibility of specialist and line managers at the top, mid and lower levels?; their views and reactions?

Supervisor perspectives
- any change in the supervisor's role?
- any change in the nature of subordinate–superordinate relations?
- supervisor's evaluation

Effects on the technical and social organization of work
- has there been any change to the technical organization of work; that is, a change to the way work is physically organised
- any change to the social organization of work, which may include:
  Quality Circles
  Quality Improvement Teams
  Other
- any change to demarcations, task structures, flexibility of labour useage?
- JIT effects

Effects on workers
- has work intensified?
- any change in staff levels?
- what have been the effects on the quality of work experience for employees and their prospects e.g. skill formation pathways?

6. Measurement of Operational Change
Qualitative and quantitative effects
- is there any meaningful measure in terms of productivity, profitability, or any other performance measure in terms of morale, employee commitment?
- impact on suppliers/customers?
- changes in the patterns of HRM/IR
  - adverbial vs co-operative IRs?
  - relations with unions?
  - what type of appraisal/evaluation/reward systems?
  - any career routes?
  - what kind of security, recruitment, dismissal, grievance procedures?
  - what use of subcontractors, casual labour?

7. Future Expectations
- where to next?

8. Assessment of Change – evaluated by the case study worker
- does the implementation and effects of TQM accord with the stated/ desired intention?

- is it possible to say that the effects are attributable to the implementation of TQM package?
- how do we assess the role of the state (if any)?
- how significant was the award restructuring process?
- how can we account for the HRM/IR changes?

References

Abrahamson, E. (1991) 'Managerial fads and fashions: the diffusion and rejection of innovations', *Academy Management Review*, 16 (3): 586–612.

Abrahamson, E. (1996) 'Management fashion', *Academy of Management Review*, 21 (1): 254–85.

A Abrahamson, E. and Fairchild, G. (1999) 'Management fashion: lifecycles, triggers, and collective learning processes', *Administrative Science Quarterly*, 44: 708–40.

Albrecht, K. (1992) *The Only Thing that Matters: Bringing the Power of the Customer into the Centre of your Business*. New York: HarperBusiness.

Aldag, R. and Stearns, T. (1991) *Management*. Cincinnati: South-Western.

B Aldrich, H. (1999) *Organizations Evolving*. London: Sage.

Aldrich, H. and Mindlin, S. (1978) 'Uncertainty and dependence: two perspectives on environment', in L. Karpik (ed.), *Organization and Environment*. London: Sage.

Alford, J. (1994) 'Cellular manufacturing: the development of the idea and its application', *New Technology, Work and Employment*, 9: 3–18.

Allan, C. (1991) 'The role of diffusion agents in the transfer of quality management in Australia'. Honours thesis, University of Griffith, Brisbane.

L Allan, C. (1995) 'The process and politics of change at Vicbank', in P. Dawson and G. Palmer (eds), *Quality Management*. Melbourne: Longman.

L Allan, C. and Dawson, P. (1995) 'The managerial politics of organisational change', in M. Patrickson, V. Bamber and G. Bamber (eds), *Organisational Change Strategies: Case Studies of Human Resource and Industrial Relations Issues*. Melbourne: Longman.

Alvesson, M. and Willmott, H. (1996) *Making Sense of Management: A Critical Introduction*. London: Sage.

Ang, C.L. and Willey, P.C. (1984) 'A comparative study of the performance of pure and hybrid group technology manufacturing systems using computer simulation techniques', *International Journal of Production Research*, 22 (2): 193–233.

Ashton, J.E. and Cook, F.X. (1989) 'Time to reform job shop manufacturing', *Harvard Business Review*, 67: 106–11.

Ashworth, J. (2002) 'International airlines emerge from a turbulent year', *The Times*, 12 January: 44.

Atkinson, J. (1984) 'Manpower strategies for flexible organisations', *Personnel Management*, 16: 28–31.

Atkinson, J. and Meager, N. (1986) *Changing Working Patterns: How Companies Achieve Flexibility to Meet New Needs*. London: National Economic Development Office.

Australian (1995) 'Struck out: the demise of US unions', 28 December: 24.

Australian (1996) 'Why downsizers risk coming unstuck', 14 January: 28.

Babbage, C. (1835) *On the Economy of Machinery and Manufacture*. London: Knight.

Bacon, N. (1999) 'Union derecognition and the "new human relations": a steel industry case study', *Work, Employment and Society*, 13 (1): 1–17.

Badham, R. (1995) 'Managing sociotechnical change: a configuration approach to technology implementation', in J. Benders, J. de Haan and D. Bennett (eds), *The Symbiosis of Work and Technology*. London: Taylor & Francis.

Badham, R. (1999) 'Frontiers of autonomy and the dynamics of teamwork: a critical approach to new forms of organizational control', 17th International Labour Process Conference, Royal Holloway, London.

Badham, R. (forthcoming) *Management of Change: A Critical Introduction*. London: B Sage.

Badham, R. and Couchman, P. (1996) 'Implementing team-based cells in Australia: a configurational process approach', *Integrated Manufacturing Systems*, 7 (5): 47–59.

Badham, R., Couchman, P. and McLoughlin, I. (1997) 'Implementing vulnerable socio-technical change projects', in I. McLoughlin and M. Harris (eds), *Innovation, Organizational Change and Technology*. London: International Thomson Business Press.

Baird, M. and Lansbury, R. (2001) 'The decline of collective bargaining in Australia: propsects for a new social settlement?' Paper presented at the Conference of the Korea Labor Institute and Cornell University, Ithaca, 5–7 October.

Baldry, C., Bain, P. and Taylor, P. (1998) '"Bright satanic offices": intensification, B control and team taylorism', in P. Thompson and C. Warhurst (eds), *Workplaces of the Future*. London: Macmillan Business.

Bartlett, C.A. and Ghoshal, S. (1991) *Managing Across Borders: The Transnational Solution*. Boston: Harvard Business School Press.

Batley, T. and Andrews, M. (1995) 'Implementing TQM in manufacturing: the route to change at Tecpak Industries', in P. Dawson and G. Palmer (eds), *Quality Management*. Melbourne: Longman.

Baty, P. (2001) 'QAA set to float new ranking hierarchy', *Times Higher Education Supplement*, 21 September: 3.

Becker, H. (1973) *Outsiders: Studies in the Sociology of Deviance*. New York: Free Press.

Beckhard, R. (1969) *Organizational Development: Strategies and Models*. Reading: Addison-Wesley.

Beckhard, R. and Harris, R.T. (1987) *Organizational Transitions: Managing Complex Change*. 2nd edn. Reading: Addison-Wesley.

Bedeian, A. (1984) *Organizations: Theory and Analysis*. 2nd edn. New York: Dryden Press.

Beer, M. and Nohria, N. (2000) 'Cracking the code of change', *Harvard Business* A *Review*, 78 (3): 133–41.

Belanger, J., Edwards, P.K. and Haiven, L. (eds) (1994) *Workplace Industrial Relations and the Global Challenge*. New York: ILR Press.

Bell, D. (1973) *The Coming of Post-Industrial Society*. New York: Basic Books.

Benders, J. and Badham, R. (2000) 'History of cell-based manufacturing', in M. Beyerlein (ed.), *Work Teams: Past, Present and Future*. Amsterdam: Kluwer Academic.

Benders, J. and Van Hootegem, G. (1999) 'Teams and their context: moving the team discussion beyond existing dichotomies', *Journal of Management Studies*, 36 (5): 609–28.

Bennington, L. and Calvert, B. (1998) 'Antidiscrimination legislation and HRM practice', in M. Patrickson and L. Hartmann (eds), *Managing an Aging Workforce*. Warriewood, NSW: Business and Professional Publishing.

Bennington, L. and Tharenou, P. (1996) 'Older workers: myths, evidence and implications for Australian managers', *Asia Pacific Journal of Human Resources*, 34 (3): 63–76.

Beynon, H. (1984) *Working for Ford*. Harmondsworth: Penguin.

Beynon, H. (1997) 'The changing practices of work', in R. Brown (ed.), *The Changing Shape of Work*. London: Macmillan.

Biddle, G. (1993) 'Group technology and batch production', *Labour and Industry*, 5 (1): 105–30.

Bijker, W. (1995) *Of Bicycles, Bakelites and Bulbs: Towards a Theory of Socio-Technical Change*. Cambridge: MIT Press.

Birdi, K. and Warr, P. (1995) 'Age differences in three components of employee well-being', *Applied Psychology: An International Review*, 44 (4): 345–73.

Blackburn, P., Coombs, R. and Green, K. (1985) *Technology, Economic Growth and the Labour Process*. London: Macmillan.

Blau, P. (1964) *Exchange and Power in Social Life*. New York: Wiley.

Blauner, R. (1964) *Alienation and Freedom: The Factory Worker and his Industry*. Chicago: University of Chicago Press.

Blewett, V. (1995a) 'Conceptualising the need for TQM at Accom Industries Pty Ltd', in P. Dawson and G. Palmer (eds), *Quality Management*. Melbourne: Longman.

Blewett, V. (1995b) 'Health and safety, customer–supplier relations and statistical process control: strategies for continuous improvement at Hendersons Automotive (SA)', in P. Dawson and G. Palmer (eds), *Quality Management*. Melbourne: Longman.

Boddy, D. and Buchanan, D. (1986) *Managing New Technology*. Oxford: Blackwell.

Bolman, L. and Deal, T. (1991) *Reframing Organizations: Artistry, Choice, and Leadership*. San Francisco: Jossey-Bass.

Boxall, P. and Haynes, P. (1997) 'Strategy and trade union effectiveness in a neo-liberal environment', *British Journal of Industrial Relations*, 35 (4): 567–91.

Bradley, H. (1999) *Gender and Power in the Workplace: Analysing the Impact of Economic Change*. Basingstoke: Macmillan.

Bradley, H., Erickson, M., Stephenson, C. and Williams, S. (2000) *Myths at Work*. Cambridge: Polity Press.

Brannen, J., Lewis, S. and Moss, P. (2000) 'The impact of organisational change on family lives: theoretical and methodological developments in an ongoing exploratory study'. Paper presented at an ESRC Seminar, The Changing Nature of Work and Family Life, University of Aberdeen, 23 November.

Braverman, H. (1974) *Labor and Monopoly Capital: The Degradation of Work in the Twentieth Century*. New York: Monthly Review Press.

ß Brown, A. (1995a) *Organisational Culture*. London: Pitman.

Brown, A. (1995b) 'The development of process improvement teams and the measurement of outcomes at Alcoa's Kwinana Refinery', in P. Dawson and G. Palmer (eds), *Quality Management*. Melbourne: Longman.

Buchanan, D. (1994) 'Cellular manufacture and the role of teams', in J. Storey (ed.), *New Wave Manufacturing Strategies: Organizational and Human Resource Management Dimensions*. London: Paul Chapman Publishing.

Buchanan, D. (2000) 'An eager and enduring embrace: the ongoing rediscovery of teamworking as a management idea', in S. Proctor and F. Mueller (eds), *Teamworking*. London: Macmillan Business.

ß Buchanan, D. and Badham, R. (1999) *Power, Politics, and Organizational Change: Winning the Turf Game*. London: Sage.

Buchanan, D. and Huczynski, A. (1997) *Organizational Behaviour: An Introductory Text*. 3rd edn. London: Prentice Hall.

Burawoy, M. (1979) *Manufacturing Consent: Changes in the Labour Process under Monopoly Capitalism.* Chicago: University of Chicago Press.

Burchell, B. (2000) 'Job insecurity and work intensification'. Paper presented to an ESRC Seminar, The Changing Nature of Work and Family Life, University of Aberdeen, 23 November.

Burnes, B. (1992) *Managing Change: A Strategic Approach to Organizational Dynamics.* London: Pitman.

Burnes, B. (2000) *Managing Change: A Strategic Approach to Organizational Dynamics.* 3rd edn. London: Pitman.

Burns, T. and Stalker, G.M. (1961) *The Management of Innovation.* London: Tavistock.

Callon, M. (1999) 'Actor–network theory: the market test', in J. Law and J. Hassard (eds), *Actor Network Theory and After.* Oxford: Blackwell.

Carnall, C. (1999) *Managing Change in Organizations.* 3rd edn. London: Prentice Hall.

Carter, B. (2000) 'Adoption of the organising model in British trade unions: some evidence from manufacturing, science and finance (MSF)', *Work, Employment and Society,* 14 (1): 117–36.

Castells, M. (1996) *The Information Age: Economy, Society and Culture. Vol. 1: The Rise of the Network Society.* Oxford: Blackwell.

Castells, M. (2000) *The Information Age: Economy, Society and Culture. Vol. 1: The Rise of the Network Society.* 2nd edn. Oxford: Blackwell.

Castells, M. (2001) 'Information technology and global capitalism', in W. Hutton and A. Giddens (eds), *On the Edge: Living with Global Capitalism.* London: Vintage.

Child, J. (1972) 'Organization structure, environment and performance: the role of strategic choice', *Sociology* 6 (1): 1–22.

Child, J. (1975) 'The industrial supervisor', in G. Esland, G. Salaman and M. Speakman (eds), *People and Work.* Edinburgh: Holmes McDougall.

Child, J. (1997) 'Strategic choice in the analysis of action, structure, organizations and environment: retrospect and prospect', *Organization Studies,* 18 (1): 43–76.

Child, J. and Partridge, B. (1982) *Lost Managers: Supervisors in Industry and Society.* Cambridge: Cambridge University Press.

Chiles, T. and Choi, T. (2000) 'Theorizing TQM: an Austrian and evolutionary economics interpretation', *Journal of Management Studies,* (37) 2: 185–212.

Clark, J. (1995a) *Managing Innovation and Change: People, Technology and Strategy.* London: Sage.

Clark, J. (1995b) 'Is there a future for industrial relations?', *Work, Employment and Society,* (6) 3: 593–605.

Clark, J., McLoughlin, I., Rose, H. and King, R. (1988) *The Process of Technological Change: New Technology and Social Choice in the Workplace.* Cambridge: Cambridge University Press.

Clausen, C. and Koch, C. (1999) 'The role of spaces and occasions in the transformation of information technologies: lessons from the social shaping of IT systems for manufacturing in a Danish context', *Technology Analysis and Strategic Management,* 11 (3): 463–82.

Clausen, C., Dawson, P. and Nielsen, K.T. (eds) (2000) 'Political processes in management, organization and the social shaping of technology', special issue, *Technology Analysis and Strategic Management,* 12 (1): 1–143.

Claydon, T. (1989) 'Union derecognition in Britain in the 1980s', *British Journal of Industrial Relations,* 27: 214–23.

Claydon, T. (1996) 'Union derecognition: a re-examination', in I. Beardwell (ed.), *Contemporary Industrial Relations: A Critical Analysis.* Oxford: Oxford University Press.

Clegg, S. (1990) *Modern Organizations: Organization Studies in the Postmodern World*. London: Sage.

Clegg, S. and Dunkerley, D. (1980) *Organization, Class and Control*. London: Routledge & Kegan Paul.

Clutterbuck, D. (1985) *New Patterns of Work*. Aldershot: Gower.

Clutterbuck, D. and Crainer, S. (1990) *Makers of Management: Men and Women Who Changed the Business World*. London: Macmillan.

Collins, D. (1998) *Organizational Change: Sociological Perspectives*. London: Routledge.

Collins, D. (2000) *Management Fads and Buzzwords: Critical-Practical Perspectives*. London: Routledge.

Collins, D. (2001) 'The fad motif in management scholarship', *Employee Relations*, 23 (1): 26–37.

Cooney, R. (1999) 'Group work and new production practices in the Australian passenger motor vehicle manufacturing industry'. Ph.D. thesis, University of Melbourne.

Cooper, R., Westcott, M. and Lansbury, R. (undated working paper) 'Labor revitalization? The case of Australia', University of Sydney, Australia.

Cowing, E. (2002) 'Ford restructuring cuts 35,000 jobs worldwide', *Scotsman*, 12 January: 22.

Crompton, R. (1976) 'Approaches to the study of white collar unionism', *Sociology*, 10 (3): 407–26.

Crompton, R. (1997) *Women and Work in Modern Britain*. Oxford: Oxford University Press.

Crosby, P. (1980) *Quality Is Free: The Art of Making Quality Certain*. New York: Mentor.

Crouch, C. (1994) *Industrial Relations and European State Traditions*. Oxford: Clarendon Press.

Cyert, R. and March, J. (1963) *A Behavioural Theory of the Firm*. Englewood Cliffs: Prentice Hall.

Daft, R.L. (1986) *Organization Theory and Design*. New York: West Publishing.

Danford, A. (1998) 'Teamworking and labour regulation in the autocomponents industry', *Work, Employment and Society*, 12 (3): 409–31.

Daniels, K., Lamond, D. and Standen, S. (2000) *Managing Telework*. London: Thomson Learning.

Dawson, P. (1991) 'Lost managers or industrial dinosaurs? A reappraisal of front-line management', *Australian Journal of Management*, 16 (1): 35–48.

Dawson, P. (1994) *Organizational Change: A Processual Approach*. London: Paul Chapman Publishing.

Dawson, P. (1995) 'Managing quality in the multi-cultural workplace', in A. Wilkinson and H. Wilmott (eds), *Making Quality Critical: New Perspectives on Organizational Change*. London: Routledge.

Dawson, P. (1996) *Technology and Quality: Change in the Workplace*. London: International Thomson Business Press.

Dawson, P. (1998) 'The rhetoric and bureaucracy of quality management: a totally questionable method?', *Personnel Review*, 27 (1): 5–19.

Dawson, P. (2002) 'Changing supervisory relations at work: behind the success stories of Quality Management', in J. Antony and D. Preece (eds), *Understanding, Managing and Implementing Quality: Frameworks, Techniques and Cases*. London: Routledge.

Dawson, P. and Palmer, G. (eds) (1995) *Quality Management: The Theory and Practice of Implementing Change*. Melbourne: Longman.

Dawson, P., Clausen, C. and Nielsen, K.T. (2000) 'Political processes in management, organisation and the social shaping of technology', *Technology Analysis and Strategic Management*, 12 (1): 5–15.

Deming, W.E. (1981) *Japanese Methods for Productivity and Quality*. Washington: George Washington University Press.

DiMaggio, P. and Powell, W. (1983) 'The iron cage revisited: institutional isomorphism and collective rationality', *American Sociological Review*, 48: 147–60.

DiMaggio, P. and Powell, W. (eds) (1991) *The New Institutionalism in Organisational Analysis*. Chicago: University of Chicago Press.

Domberger, S. and Hensher, D. (1993) 'Private and public sector regulation of competitive tendered contracts', *Empirica*, 20: 221–40.

Donovan, P. and Tweddell, E. (1995) *F.H. Faulding & Co. Limited: 150 Years, 1845–1995*. Adelaide: Wakefield Press.

Drew, E., Emerek, R. and Mahon, E. (eds) (1998) *Women, Work and the Family in Europe*. London: Routledge.

Dunford, R.W. (1990) 'A reply to Dunphy and Stace', *Organization Studies*, 11 (1): 131–4.

Dunphy, D. (1981) *Organizational Change by Choice*. Sydney: McGraw-Hill.

Dunphy, D. and Griffiths, A. (1998) *The Sustainable Corporation: Organisational Renewal in Australia*. St Leonards: Allen & Unwin.

Dunphy, D. and Stace, D. (1990) *Under New Management: Australian Organizations in Transition*. Sydney: McGraw-Hill.

Dyerson, R. and Mueller, F. (1999) 'Learning, teamwork and appropriability: managing technological change in the Department of Social Security', *Journal of Management Studies*, 36 (5): 629–52.

Eccles, T. (1994) *Succeeding with Change: Implementing Action-Driven Strategies*. London: McGraw-Hill.

The Economist (1996) 'Why downsizers risk coming unstuck', *The Australian*, January 14: 28.

Edwards, R. (1979) *Contested Terrain: The Transformation of the Workplace in the Twentieth Century*. London: Heinemann.

Emerson, R. (1962) 'Power-dependence relations', *American Sociological Review*, 27: 31–41.

Encel, S. (1998) 'Age discrimination', in M. Patrickson and L. Hartmann (eds), *Managing an Ageing Workforce*. Warriewood, NSW: Business & Professional Publishing.

Eriksson, A. and Hunt, J. (1997) 'Reflections on conducting processual research on management and organizations', *Scandinavian Journal of Management*, 13 (4): 331–5.

Feigenbaum, A. (1956) 'Total quality control', *Harvard Business Review*, 34 (6): 93–101.

Feigenbaum, A. (1961) *Total Quality Control*. New York: McGraw-Hill.

Felstead, A. and Jewson, N. (eds) (1999) 'Flexible labour and non-standard employment: an agenda of issues', in *Global Trends in Flexible Labour*. London: Macmillan Business.

Forrest, A. (1993) 'A view from outside the whale: the treatment of women and unions in industrial relations', in L. Briskin and P. McDermott (eds), *Women Challenging Unions: Feminism, Democracy and Militancy*. Toronto: University of Toronto Press.

Fox, A. (1974) *Beyond Contract: Work, Power and Trust Relations*. London: Faber & Faber.

French, W. and Bell, C. (1983) *Organization Development: Behavioural Science Interventions for Organization Improvement*. Englewood Cliffs: Prentice Hall.

French, W. and Bell, C. (1995) *Organizational Development and Change*. 5th edn. Minneapolis: West Publishing.

Friedman, A. (1977) *Industry and Labour: Class Struggle at Work and Monopoly Capitalism*. London: Macmillan.

Gabor, S.C. and Petersen, P.B. (1991) 'Book review: *When Giants Learn to Dance: Mastering the Challenges of Strategy, Management, and Careers in the 1990s*', *Academy of Management Executive*, 5 (1): 97–9.

Gall, G. and McKay, S. (1999) 'Developments in union recognition and derecognition in Britain, 1994–1998', *British Journal of Industrial Relations*, 37 (4): 601–14.

Gall, G. and McKay, S. (internal working paper, undated) 'Trade union recognition in Britain: the dawn of a new era?' Department of Management and Organisation, University of Stirling.

Gallagher, C. and Knight, W. (1973) *Group Technology*. London: Butterworth.

Gallie, D. (1998) 'The flexible workforce? The employment conditions of part-time and temporary workers'. Paper presented at Social Stratification Workshop, University of Essex, January.

Gardener, B. and Whyte, W. (1945) 'The man in the middle: positions and problems of the foreman', *Applied Anthropology: Problems of Human Organization*, 4 (2): 1–28.

Garraham, P. and Stewart, P. (1991) 'Flexible systems and the international automobile industry: a case of lean or mean production?'. Paper presented to the 9th ASTON/UMIST Annual Labour Process Conference, UMIST, Manchester, April.

Garraham, P. and Stewart, P. (1992) *The Nissan Enigma*. London: Mansell.

Ghoshal, S. and Bartlett, C. (1998) *Managing Across Borders: The Transnational Solution*. London: Random House.

Giddens, A. and Hutton, W. (2001) 'In conversation', in W. Hutton and A. Giddens (eds), *On the Edge: Living with Global Capitalism*. London: Vintage.

Gill, J. and Johnson, J. (1991) *Research Methods for Managers*. London: Paul Chapman Publishing.

Goddard, A. (2001) 'A high five for British research', *Times Higher Education Supplement*, 14 December: 1.

Gray, E.R. and Smeltzer, L.R. (1990) *Management: The Competitive Edge*. New York: Macmillan.

Gray, L.G. and Starke, F.A. (1988) *Organizational Behavior: Concepts and Applications*. 4th edn. Columbus: Merrill Publishing.

Grint, K. and Woolgar, S. (1997) *The Machine at Work*. Oxford: Polity Press.

Grun, B. (1991) *The Timetale of History*. New York: Simon & Schuster.

Guest, D. (1992) 'Right enough to be dangerously wrong: an analysis of the search of excellence phenomenon', in G. Salaman (ed.), *Human Resource Strategies*. London: Sage.

Hackman, R.J. and Wageman, R. (1995) 'Total quality management: empirical, conceptual, and practical issues', *Administrative Science Quarterly*, 40 (2): 309–42.

Ham, I., Hitomi, K. and Yoshida, T. (1985) *Group Technology: Applications to Production Management*. Boston: Kluwer-Nijhoff.

Hamel, G. (2000) *Leading the Revolution*. Boston: Harvard Business School Press.

Hamel, G. and Prahalad, C.K. (1994) *Competing for the Future*. Boston: Harvard Business School Press.

Hammer, M. and Champy, J. (1993) *Reengineering the Corporation: A Manifesto for Business Revolution*. New York: HarperBusiness.

Handy, C. (1984) *The Future of Work*. Oxford: Blackwell.

Handy, C. (1994) *The Empty Raincoat*. London: Hutchinson.

Handy, C. (1996) *Beyond Certainty: The Changing World of Organizations*. Boston: Harvard Business School Press.

Handy, C. (1999) *The New Alchemists*. London: Hutchinson.

Handy, C. (2001) *The Elephant and the Flea*. London: Hutchinson.

Harrison, N. and Samson, D. (1997) *International Best Practice in the Adoption and Management of New Technology*. Canberra: Commonwealth of Australia.

Hatch, J. (1997) *Organization Theory*. Oxford: Oxford University Press.

Hayes, J. (2002) *The Theory and Practice of Change Management*. Basingstoke: Palgrave. B

Hazelmere Group (1978) *Who Needs the Drug Companies?*. London: Hazelmere Group.

Healy, G. and Kirton, G. (2000) 'Women, power and trade union government in the UK', *British Journal of Industrial Relations*, 38 (3): 343–60.

Heath, C. and Luff, P. (2000) *Technology in Action*. Cambridge: Cambridge University Press.

Hellriegel, D., Slocum, J. and Woodman, R. (1995) *Organizational Behaviour*. 7th edn. New York: West Publishing.

Henry, J. and Mayle, D. (2002) *Managing Innovation and Change*. 2nd edn. London: Sage. B

Hill, S. (1991) 'Why quality circles failed but total quality management might succeed', *British Journal of Industrial Relations*, 29 (4): 541–68.

Hill, S. (1995) 'From quality circles to total quality management', in A. Wilkinson and H. Willmott (eds), *Making Quality Critical: New Perspectives on Organizational Change*. London: Routledge.

Hirst, P. and Thompson, G. (1999) *Globalization in Question*. London: Polity Press.

Hobsbawm, E.J. (1964) *Labouring Men*. London: Weidenfeld & Nicolson.

Hodgetts, R. and Luthans, F. (1997) *International Management*. 3rd edn. Singapore: McGraw-Hill.

Homstein, Z. (2001) *Outlawing Age Discrimination: Foreign Lessons, UK Choices*. York: Joseph Rowntree Foundation/Policy Press.

Howard, W. (1987) 'Australian trade unions in the context of union theory', in G. Ford, J. Hearn and R. Lansbury (eds), *Australian Labour Relations: Readings*. 3rd edn. Melbourne: Longman.

Huczynski, A. (1993) *Management Gurus: What Makes them and How to Become One*. London: Routledge.

Hundley, G. (1989) 'Things unions do: job attributes and union membership', *Industrial Relations*, 28 (3): 335–55.

Hunter, J. and Gates, G. (1998) 'Outsourcing: "functional", "fashionable" or "foolish"?', in G. Griffin (ed.), *Management Theory and Practice: Moving to a New Era*. Melbourne: Macmillan. L

Huq, F., Hensler, D. and Mohamed, Z. (2001) 'A simulation analysis of factors influencing the flow time and through-put performance of functional and cellular layouts', *Integrated Manufacturing Systems*, 12 (4): 285–95.

Huse, E. (1982) *Management*. New York: West.

Hutton, W. (1995) *The State We're in*. London: Vintage.

Hutton, W. and Giddens, A. (eds) (2001) *On the Edge: Living with Global Capitalism*. London: Vintage.

Hyman, R. (1989) *The Political Economy of Industrial Relations*. Basingstoke: Macmillan.

Hyman, R. (1994) 'Changing trade union identities and strategies', in R. Hyman and A. Ferner (eds), *New Frontiers in European Industrial Relations*. Oxford: Blackwell.

Hyman, R. and Ferner, A. (eds) (1994) *New Frontiers in European Industrial Relations*. Oxford: Blackwell.

Imai, M. (1986) *Kaizen: The Key to Japan's Competitive Success*. New York: McGraw-Hill.

Ishikawa, K. (1985) *What is Total Quality Control? The Japanese Way*. Englewood Cliffs: Prentice Hall.

Itzin, C. and Newman, J. (eds) (1995) *Gender, Culture and Organizational Change: Putting Theory into Practice*. London: Routledge.

Itzin, C. and Phillipson, C. (1995) 'Gendered ageism: a double jeopardy for women in organizations', in C. Itzin and J. Newman (eds), *Gender, Culture and Organizational Change: Putting Theory into Practice*. London: Routledge.

Jackson, B. (2001) *Management Gurus and Management Fashions*. London: Routledge.

Jackson, P. and Van der Wielen, J. (1998) *Teleworking: International Perspectives. From Telecommuting to the Virtual Organisation*. London: Routledge.

Jaffee, D. (2001) *Organization Theory: Tension and Change*. New York: McGraw-Hill.

James, H. (2001) *The Ends of Globalization*. Cambridge: Harvard University Press.

Juran, J.M. (1988) *Quality Control Handbook*. New York: McGraw-Hill.

Kaemar, K. and Ferris, G. (1989) 'Theoretical and methodological considerations in age-job satisfaction relationship', *Journal of Applied Pychology*, 79: 767–82.

Kamp, A. (2000) 'Breaking up old marriages: the political process of change and continuity at work', *Technology Analysis and Strategic Management*, 12 (1): 75–90.

Kanter, R.M. (1985) *The Change Masters: Corporate Entrepreneurs at Work*. London: Allen & Unwin.

Kanter, R.M. (1990) *When Giants Learn to Dance: Mastering the Challenges of Strategy, Management, and Careers in the 1990s*. London: Unwin Hyman.

Kanter, R.M., Stein, B.A. and Jick, T.D. (1992) *The Challenge of Organizational Change: How Companies Experience it and Leaders Guide it*. New York: Free Press.

Kelly, D. and Amburgey, T.L. (1991) 'Organizational inertia and momentum: a dynamic model of strategic change', *Academy of Management Journal*, 34 (3): 591–612.

Kelly, J. (1990) 'British trade unionism 1979–89: change continuity and contradictions' special issue: *Work, Employment and Society*, 29–60.

Kelly, J. (1996) 'Union militancy and social partnership', in P. Ackers, C. Smith and P. Smith (eds), *The New Workplace and Trade Unionism*. London: Routledge.

Kelly, J. (1998) *Rethinking Industrial Relations: Mobilization, Collectivism and Long Waves*. London: Routledge.

Knight, D.O. and Wall, M.L. (1989) 'Using group technology for improving communication and co-ordination among teams of workers in manufacturing cells', *Industrial Engineering*, 21 (1): 28–34.

Knights, D. and McCabe, D. (1998) 'Dreams and designs on strategy: a critical analysis of TQM and management control', *Work, Employment and Society*, 12 (3): 433–56.

Knights, D. and Murray, F. (1994) *Managers Divided: Organisation Politics and Information Technology Management*. Chichester: Wiley.

Knights, D. and Willmott, H. (eds) (2000) *The Reengineering Revolution: Critical Studies of Corporate Change*. London: Sage.

Kochan, T., Katz, H. and McKersie, R. (1986) *The Transformation of American Industrial Relations*. New York: Basic Books.

Korczynski, M. and Ritson, N. (2000) 'Derecognising unions and centralising bargaining: analysing dualism in the oil and chemicals industries', *Work, Employment and Society*, 14 (3): 419–37.

Kotter, J. (1995) 'Leading change: why transformation efforts fail', *Harvard Business Review*, 73 (2): 59–67.

Kotter, J. (1996) *Leading Change*. Cambridge: Harvard Business School Press.

Kreitner, R. and Kinicki, A. (1992) *Organizational Behaviour*. 2nd edn. Homewood: Irwin.

Lamond, D., Standen, P. and Daniels, K. (1998) 'Contexts, cultures and forms of teleworking', in G. Griffin (ed.), *Management Theory and Practice: Moving to a New Era*. Melbourne: Macmillan.

Latour, B. (1991) 'Technology is society made durable', in J. Law (ed.), *A Sociology of Monsters: Essays on Power, Technology and Domination*. London: Routledge.

Lawler, E. and Mohrman, S. (1985) 'Quality circles after the fad', *Harvard Business Review*, 63 (1): 65–71.

Lawrence, P. and Lorsch, J. (1967) *Organization and Environment*, Cambridge: Harvard University Press.

Leavitt, H.J. (1964) 'Applied organizational change in industry: structural, technical and human approaches', in W.W. Cooper, H.J. Leavitt and M.W. Shelly (eds), *New Perspectives in Organization Research*. New York: Wiley.

Ledford, G.E., Mohram, S.A., Mohrman, A.M. and Lawler, E.E. (1990) 'The phenomenon of large-scale organizational change', in A.M. Mohrman, S.A. Mohram, G.E. Ledford, T.G. Cummings and E.E. Lawler, *Large-Scale Organizational Change*. San Francisco: Jossey-Bass.

Leisink, P., van Leemput, J. and Vilrokx, J. (eds) (1996) *The Challenge of Trade Unions in Europe: Innovation or Adaptation*. Cheltenham: Edward Elgar.

Lewin, K. (1947) 'Frontiers in group dynamics', *Human Relations*, 1: 5–42.

Lewin, K. (1951) *Field Theory in Social Science*. New York: Harper & Row.

Linstead, S. (2000) 'Gender blindness or gender suppression? A comment on Fiona Wilson's research note', *Organization Science*, 21 (1): 297–303.

Littler, C. (1982) *The Development of the Labour Process in Capitalist Societies*. London: Heinemann.

Littler, C.R. and Bramble, T. (1995) 'Conceptualising organisational restructuring in the 1990s', *Journal of the Australian and New Zealand Academy of Managment*, 1 (1): 45–56.

Luff, P., Hindmarsh, J. and Heath, C. (eds) (2000) *Workplace Studies: Recovering Work Practice and Informing System Design*. Cambridge: Cambridge University Press.

Lumley, R. (1973) *White Collar Unionism in Britain*. London: Methuen.

McCabe, D. (1996) 'The best laid schemes o' TQM: strategy, politics and power', *New Technology, Work and Employment*, 11 (1): 28–38.

McCabe, D. (2000) 'The team dream: the meaning and experience of teamworking for employees in an automobile manufacturing company', in S. Procter and F. Mueller (eds), *Teamworking*. London: Macmillan Business.

McLoughlin, I. (1999) *Creative Technological Change: The Shaping of Technology and Organisations*. London: Routledge.

McLoughlin, I. and Clark, J. (1994) *Technological Change at Work*. 2nd edn. Buckingham: Open University Press.

McLoughlin, I., Badham, R. and Couchman, P. (2000) 'Rethinking political process in technological change: socio-technical configurations and frames', *Technology Analysis and Strategic Management*, 12 (1): 17–37.

Machin, S. (2000) 'Union decline in Britain', *British Journal of Industrial Relations*, 38 (4): 631–45.

Main, J. (1989) 'How to go global – and why?', *Fortune*, 28 August: 70.

Mangham, I. (1979) *The Politics of Organizational Change*. Westport: Greenwood Press.

Marginson, P. and Wood, S. (2000) 'WERS98 special issue: editors' introduction', *British Journal of Industrial Relations*, 38 (4): 489–96.

Mauthner, N., McKee, L. and Strell, M. (2001) *Work and Family Life in Rural Communities*. York: Joseph Rowntree Foundation.

Melling, J. (1980) 'Non-commissioned officers: British employers and their supervisory workers, 1880–1920', *Social History*, 5: 183–221.

Meyer, J. and Rowan, B. (1977) 'Institutionalised organizations: formal structure as myth and ceremony', *American Journal of Sociology*, 83: 340–63.

Millward, N. (1994) *The New Industrial Relations?* London: Policy Studies Institute.

Mintz, B. and Schwartz, M. (1985) *The Power Structure of American Business*. Chicago: University of Chicago Press.

Mitroff, I. and Bennis, W. (1989) *The Unreality Industry*. New York: Oxford University Press.

Mitroff, I. and Mohrman, S. (1987) 'The slack is gone: how the United States lost its competitive edge in the world economy', *Academy of Management Executive*, 1: 65–70.

Morgan, G. (1997) *Images of Organization*. Thousand Oaks: Sage.

Mortished, C. (2002) 'Grounded: the big spenders of business class', *The Times*, 12 January: 44.

Moser, I. and Law, J. (1999) 'Good passages, bad passages', in J. Law and J. Hassard (eds), *Actor Network Theory and After*. Oxford: Blackwell

Navaratnam, K.K. (1993) 'Organizations serving the quality movement in Australia: a guide for human resource practitioners', *Asia Pacific Journal of Human Resources*, 31 (3): 83–91.

NEDO (National Economic Development Office) (1986) *Changing Working Patterns: How Companies Achieve Flexibility to Meet New Needs*. London: NEDO.

Newman, J. and Williams, F. (1995) 'Diversity and change: gender, welfare and organizational relations', in C. Itzin and J. Newman (eds), *Gender, Culture and Organizational Change: Putting Theory into Practice*. London: Routledge.

Nilakant, V. and Ramnarayan, S. (1998) *Managing Organisational Change*. New Delhi: Response Books.

Niland, J., Lansbury, R. and Verevis, C. (eds) (1994) *The Future of Industrial Relations: Global Change and Challenges*. London: Sage.

O'Donnell, F. (2002) 'After 154 years, is this the final chapter for a literary institution?', *Scotsman*, 12 January: 5.

Ohmae, K. (1990) *The Borderless World: Power and Strategy in the Global Market Place*. London: HarperCollins.

Ohmae, K. (1994) 'The global logic of strategic alliances', in *Going Global: Succeeding in World Markets*. Boston: Harvard Business Review. pp. 51–62.

Oliver, N. and Wilkinson, B. (1988) *The Japanization of British Industry*. Oxford: Blackwell.

Opitz, H. and Wiendahl, H. (1971) 'Group technology and manufacturing systems for small and medium quantity production', *International Journal of Production Research*, 9 (1): 181–203.

Pascale, R. (1990) *Managing on the Edge*. New York: Touchstone.

Paton, R. and McCalman, J. (2000) *Change Management: A Guide to Effective Implementation*. 2nd edn. London: Sage.

Patrickson, M. and Hartmann, L. (1996) 'Older women: retailing utilizes and neglected workforce resource', *Asia Pacific Journal of Human Resources*, 34 (2): 88–98.

Patrickson, M. and Hartmann, L. (eds) (1998) *Managing an Ageing Workforce.* B HRM
Warriewood, NSW: Business and Professional Publishing.

Peetz, D. (1997) 'Deunionisation and union establishment: the impact of workplace
change, HRM strategies and workplace unionism', *Labour and Industry,* 8 (1):
21–36.

Peetz, D. (1998) *Unions in a Contrary World: The Future of the Australian Trade
Union Movement.* Melbourne: Cambridge University Press.

Perrow, C. (1970) *Organizational Analysis.* Belmont: Wadsworth.

Peters, T. (1989) *Thriving on Chaos.* London: Pan Books.

Peters, T. (1993) *Liberation Management: Necessary Disorganisation for Nano-
second Nineties.* London: Pan Books.

Peters, T. (1997) *The Circle of Innovation.* New York: Knopf.

Peters, T. and Waterman, R. (1982) *In Search of Excellence: Lessons from America's
Best Run Companies.* New York: Harper & Row.

Pettigrew, A. (1973) *The Politics of Organizational Decision-Making.* London:
Tavistock.

Pettigrew, A. (1985) *Awakening Giant: Continuity and Change in ICI.* Oxford:
Blackwell.

Pettigrew, A. (1990) 'Longitudinal field research on change: theory and practice',
Organization Science, 1 (3): 267–92.

Pettigrew, A. (1997) 'What is a processual analysis?', *Scandinavian Journal of
Management,* 13 (4): 337–48.

Pfeffer, J. (1981) *Power in Organizations.* Boston: Pitman.

Pfeffer, J. and Salancik, G. (1978) *The External Control of Organizations: A
Resource Dependence Perspective.* New York: Harper & Row.

Pinch, T. and Bijker, W. (1987) 'The social construction of facts and artefacts: or how
the sociology of science and sociology of technology might benefit each other', in
W. Bijker, T. Hughes and T. Pinch (eds), *The Social Construction of Technological
Systems: New Directions in the Sociology of History.* Cambridge: MIT Press.

Pinch, T. and Bijker, W. (2000) 'The social construction of facts and artefacts: or how
the sociology of science and the sociology of technology might benefit each other',
in D. Preece, I. McLoughlin and P. Dawson (eds), *Technology, Organizations and
Innovation: Critical Perspectives on Business and Management. Vol. II: Theories,
Concepts and Paradigms.* London: Routledge.

Piore, M. and Sabel, C. (1984) *The Second Industrial Divide: Possibilities for
Prosperity.* New York: Basic Books.

Pocock, B. (1997) 'Gender and industrial relations theory and research practice',
Labour and Industry, 8 (1): 1–19.

Pollert, A. (1988) 'The flexible firm: fixation or fact?', *Work, Employment and
Society,* 2 (3): 218–316.

Preece, D. (1995) *Organizations and Technical Change: Strategy, Objectives and
Involvement.* London: Routledge.

Preece, D., McLoughlin, I. and Dawson, P. (eds) (2000) *Technology, Organizations
and Innovation: Critical Perspectives on Business and Management, Vols 1–4.*
London: Routledge.

Preece, D., Steven, G. and Steven, V. (1999) *Work, Change and Competition:
Managing for Bass.* London: Routledge.

Procter, S. and Mueller, F. (2000) *Teamworking.* London: Macmillan Business.

Pugh, D. (ed.) (1990) *Organization Theory: Selected Readings.* 3rd edn. London:
Penguin.

Pugh, D. and Hickson, D. (1976) *Organizational Structure in its Context: The Aston
Programme I.* London: Saxon House.

Quinlan, M. (1996) 'The reform of Australian industrial relations: contemporary
issues and trends', *Asia Pacific Journal of Human Resources,* 34 (2): 3–27.

Quinn, J.B. (1980) *Strategies for Change: Logical Incrementalism*. Homewood: Irwin.

Reed, M. (1989) *The Sociology of Management*. Hemel Hempstead: Harvester Wheatsheaf.

Ridderstrale, J. and Nordstrom, K. (2000) *Funky Business: Talent Makes Capital Dance*. Edinburgh: Pearson Education.

Roethlisberger, F. (1945) 'The foreman: master and victim of double talk', *Harvard Business Review*, 23 (3): 283–98.

Roethlisberger, F. and Dickson, W. (1950) *Management and the Worker: An Account of a Research Program Conducted by the Western Electric Company, Hawthorne Works, Chicago*. Cambridge: Harvard University Press.

Ropo, A., Eriksson, P. and Hunt, J. (eds) (1997a) 'Reflections on conduction processual research on management and organizations', special issue, *Scandinavian Journal of Management*, 13 (4).

Ropo, A., Eriksson, P. and Hunt, J. (1997b) 'Reflections on conducting processual research on management and organizations', *Scandinavian Journal of Management*, 13 (4): 331–5.

Rose, M. (1988) *Industrial Behaviour: Research and Control*. 2nd edn. Harmondsworth: Penguin.

Schein, E.H. (1985) *Organizational Culture and Leadership*. San Francisco: Jossey-Bass.

Schonberger, R.J. (1982) *Japanese Manufacturing Techniques: Nine Hidden Lessons in Simplicity*. New York: Free Press

Senior, B. (1997) *Organizational Change*. London: Pitman.

Sennett, R. (2001) 'Street and office: two sources of identity', in W. Hutton and A. Giddens (eds), *On the Edge: Living with Global Capitalism*. London: Vintage.

Sewell, G. (1998) 'The discipline of teams: the control of team-based industrial work through electronic and peer surveillance', *Administrative Science Quarterly*, 43 (2): 397–428.

Sewell, G. and Wilkinson, B. (1992) ' "Someone to watch over me": surveillance, discipline and the just-in-time labour process', *Sociology*, 26 (2): 271–89.

Shapiro, E. (1995) *Fad Surfing in the Boardroom*. Reading: Addison-Wesley.

Shaw, M. (2000) *Theory of the Global State*. Cambridge: Cambridge University Press.

Shtub, A. (1989) 'Estimating the effect of conversion to a group technology layout on the cost of material handling', *Engineering Costs and Production Economics*, 16 (2): 103–9.

Simon, H. (1972) 'Theories of bounded rationality', in C. McGuire and R. Radner (eds), *Decision and Organization*. Amsterdam: Elsevier.

Smith, J.H. (1987) 'Elton Mayo and the hidden Hawthorne', *Work, Employment and Society*, 1 (1): 107–20.

Sohal, A., Fitzpatrick, P. and Power, D. (2001) 'A longitudinal study of a flexible manufacturing cell operation', *Integrated Manufacturing Systems*, 12 (4): 236–45.

Spence, R. (2001) 'When flexible', *Guardian*, 13 January: 28.

Stace, D. and Dunphy, D. (1994) *Beyond the Boundaries: Leading and Re-Creating the Successful Enterprise*. Sydney: McGraw-Hill.

Steinberg, M., Walley, L., Tyman, R. and Donald, K. (1998) 'Too old to work?', in M. Patrickson and L. Hartmann (eds), *Managing an Ageing Workforce*. Warriewood, NSW: Business & Professional Publishing.

Storey, J. (1992) *Developments in the Management of Human Resources*. Oxford: Blackwell.

Storey, J. (ed.) (1994) *New Wave Manufacturing Strategies: Organizational and Human Resource Management Dimensions*. London: Paul Chapman Publishing.

Sunday Times (2002) 'Enron nightmare kills an American dream', 20 January: 4–5.

Taplin, I.M. (1990) 'The contradictions of business unionism and the decline of organised labour', *Economic and Industrial Democracy*, 11: 249–78.

Taylor, F. (1911) *The Principles of Scientific Management*. New York: Harper.

Taylor, P. and Bain, P. (1999) 'An assembly line in the head: work and employee relations in the call centre', *Industrial Relations Journal*, 30 (2): 101–16.

Thomas, R. (1994) *What Machines Can't Do: Politics and Technology in the Industrial Enterprise*. Berkeley: University of California Press.

Thompson, J.D. (1967) *Organizations in Action*. New York: McGraw-Hill.

Thompson, P. and Ackroyd, S. (1995) 'All quiet on the workplace front? a critique of recent trends in British industrial sociology', *Sociology*, 29 (4): 615–33.

Thompson, P. and Warhurst, C. (eds) (1998) *Workplace of the Future*. Basingstoke: Macmillan.

Thurley, K. and Hamblin, A. (1963) 'The supervisor and his job', *Problems of Progress in Industry*, no. 13. London: HMSO.

Thurley, K. and Wirdenius, H. (1973) *Supervision: A Reappraisal*. London: Heinemann.

Times Business (2002) 'Marconi sheds more jobs', 9 August: 25.

Times Higher Education Supplement (2001) 'Russell elite go for jugular of ailing QAA', 9 November: 1.

Tingle, L. (1995) 'The little general's losing battle', *Australian*, 23–4 December: 14–17.

Trist, E. and Murray, H. (eds) (1993) 'Historical overview: the foundation and development of the Tavistock Institute', in *The Social Engagement of Social Science. Vol. 2: The Socio-Technical Perspective*. Philadelphia: University of Pennsylvania Press.

Tuckman, A. (1994) 'The yellow brick road: TQM and the restructuring of organisational culture', *Organisation Studies*, 15 (5): 727–51.

Tuckman, A. (1995) 'Ideology, quality and TQM', in A. Wilkinson and H. Willmott (eds), *Making Quality Critical: New Perspectives on Organizational Change*. London: Routledge.

Turnbull, P. (1988) 'The limits to Japanisation: "just-in-time", labour relations and the UK automotive industry', *New Technology, Work and Employment*, 3 (1): 7–20.

Ulrich, D. and Lake, D. (1991) 'Organizational capability: creating competitive advantage', *Academy of Management Executive*, (5) 1: 77–92.

Valentine, R. and Knights, D. (1998) 'Research note: TQM and BPR – can you spot the difference?', *Personnel Review*, 27 (1): 78–85.

Van de Ven, A. and Huber, G.P. (1990) 'Longitudinal field research methods for studying processes of organizational change', *Organization Science*, 1 (3): 213–19.

Venkatraman, N. and Henderson, J. (1998) 'Real strategies for virtual organizing', *Sloan Management Review*, 40: 33–48.

Venugopal, V., Suresh, N. and Slomp, J. (eds) (2001) 'Manufacturing cells: design, implementation and analysis', *Integrated Manufacturing Systems*, 12 (4): 230–325.

Vesey, J.T. (1991) 'The new competitors: they think in terms of "speed-to-market"', *Academy of Management Executive*, 5 (2): 23–33.

Wajcman, J. (2000) 'Feminism facing industrial relations in Britain', *British Journal of Industrial Relations*, 38 (2): 183–201.

Walby, S. (1997) *Gender Transformations*. London: Routledge.

Walker, C., Guest, R. and Turner, A. (1956) *The Foreman on the Assembly Line*. Cambridge: Harvard University Press.

Warr, P. (1997) 'Age, work and mental health', in K. Shaie and C. Schooler (eds), *The Impact of Work on Older Adults*. New York: Springer.

Weick, K. (1969) *The Social Psychology of Organizing*. Reading: Addison-Wesley.

Weisbord, M.R. (1988) *Productive Workplaces: Organizing and Managing for Dignity, Meaning and Community*. San Francisco: Jossey-Bass.

Wellins, R., Byham, W. and Wilson, J. (1991) *Empowered Teams: Creating Self-Directed Work Groups that Improve Quality, Productivity and Participation*. San Francisco: Jossey-Bass.

Wemmerlov, U. and Hyer, N.L. (1989) 'Cellular manufacturing in the US industry: a survey of users', *International Journal of Production Research*, 27 (9): 1511–30.

Wilkinson, A. (1998) 'Empowerment: theory and practice', *Personnel Review*, 27 (1): 40–56.

Wilkinson, A. and Willmott, H. (eds) (1995) *Making Quality Critical: New Perspectives on Organizational Change*. London: Routledge.

Wilkinson, A., Redman, T., Snape, E. and Marchington, M. (1998) *Managing with Total Quality Management: Theory and Practice*. Basingstoke: MacMillan Business.

Willcocks, L. and Mason, D. (1987) *Computerising Work: People, Systems Design and Workplace Relations*. London: Paradigm Publishing.

Williams, G. and Macalpine, M. (1995) 'The gender lens: management development for women in "developing countries"', in C. Itzin and J. Newman (eds), *Gender, Culture and Organizational Change: Putting Theory into Practice*. London: Routledge.

Williams, R. and Edge, D. (1996) 'The social shaping of technology', *Research Policy*, 25: 865–99.

Willmott, H. (1995) 'The odd couple? Re-engineering business processes, managing human resources', *New Technology, Work and Employment*, 10 (2): 89–98.

Wilson, D.C. (1992) *A Strategy of Change: Concepts and Controversies in the Management of Change*. London: Routledge.

Wilson, F. (1996) 'Research note: organization theory: blind and deaf to gender', *Organization Studies*, 17 (5): 825–42.

Wojtas, O. (2002) 'Scottish watchdog puts its faith in trust', *Times Higher Education Supplement*, 9 August: 4.

Womack, J.P., Jones, D.T. and Roos, D. (1990) *The Machine that Changed the World*. New York: Rawson Associates.

Wood, S. (1979) 'A reappraisal of the contingency approach to organization', *Journal of Management Studies*, 16 (3): 334–54.

Woodside, A.G. and Pitts, R.E. (eds) (1996) *Creating and Managing International Joint Ventures*. Westport: Quorum Books.

Woodward, J. (1980) *Industrial Organization: Theory and Practice*. 2nd edn. Oxford: Oxford University Press.

Wray, D. (1949) 'Marginal men of industry: the foremen', *American Journal of Sociology*, (54) 4: 298–301.

Zuboff, S. (1988) *In the Age of the Smart Machine*. New York: Heinemann.

Author Index

Abrahamson, E. 37, 39–40, 42
Ackroyd, S. 51
Albrecht, K. 151
Aldag, R. 32
Aldrich, H. 75, 178
Alford, J. 98
Allan, C. 89, 149, 150, 158
Alvesson, M. 41
Amburgey, T. L. 47
Andrews, M. 155
Ang, C. L. 98
Arkwright, R. 27
Ashton, J. E. 98
Ashworth, J. 172
Atkinson, J. 23, 53, 54

Babbage, C. 28
Bacon, N. 129
Badham, R. 16–18, 20, 32, 33, 35, 44, 47, 99, 101, 110–11, 176
Bain, P. 22, 53
Baird, M. 127, 128
Baldry, C. 22, 101
Bartlett, C. A. 115–16, 120
Batley, T. 155
Baty, P. 148
Becker, H. 58
Beckhard, R. 16, 31, 42
Bedeian, A. 19
Beer, M. 2, 173
Belanger, J. 127
Bell, C. 29, 31
Bell, D. 26
Benders, J. 99, 100, 110
Bennington, L. 90, 91
Bennis, W. 39
Beynon, H. 54
Biddle, G. 99
Bijker, W. 70–1, 82
Birdi, K. 91
Blackburn, P. 99
Blauner, R. 69
Blau, P. 75
Blewett, V. 149, 153, 156, 162
Boddy, D. 43

Bolman, L. 13
Boulton, M. 28
Boxall, P. 131, 132
Bradley, H. 21, 52, 62–3, 83, 113, 114, 129, 146, 170
Bramble, T. 21
Brannen, J. 24
Braverman, H. 46, 70
Brown, A. 13, 154
Buchanan, D. 16–18, 20, 29, 32, 33, 35, 43, 44, 47, 100–1, 110–11, 176
Burawoy, M. 70
Burchell, B. 22
Burnes, B. 16, 23, 28, 36, 39
Burns, T. 34, 69, 100

Callon, M. 71
Calvert, 90
Carnall, C. 19, 178
Carter, B. 128, 130
Castells, M. 113, 144
Champy, J. 23, 29
Child, J. 27, 70, 81, 84
Chiles, T. 151
Choi, T. 151
Clark, J. 14, 22, 40, 80, 127, 151
Clausen, C. 45, 70, 71
Claydon, T. 129
Clegg, S. 75, 100
Clutterbuck, D. 23, 30, 54
Collins, D. 14, 20, 39, 40–1, 42, 114, 116, 129, 173
Cook, F. X. 98
Cooney, R. 110
Cooper, R. 127, 128, 129, 131, 146
Couchman, P. 99
Cowing, E. 172
Crainer, S. 30
Crompton, R. 51, 130
Crosby, P. 36, 148, 151, 161
Crouch, C. 127
Cyert, R. 81

Daft, R. L. 43
Danford, A. 101

Daniels, K. 53
Deal, T. 13
Deming, W. E. 36, 148, 150, 161
Dickson, W. 29
DiMaggio, P. 39, 42
Domberger, S. 52–3
Donovan, P. 117
Drew, E. 51
Dunford, R. W. 35
Dunkerley, D. 75
Dunphy, D. 16, 18, 32, 33, 34–5, 37, 46
Dyerson, R. 100

Eccles, T. 19
Edge, D. 70
Edwards, R. 45, 84
Emerson, R. 75
Encel, S. 90, 91

Fairchild, G. 39
Feigenbaum, A. 148, 150
Felstead, A. 23–4
Ferner, A. 127
Ferris, G. 91
Forrest, A. 134
Fox, A. 129
French, W. 29, 31
Friedman, A. 70, 100

Gabor, S. C. 38
Gallagher, C. 98
Gall, G. 128, 130
Gallie, 54
Gardener, B. 84, 88
Garraham, P. 23, 54
Gates, G. 52, 53
Ghoshal, S. 115–16, 120
Giddens, A. 112, 113–14, 146, 170, 177
Gill, J. 5
Goddard, A. 149
Gray, E. R. 37
Gray, L. G. 30
Griffiths, A. 32, 33
Grint, K. 70, 71
Grun, B. 150
Guest, D. 37

Hackman, R. J. 148, 152
Hamblin, A. 85
Hamel, G. 39, 171–2, 176
Ham, I. 99
Hammer, M. 23, 29
Handy, C. 23, 36, 53–4, 170–1
Harrison, N. 23, 41
Harris, R. T. 16, 42
Hartmann, L. 91, 92
Hatch, J. 40
Hawke, R. 151
Hayes, J. 178
Haynes, P. 131, 132
Hazelmere Group 114

Healy, G. 128, 133
Heath, C. 72
Hellriegel, D. 30
Henderson, J. 53
Henry, J. 178
Hensher, D. 53
Hickson, D. 34
Hill, S. 151
Hirst, P. 114
Hobsbawn, E. J. 27
Hodgetts, R. 115
Homstein, Z. 90
Howard, 127
Huber, G. P. 41
Huczynski, A. 29, 36, 37
Hundley, G. 130
Hunter, J. 52, 53
Huq, F. 99
Huse, E. 31
Hutton, W. 53, 112, 114, 146, 170, 177
Hyer, N. L. 98–9
Hyman, R. 127, 131–2

Imai, M. 151
Ishikawa, K. 151
Itzin, C. 51, 92

Jackson, B. 39, 40, 42, 43
Jackson, P. 53
Jaffee, D. 13–14, 22, 178
James, H. 114
Jewson, N. 23–4
Johnson, J. 5
Juran, J. M. 36, 148, 150, 161

Kaemar, K. 91
Kamp, A. 81
Kanter, R. M. 13, 36, 37–8, 39
Kelly, D. 47
Kelly, J. 128, 129, 130, 135
Kinicki, A. 30
Kirton, G. 128, 133
Knight, D. O. 98
Knight, W. 98
Knights, D. 2, 23, 33, 41, 148, 152
Kochan, T. 129
Koch, C. 70
Korczynski, M. 128, 129–30
Kotter, J. 36, 38–9, 177
Kreitner, R. 30

Lake, D. 37
Lamond, D. 53
Lansbury, R. 127, 128
Latour, B. 71
Law, J. 71
Lawler, E. 42
Lawrence, P. 34
Leavitt, H. J. 15, 47
Ledford, G. E. 32, 41
Leisink, P. 144

Lewin, K. 30, 35
Linstead, S. 147
Littler, C. 21, 27–8, 84
Lorsch, J. 34
Luff, P. 44, 71–2
Lumley, R. 130
Luthans, F. 115

Macalpine, M. 61
McCabe, D. 101–2, 152
McCalman, J. 178
Machin, S. 128
McKay, S. 128, 130
McLoughlin, I. 14, 43, 44, 70, 71, 80
Main, J. 115
Mangham, I. 35
March, J. 81
Marginson, P. 128, 129, 130
Mason, D. 33
Mauthner, N. 66, 67
Mayle, D. 178
Mayo, E. 30
Meager, N. 23, 53, 54
Melling, J. 27
Meyer, J. 12
Millward, N. 129
Mindlin, S. 75
Mintz, B. 79–80
Mitroff, I. 36, 39, 42
Mohrman, S. 36, 42
Morgan, G. 13
Mortished, C. 172
Moser, 71
Mueller, F. 22, 24, 100
Murray, F. 33, 41
Murray, H. 32, 100

Navaratnam, K. K. 151
Newcombe, T. 27
Newman, J. 51
Nilakant, V. 3
Niland, J. 127
Nohria, N. 2, 173
Nordstrom, K. 39

O'Donnell, F. 173
Ohmae, K. 114
Oliver, N. 22, 23
Opitz, H. 99

Palmer, G. 13, 23, 41, 148, 149, 152, 153
Partridge, B. 84
Pascale, R. 37
Paton, R. 178
Patrickson, M. 91, 92, 112
Peetz, D. 129, 130
Perrow, C. 34
Petersen, P. B. 38
Peters, T. 13, 35, 36, 37, 176
Pettigrew, A. 14, 35, 40, 41
Pfeffer, J. 35, 75

Phillipson, C. 51, 92
Pinch, T. 70–1
Piore, M. 70, 100
Pitts, R. E. 115
Pocock, B. 133, 134
Pollert, A. 54
Powell, W. 39, 42
Prahalad, C. K. 39
Preece, D. 40, 44, 69
Procter, S. 22, 24, 100
Pugh, D. 34

Quinlan, M. 131
Quinn, J. 16, 44

Ramnarayan, S. 3
Reed, M. 12, 13
Ridderstrale, J. 39
Ritson, N. 128, 129–30
Roethlisberger, F. 29, 84
Ropo, A. 41
Rose, M. 12, 30
Rowan, B. 12

Sabel, C. 70, 100
Salancik, G. 75
Samson, D. 23, 41
Scammell, W. 119–20
Schein, E. H. 14
Schonberger, R. J. 36
Schwartz, M. 79–80
Senior, B. 178
Sennett, R. 178
Sewell, G. 84, 100
Shapiro, E. 37, 40
Shaw, M. 114
Shtub, A. 98
Simon, H. 12
Skilling, J. 172
Smeltzer, L. R. 37
Smith, A. 28
Smith, J. H. 30
Sohal, A. 100
Spence, R. 22
Stace, D. 16, 18, 32, 34–5, 37, 46
Stalker, G. M. 34, 69, 100
Starke, F. A. 30
Stearns, T. 32
Steinberg, M. 91
Stephenson, G. 27
Stewart, P. 23, 54
Storey, J. 14, 22

Taplin, I. M. 131
Taylor, F. 28–9
Taylor, P. 53
Tharenou, P. 91
Thomas, R. 80–1
Thompson, G. 114
Thompson, J. D. 34, 42
Thompson, P. 22, 23, 51

Thurley, K. 85
Tingle, L. 21
Trist, E. 32, 100
Tuckman, A. 148, 151
Turnbull, P. 22
Tweddell, E. 117, 124–5

Ulrich, D. 37

Valentine, R. 148, 152
Van Der Wielen, J. 53
Van de Ven, A. 41
Van Hootegem, G. 100
Venkatraman, N. 53
Venugopal, V. 99
Vesey, J. T. 37

Wageman, R. 148, 152
Wajcman, J. 128, 133, 134, 145
Walby, S. 51
Walker, C. 85
Wall, M. L. 98
Warhurst, C. 22, 23
Warr, P. 91, 92
Waterman, R. 13, 35, 36, 176
Watt, J. 27, 28
Wedgewood, Josiah 28

Weick, K. 75
Weisbord, M. R. 30
Wellins, R. 100
Wemmerlov, U. 98–9
Whyte, W. 84, 88
Wiendahl, H. 99
Wilkinson, A. 148, 152
Wilkinson, B. 22, 23, 100
Willcocks, L. 33
Willey, P. C. 98
Williams, F. 51
Williams, G. 61
Williams, R. 70
Willmott, H. 2, 23, 29, 41, 148, 152
Wilson, D. 35
Wilson, F. 147
Wirdenius, H. 85
Wojtas, 149
Womack, J. P. 23
Wood, S. 34, 35, 128, 129, 130
Woodside, A. G. 115
Woodward, J. 34, 69–70
Woolgar, S. 70, 71
Wray, D. 84, 88

Zuboff, S. 143

Subject Index

Accom Industries 153, 157
Actor Network Theory (ANT) 71
administrative structures 15, 16, 47
age
    discrimination 90
    older employees 7, 83–97
ageism 51
airline industry 172
Air New Zealand 172
Alcoa 153–4, 161
Ansett Australia 58–9
Australian Services Union (ASU) 7–8, 128,
    134–46, 175
Australia for Quality Campaign 151
Austyn 117
automation 72–3, 76–9, 80–1
autonomy 36, 100, 101, 113

bargaining position 66–7
Bergen loaf 78
best practice management 12
bicycle development 70–1
Blakemore Consulting 154
bottom–up view 14
bounded rationality 12
Breadcoop 73
breaks 64
British Airways 172
bureaucratic perspective 24
business concept innovation 171
Business Process Reengineering (BPR) 2, 23,
    29, 152

call centres 53, 131, 144–5
casual work 21, 51, 52, 62–7
    unions 132–3, 144, 146
    women 91
celebrity professors 14, 35–9
cellular manufacture 7, 57, 93–4, 98–111, 175
centrality, perceived 48
centralized bargaining 129
Central Linen Services 55–6
charismatic transformation 34
child care 64, 66
classic unionism 132

coercive strategies 17, 20
collaborative models 35
collaborative system 21
collective bargaining 127, 128–30, 131
collective identity 65
collective solidarity 67
Comalco 131
Community and Public Sector Union (CPSU)
    131
complacency 38
computers
    see also technology
    cellular manufacturing 105–6
    employment 143–4
    supervision 84
conflict theory 13–14
consultancy unionism 132
consultants 18, 35–9, 161
consumers
    demand 73–6, 78
    loyalty 75
contested change 17
context of change 13, 47, 110, 163–5, 174–5
contingency models 20, 34–5, 50
continuity 39
continuous improvement 153
contract-based system 21, 127
core workers 23, 53, 54
CRA Ltd 131
critical change 17–18
cultural heterogeneity 152
cultural perspective 12, 13, 24
culture of organizations 47
customers
    power 6, 73–6, 79–80
    supplier relations 156–7, 165, 175

Dalebake Bakeries 6, 69, 72–82, 175
data analysis 45–9
data categories 46
David Bull Laboratories (DBL) 112, 117,
    121–3
defining characteristics 48
dictatorial transformation 34, 35
distancing 54

division of labour 28
dominant coalition 81
Doryx 117, 121
downsizing 21, 142, 158

economic rationalism 142–3
economic security 19
economy, global 113
education, quality management 149
efficiency 28
Egyptians 26
electronic surveillance 98, 102, 103, 110
employees
   communication 174
   consultation with 29, 30
   critical reflection 10
   empowerment 129, 152, 164
   experience 54–8, 169
   flexibility 22–4
   globalization 122
   involvement 106, 108, 110, 157
   morale 10
   older 7, 83–97
   recruitment 121
   representation 62–7
   resistance 18–20, 24–5, 29–30, 45, 106–8,
      109, 110, 177
   staff turnover 120
employment, post–war 29
Employment Relations Act (1999) 130
enacted environment 75
Enron 172, 176
Eryc (erythromycin) 112, 117, 121, 125
European Commission, age discrimination 90
Excellence 40
extensive participation 17, 18
external context 47, 175
external relations 156
external triggers 15–16
external workers 23, 54

fad surfing 40
familial system 27
Faulding Company 7, 112–13, 116–26
flexibility 21–4, 25
   Dalebake 78
   functional 54
   interpretative 70, 71, 82
   non-standard employment 51–68
   numerical 53, 54
   teamworking 100–1
forced evolution 34
force–field analysis 30
Ford 172
Fortex 57
functional flexibility 54
functionalism 13–14

gang boss system 27
gender
   child care 64, 66

maternity leave 63
older employees 91–2
part-time work 51, 61–2
unions 133–4, 137–41, 142, 146–7
General Motors 57, 93–4
geographical dispersal 143–5, 146
global approach 115
globalization 7, 170
   myth 52
   strategic change 112–26
   as a trigger 15
goal-directed rational decision-making 12
group pressure 104
group problem-solving 155
Group Technology (GT) 99
guru managers 14, 35–9, 168

Hendersons Automotive 156, 161–2, 163
home working 143–4
human choice 114
Human Relations 29, 30, 31, 32, 50
Human Resource Management (HRM)
   competitive 14
   Faulding Co 118–19
   unions 129, 130
human resources 21, 47
   shamrock organizations 23
   teamworking 99–100
   as a trigger 15, 16

incremental change 17
Industrial Revolution 26–8
in-store bakeries 74
internal context 47, 175
internal contractor 27–8
internal relations 156
internal triggers 15–16
internationalization 15, 42, 113, 114–15
international model 115
Internet 113
interpretative flexibility 70, 71, 82
irrelevancy 39

James Thin stores 173
Japan 36, 150, 155–6
job (in)security 51, 55, 58
   see also redundancy
   casualization of work 62–7
   change resistance 19
   downsizing 21
   flexibility 22, 24
   older employees 86, 89, 91–2
   teleworking 53
   TQM 87
   traditional employment 54
   unions 142
   work force compliance 60–1, 68
   work intensification 57
job mobility 29, 84
job satisfaction, age 91
Just-In-Time (JIT) 12, 36, 108

Kapanol 117
knowledge management 12
knowledge workers 21

Laubman and Pank 157, 163, 164
laws, as a trigger 15
leadership
  democratic 29
  style 34
lean manufacturing/production 56, 108
learning organizations 12
logical incrementalism 44

Machiavellian politics 111
McKinsey Seven S Framework 36
management
  anti–union ideology 129
  cellular manufacture 103–9
  Faulding 119–21, 122–6
  older employees 94–5, 96
  organizational action 37–8
  power 65–7
  TQM 153, 154, 157–8, 160
  as united group 70
Marconi 173
Marks & Spencer 173
master craftsman system 27
Mitsubishi Motors 60–1, 64
moral order 13
multicultural workplaces 152
multinational model 115
multinationals 170, 172
multiskilling 21, 54
myths 52, 58, 67, 83, 88, 92, 96, 102

National Category Managers (NCM) 75
National Economic Development Office
  (NEDO) 23
natural attrition 86
natural teams 154
negotiated settlements 17
network society 113, 114
new product development 115, 123–4
non-standard employment
  see also casual work; part–time work
  flexibility 51–68
n–step guides 40
numerical flexibility 53, 54

onion model 71
organizational action 37–8
Organizational Development (OD) 20, 29,
  30–2, 35, 50
organizational excellence 36–7
organizational growth/expansion 15, 118–19
organization theory 12
organizing model 130, 131–2
outsiders 57–8, 67
outsourcing 21, 52–3, 58–62, 142
over-socialized models 14

paper tiger unionism 132

Parke–Davis 121
participative evolution 34
participative methods 20
partnership arrangements 115
partnership unionism 132
part-time work 21
  flexibility 51–3, 58–62
  increase 54
  unions 132–3, 142–3, 146
peripheral workers 23, 53, 54
pharmaceuticals 7, 112–13, 114, 115, 116–26
Pirelli 86, 87, 154, 155, 158, 161, 163
politics 12, 13, 17, 18, 35, 46–7, 175
  cellular manufacture 98–111
  Machiavellian 111
  quality management 164
  sensitivity 174
  as a trigger 15
  Washdale Manufacturing 108–9
  winning the turf 110
power 35
  customers 6, 73–6, 79–80
  dependence relationship 75
  management 65–7
power-assisted steering 17, 20
power-coercive resolutions 17
power relations 13, 69–82
primary tasks 15, 16
Process Improvement Teams (PIT) 153, 154
processual perspective 4, 10, 14, 40–50, 153–9,
  175, 178–9
psychological threat 19

Quality Assurance Agency (QAA) 149
quality management 8–9, 13, 148–66, 173, 178
  see also Total Quality Management (TQM)

radical change 17
rational decision–making 12–13, 24
redundancy, older employees 87–8, 94–5, 96
refreezing 31
representative participation 17, 18
Research Assessment Exercise 149
resource dependence perspective 75

Savings & Loans Credit Union 60, 63, 64
scale
  of change 18, 34
  substance of change 48
scientific management 28–9, 50, 152
scope, substance of change 48
Scottish Higher Education Funding Council
  (SHEFC) 149
security 120
September Eleventh 172
Service Excellence Programme (SEP) 157
servicing model 130, 131–2
sexism 51
shamrock organizations 23, 53–4
shift work 98, 102, 103–4, 110
situational approach 34–5

social arrangements 19
Social Construction of Technology (SCOT) 70
social constructivism 70
social events, as a trigger 15
Social Technical Systems (STS) 32–3, 100
South Australian & Northern Territory Branch
  (SANTB) 8, 128, 134–40, 142, 144, 145
State Bank of Australia 159–60, 162, 163
Statistical Process Control (SPC) 162
status lowering 19
strategic change 112–26
strategic choice 70, 81
strategic objectives 43–4, 123–5
structural perspective 24
students 66
sub-contracting 27–8
substance of change 47–9, 161–3, 174–5
substantive change 18, 19
supermarkets 73–5, 78, 79–80
supervisors 7, 21, 27–8, 83–97, 107
surveillance
  electronic 98, 102, 103, 110
  teamworking 100
Sydbank 89
symbolic interactionism 13–14
system selection 44

TAB 64–6
tacit knowledge 93
Tavistock Institute of Human Relations 32, 50
team-based cellular manufacturing (TBCM)
  101
team leaders 86, 102
teamworking 24, 93–4, 98–111
technical-bureaucratic perspective 13
technical organization 12
technical-theoretical perspective 12
technological determinism 70, 80–1
technology 21
  context of change 47
  network society 113
  power relations 69–82
  processual perspective 43, 44
  STS 32–3
  supervision 84
  as a trigger 15–16

unions 143–5
  Washdale Manufacturing 102
Tecpak 154–5, 162, 163
Telecom Australia 94–5, 96
teleworking 53
temporal element 18
test marketing 120
timeframe, substance of change 48
time and motion studies 28
top-down consensus-oriented views 14
top-down strategies 31
Total Quality Management (TQM) 8–9, 40,
  149–66
  case study programme 180–5
  Fortex 57
  Pirelli Cables 87
  problems with 152
  Sydbank 89
training 162–3, 174
transnational solution 115–16, 126
triggers 15–16, 24
tyres development 70–1

under-socialized models 14
unfreezing 30
unions 7–8, 46
  casualization of work 67
  General Motors 57
  membership decline 21, 127, 128–32
  outsourcing 59–60
  part-time work 61, 62
  shifting industrial landscape 127–47
  TAB 64–5
  teleworking 53
  TQM 164
  Washdale Manufacturing 108, 109
upskilling 21

Vicbank 157–8, 159–60, 162–3, 164
Volkswagen 99–100
Volvo 33

Washdale Manufacturing 7, 98, 102–11
well-being, age effects 91, 92
work intensification 22, 56–7, 146
Workplace Relations Act (1996) 128